EFFECTIVE

ORGANIZATIONAL

BEHAVIOUR

Effective Management
Series Editor: Alan H. Anderson

Effective Personnel Management
Alan H. Anderson

Effective Business Policy
Alan H. Anderson and Dennis Barker

Effective General Management
Alan H. Anderson

Effective Organizational Behaviour
Alan H. Anderson and Anna Kyprianou

Effective Labour Relations
Alan H. Anderson

Effective Marketing
Alan H. Anderson and Thelma Dobson

Effective International Marketing
Alan H. Anderson, Thelma Dobson and James Patterson

Effective Marketing Communications
Alan H. Anderson and David Kleiner

Effective Entrepreneurship
Alan H. Anderson and Peter Woodcock

Effective Enterprise Management
Alan H. Anderson and Dennis Barker

Effective Accounting Management
Alan H. Anderson and Eileen Nix

Effective Financial Management
Alan H. Anderson and Richard Ciechan

EFFECTIVE ORGANIZATIONAL BEHAVIOUR

*a skills and
activity-based approach*

ALAN H. ANDERSON
and
ANNA KYPRIANOU

Copyright © Alan H. Anderson and Anna Kyprianou 1994

The right of Alan H. Anderson and Anna Kyprianou to be identified as authors of this work has been asserted in accordance with the Copyright, Designs and Patents Act 1988.

First published 1994

Blackwell Publishers
108 Cowley Road
Oxford OX4 1JF
UK

238 Main Street
Cambridge, Massachusetts 02142
USA

British Library Cataloguing in Publication Data

A CIP catalogue record for this book is available from the British Library.

Library of Congress Cataloging-in-Publication Data

Anderson, Alan H., 1950-
    Effective organizational behaviour: a skills and activity-based approach / Alan H. Anderson and Anna Kyprianou.
        p. cm. – (Effective management)
    Includes bibliographical references and index.
    ISBN 0-631-19128-3 (acid-free paper: pbk)
    1. Organizational effectiveness. 2. Organizational behaviour. I. Kyprianou, Anna. II. Title. III. Series. IV. Series: Effective management (Oxford, England)
    HD58. 9 A537 1994   94-1777
    658.4–dc20   CIP

Designed and typeset by VAP Group Ltd., Kidlington, Oxfordshire

Printed in Great Britain by TJ Press Ltd., Padstow, Cornwall

This book is printed on acid-free paper

We would both like to dedicate this book to our partners.
Alan Anderson
Anna Kyprianou

Contents

Figures

Boxes

Activities

Introduction to the Series

❝ He that has done nothing has known nothing. **❞**

Carlyle

The Concept

In this series 'effective' means getting results. By taking an action approach to management, or the stewardship of an organization, the whole series allows people to create and develop their skills of effectiveness. This interrelated series gives the underpinning knowledge base and the application of functional and generic skills of the effective manager who gets results.

Key qualities of the effective manager include:

- **functional expertise** in the various disciplines of management;
- an understanding of the **organizational context**;
- an appreciation of the **external environment**;
- **self-awareness** and the power of **self-development**.

These qualities must fuse in a climate of **enterprise**.

Management is results-oriented so action is at a premium. The basis of this activity is **skills** underpinned by our qualities. In turn these skills can be based on a discipline or a function, and be universal or generic.

The Approach of the Series

These key qualities of effective management are the core of the current twelve books of the series. The areas covered by the series at present are:

People	*Effective Personnel Management*
	Effective Labour Relations
	Effective Organizational Behaviour
Finance	*Effective Financial Management*
	Effective Accounting Management
Marketing and sales	*Effective Marketing*
	Effective International Marketing
	Effective Marketing Communications
Operations/Enterprise	*Effective Enterprise Management*
	Effective Entrepreneurship
Policy/General	*Effective Business Policy*
	Effective General Management

The key attributes of the effective manager are all dealt with in the series, and we will pinpoint where they are emphasized:

- *Functional expertise.* The four main disciplines of management – finance, marketing, operations and personnel management – make up nine books. These meet the needs of specialist disciplines and allow a wider appreciation of other functions.

- *Organizational context.* All the 'people' books – the specialist one on *Effective Organizational Behaviour*, and also *Effective Personnel Management* and *Effective Labour Relations* – cover this area. The resourcing/control issues are met in the 'finance' texts, *Effective Financial Management* and *Effective Accounting Management*. Every case activity is given some organizational context.

- *External environment.* One book, *Effective Business Policy*, is dedicated to this subject. Environmental contexts apply in every book of the series: especially in *Effective Entrepreneurship*, *Effective General Management*, and in all of the 'marketing' texts – *Effective Marketing*, *Effective International Marketing* and *Effective Marketing Communications*.

- *Self-awareness/self-development.* To a great extent management development is manager development, so we have one generic skill (see later) devoted to this topic running through each book. The subject is examined in detail in *Effective General Management*.

- *Enterprise.* The *Effective Entrepreneurship* text is allied to *Effective Enterprise Management* to give insights into this whole area through all the developing phases of the firm. The marketing and policy books also revolve around this theme.

Skills

The functional skills are inherent within the discipline-based texts. In addition, running through the series are the following generic skills:
- self-development
- teamwork
- communications
- numeracy/IT
- decisions

These generic skills are universal managerial skills which occur to some degree in every manager's job.

Format/Structure of Each Book

Each book is subdivided into six units. These are self-contained, in order to facilitate learning, but interrelated, in order to give an effective holistic view. Each book also has an introduction with an outline of the book's particular theme.

Each unit has *learning objectives* with an overview/summary of the unit.

Boxes appear in every unit of every book. They allow a different perspective from the main narrative and analysis. Research points, examples, controversy and theory are all expanded upon in these boxes. They are numbered by unit in each book, e.g. 'Box PM1.1' for the first box in Unit One of *Effective Personnel Management.*

Activities, numbered in the same way, permeate the series. These action-oriented forms of learning cover cases, questionnaires, survey results, financial data, market research information, etc. The skills which can be assessed in each one are noted in the code at the top right of the activity by having the square next to them ticked. That is, if we are assuming numeracy then the square beside Numeracy would be ticked (✓), and so on. The weighting given to these skills will depend on the activity, the tutors'/learners' needs, and the overall weighting of the skills as noted in the appendix on 'Generic Skills', with problem solving dominating in most cases.

Common cases run through the series. Functional approaches are added to these core cases to show the same organization from different perspectives. This simulates the complexity of reality.

Workbook

The activities can be written up in the *workbook* which accompanies each book in the series.

Handbook

For each book in the series, there is a *handbook*. This is not quite the 'answers' to the activities, but it does contain some indicative ideas for them (coded accordingly), which will help to stimulate discussion and thought.

Test bank

We are developing a bank of tests in question-and-answer format to accompany the series. This will be geared to the knowledge inputs of the books.

The Audience

The series is for all those who wish to be effective managers. As such, it is a series for management development on an international scale, and embraces both management education and management training. In management education, the emphasis still tends to be on cognitive or knowledge inputs; in management training, it still tends to be on skills and techniques. We need both theory and practice, with the facility to try out these functions and skills through a range of scenarios in a 'safe' learning environment. This series is unique in encompassing these perspectives and bridging the gulf between the academic and vocational sides of business management.

Academically the series is pitched at the DMS/DBA types of qualification, which often lead on to an MA/MBA after the second year. Undergraduates following business degrees or management studies will benefit from the series in their final years. Distance learners will also find the series useful, as will those studying managerial subjects for professional examinations. The competency approach and the movement towards Accredited Prior Learning and National Vocational Qualifications are underpinned by the knowledge inputs, while the activities will provide useful simulations for these approaches to management learning.

This developmental series gives an opportunity for self-improvement. Individuals may wish to enhance their managerial potential by developing themselves without institutional backing by working through the whole series. It can also be used to underpin corporate training programmes, and acts as a useful design vehicle for specialist inputs from organizations. We are happy to pursue these various options with institutions or corporations.

The approach throughout the series combines skills, knowledge and application to create and develop the effective manager. Any comments or thoughts from participants in this interactive process will be welcomed.

Alan H. Anderson
Melbourn, Cambridge

The Series: Learning, Activities, Skills and Compatibility

The emphasis on skills and activities as vehicles of learning makes this series unique. Behavioural change, or learning, is developed through a two-pronged approach.

First, there is the **knowledge-based (cognitive)** approach to learning. This is found in the main text and in the boxes. These cognitive inputs form the traditional method of learning based on the principle of receiving and understanding information. In this series, there are four main knowledge inputs covering the four main managerial functions: marketing/sales, operations/enterprise, people, and accounting/finance. In addition, these disciplines are augmented by a strategic overview covering policy making and general management. An example of this first approach may be illustrative. In the case of marketing, the learner is confronted with a model of the internal and external environments. Thereafter the learner must digest, reflect, and understand the importance of this model to the whole of the subject.

Second, there is the **activity-based** approach to learning, which emphasizes the application of knowledge and skill through techniques. This approach is vital in developing effectiveness. It is seen from two levels of learning:

1 The use and application of *specific skills*. This is the utilization of your cognitive knowledge in a practical manner. These skills emanate from the cognitive aspect of learning, so they are functional skills, specific to the discipline.

   For example, the learner needs to understand the concept of job analysis before he or she tackles an activity that requires the drawing up of a specific job evaluation programme. So knowledge is not seen for its own sake, but is applied and becomes a specific functional skill.

2 The use and application of *generic skills*. These are universal skills which every manager uses irrespective of the wider external environment, the organization, the function and the job. This is seen, for example, in the ability to make clear decisions on the merits of a case. This skill of decision making is found in most of the activities.

There is a relationship between the specific functional skills and the generic skills. The specific functional skills stand alone, but the generic skills cut across them. See figure SK.1.

In this series we use activities to cover both the specific functional and the generic skills. There are five generic skills. We shall examine each of them in turn.

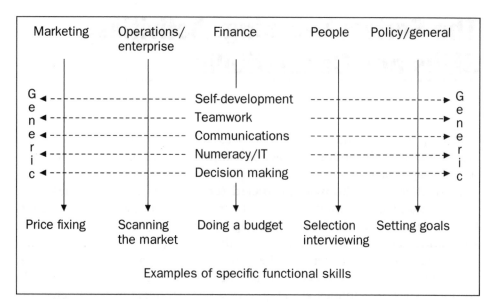

Figure SK.1 Series skills matrix: functional and generic skills.

Self-development

The learner must take responsibility for his or her learning as well as 'learning how to learn'. Time management, work scheduling and organizing the work are involved in the procedural sense. From a learning perspective, sound aspects of learning, from motivation to reward, need to be clarified and understood. The physical process of learning, including changing knowledge, skills and attitudes, may be involved. Individual goals and aspirations need to be recognized alongside the task goals. The ultimate aim of this skill is to facilitate learning transfer to new situations and environments.

Examples of this skill include:

● establishing and clarifying work goals;

● developing procedures and methods of work;

● building key learning characteristics into the process;

● using procedural learning;

● applying insightful learning;

● creating personal developmental plans;

● integrating these personal developmental plans with work goals.

Teamwork

Much of our working lives is concerned with groups. Effective teamwork is thus at a premium. This involves meeting both the task objectives and the socio-emotional processes within the group. This skill can be used for groups in a training or educational context. It can be a bridge between decision making and an awareness of self-development.

Examples of this skill include:

- clarifying the task need of the group;
- receiving, collating, ordering and rendering information;
- discussing, chairing and teamwork within the group;
- identifying the socio-emotional needs and group processes;
- linking these needs and processes to the task goals of the group.

Communications

This covers information and attitude processing within and between individuals. Oral and written communications are important because of the gamut of 'information and attitudinal' processing within the individual. At one level communication may mean writing a report, at another it could involve complex interpersonal relationships.

Examples of this skill include:

- understanding the media, aids, the message and methods;
- overcoming blockages;
- listening;
- presenting a case or commenting on the views of others;
- writing;
- designing material and systems for others to understand your communications.

Numeracy/IT

Managers need a core mastery of numbers and their application. This mastery is critical for planning, control, co-ordination, organization and, above all else, for decision making. Numeracy/IT are not seen as skills for their own sake. Here, they are regarded as the means to an end. These skills enable information and data to be utilized by the effective manager. In particular these skills are seen as an adjunct to decision making.

Examples of this skill include:

- gathering information;
- processing and testing information;

- using measures of accuracy, reliability, probability etc.;
- applying appropriate software packages;
- extrapolating information and trends for problem solving.

Decision making

Management is very much concerned with solving problems and making decisions. As group decisions are covered under teamwork, the emphasis in this decision-making skill is placed on the individual.

Decision making can involve a structured approach to problem solving with appropriate aims and methods. Apart from the 'scientific' approach, we can employ also an imaginative vision towards decision making. One is rational, the other is more like brainstorming.

Examples of this skill include:

- setting objectives and establishing criteria;
- seeking, gathering and processing information;
- deriving alternatives;
- using creative decision making;
- action planning and implementation.

This is *the* skill of management and is given primary importance in the generic skills within the activities as a reflection of everyday reality.

Before we go about learning how to develop into effective managers, it is important to understand the general principles of learning. Both the knowledge-based and the activity-based approaches are set within the environment of these principles. The series has been written to relate to Anderson's sound principles of learning which were developed in *Successful Training Practice*.

- *Motivation* – intrinsic motivation is stimulated by the range and depth of the subject matter and assisted by an action orientation.
- *Knowledge of results* – ongoing feedback is given through the handbook for each book in the series.
- *Scale learning* – each text is divided into six units, which facilitates part learning.
- *Self-pacing* – a map of the unit with objectives, content and an overview helps learners to pace their own progress.
- *Transfer* – realism is enhanced through lifelike simulations which assist learning transfer.
- *Discovery learning* – the series is geared to the learner using self-insight to stimulate learning.
- *Self-development* – self-improvement and an awareness of how we go about learning underpin the series.

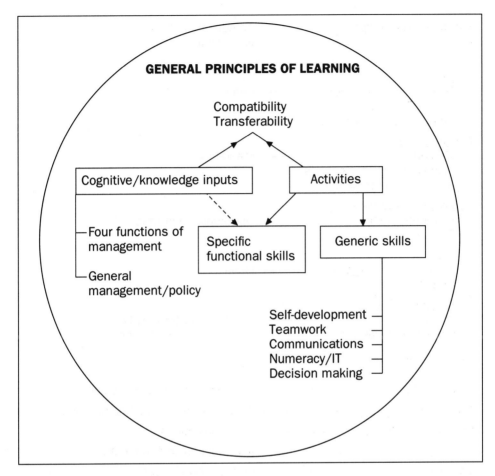

Figure SK.2 Series learning strategy.

- *Active learning* – every activity is based upon this critical component of successful learning.

From what has been said so far, the learning strategy of the series can be outlined in diagrammatic form. (See figure SK.2.)

In figure SK.2, 'compatibility and transferability' are prominent because the learning approach of the series is extremely compatible with the learning approaches of current initiatives in management development. This series is related to a range of learning classification being used in education and training. Consequently it meets the needs of other leading training systems and learning taxonomies. See figures SK.3–SK.6.

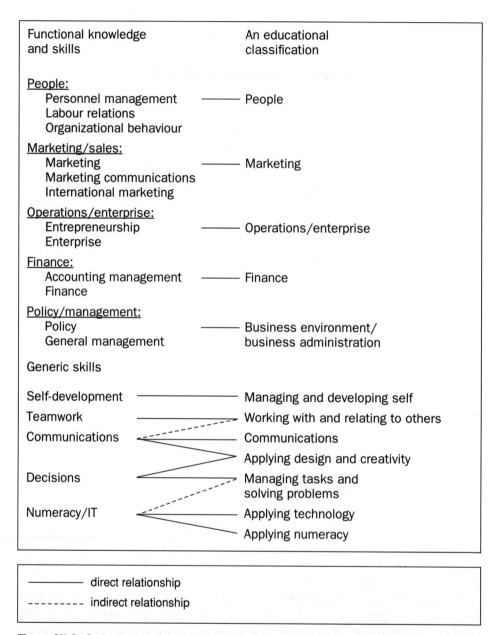

Figure SK.3 appears with the following content:

Functional knowledge
and skills

An educational
classification

People:
   Personnel management ——— People
   Labour relations
   Organizational behaviour

Marketing/sales:
   Marketing ——— Marketing
   Marketing communications
   International marketing

Operations/enterprise:
   Entrepreneurship ——— Operations/enterprise
   Enterprise

Finance:
   Accounting management ——— Finance
   Finance

Policy/management:
   Policy ——— Business environment/
   General management   business administration

Generic skills

Self-development ——————— Managing and developing self
Teamwork ————————— Working with and relating to others
Communications <---------- Communications
                          Applying design and creativity
Decisions ————————— Managing tasks and
                          solving problems
Numeracy/IT <---------- Applying technology
                          Applying numeracy

——— direct relationship
- - - - - indirect relationship

Figure SK.3 Series knowledge and skills related to an educational classification.

Source: Adapted from Business Technician and Education Council, 'Common skills and experience of BTEC programmes'.

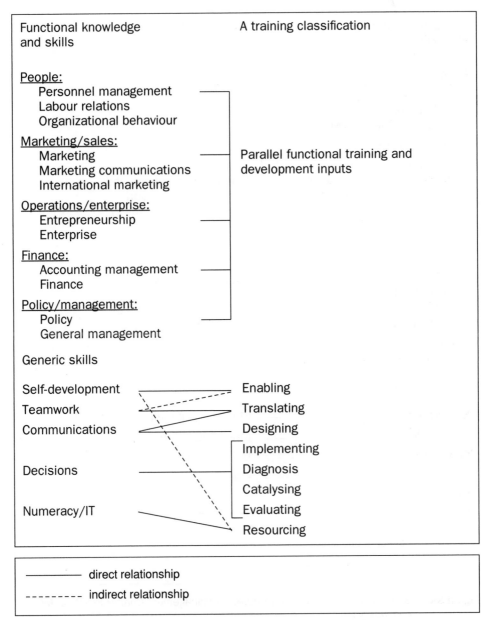

Figure SK.4 Series knowledge and skills related to a training classification.

Source: Adapted from J.A.G. Jones, 'Training intervention strategies' and experience of development programmes.

Functional knowledge and skills	MCI competency
People:	Managing people
Personnel management	
Labour relations	
Organizational behaviour	
Marketing/sales:	Managing operations and managing information (plus new texts pending)
Marketing	
Marketing communications	
International marketing	
Operations/enterprise:	
Entrepreneurship	
Enterprise	
Finance:	Managing finance
Accounting management	
Finance	
Policy/management:	Managing context
Policy	
General management	
Generic skills	
Self-development	Managing oneself
Teamwork	Managing others
Communications	Using intellect
Decisions	Planning
Numeracy/IT	

——————— direct relationship

- - - - - - - - indirect relationship

Figure SK.5 Series knowledge and skills related to Management Charter Initiative (MCI) competencies.

Source: Adapted from MCI diploma guidelines.

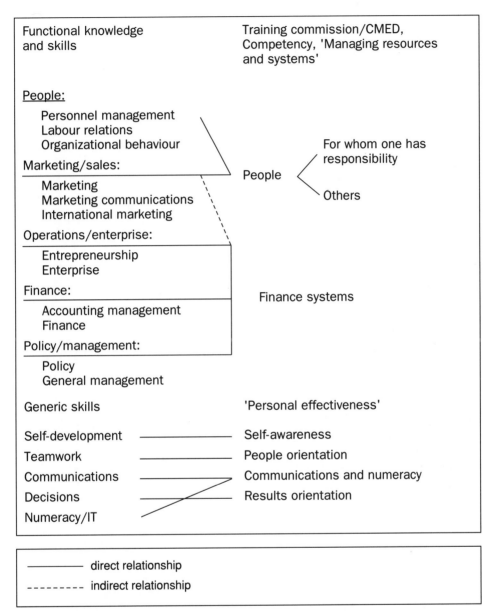

Figure SK.6 Series knowledge and skills related to Training Commission/Council for Management Education (CMED) competencies.

Source: Adapted from Training Commission/CMED, 'Classifying the components of management competencies'.

Preface

> ❝ People don't want to be subservient to machines and systems. They react to inhuman working conditions in very human ways: by job-hopping, absenteeism, apathetic attitudes, antagonisms and even malicious mischief. From the workers' point of view, this is perfectly reasonable.
>
> ... we have educated them [the workers] to regard themselves as mature adults, capable of making their own choices. Then we offer them virtually no choice in over-organised industrial units. For eight hours a day they are regarded as children, ciphers or potential problems and managed and controlled accordingly. ❞
>
> *P. Gyllenhammar, then President of Volvo*[1]

It is a commonly held belief that the people who make up an organization are the most valuable asset of the organization, and yet, like Mr Gyllenhammar, we can all cite organizational instances where this is not always apparent. The fact still remains that people are an essential component of any organization, and the *difference* between an effective organization and an ineffective one is its workforce.[2] Therefore, understanding human behaviour in an organizational context is of vital importance to the effectiveness of both managers and the organization itself.

Essentially, organizational behaviour seeks to analyse and interpret human behaviour in work organizations. That sounds simple enough: as many of our students have often said, 'effective organizational behaviour is just a question of common sense'. And to some extent they are right. Organizational behaviour is, however, a little more than just common sense. It provides a deeper understanding of the reasons why people behave the way they do at work, as well as testing our commonly held assumptions. It may also give behaviour some predictability.

Hence, this subject deals with the application of the behavioural sciences to the workplace. The book is tackled on three related dimensions: the individual, the group and the organization. Yet almost as important as the subject matter, with the requisite generic and specific skills, is the *approach*. The aim, here, is also to provide an objective vision of behaviour at work, with investigation, understanding and explanation, if not prediction, to the fore.

The overriding theme of this book is, therefore, to focus on the most valuable asset of an organization – the people who work for it – in an attempt to understand their behaviour in an objective if not 'scientific' manner, and to provide the tools and insights necessary to create an effective organization.

This book provides a basis for managing people in the whole enterprise – large or small – and relates to two other books in the series, *Effective Labour Relations* and *Effective Personnel Management.*[3]

Learning Aims

Specifically, *Effective Organizational Behaviour* aims to:

- develop a clear and meaningful understanding of the field of organizational behaviour;
- help you to acquire knowledge and insights concerning the behaviour of individuals and groups in the work situation;
- develop an appreciation of how an effective organization is managed, organized and structured.

These 'macro' learning aims can be translated into 'micro' objectives:

- to give an overview of the scope of the behavioural sciences at the place of work;
- to apply the models and approaches of the behavioural sciences to the place of work;
- to examine different organizational types, cultures and structures;
- to identify key organizational processes, for example, communication systems;
- to review individual differences at work;
- to review group working in organizations;
- to examine change in individuals, groups and organizations (for example, motivation, dynamics of a team, conflict and organizational development).

The key to understanding behaviour in organizations is knowing what to focus upon. Studying the entire organization or concentrating on small parts of it (such as individuals, work groups or departments) are good starting points. However, examining one part of the organization or even the whole is not enough; eventually, it is necessary to know something about how the parts relate to other parts within the whole. This is the integrated approach used in this book.

Format and Content

This book focuses on six discrete areas in the six units:

1 *Organizational behaviour approaches and perspectives.* Historically, there have been a number of different approaches to organizational behaviour. This unit reviews the nature of the behavioural sciences and their influence in organizations, as well as considering a range of organizational behaviour approaches and perspectives.

2 *The individual.* Individual performance is the foundation of organizational performance. Understanding individual behaviour, therefore, is crucial for effective management and consequently for effective organizations. As organizational effectiveness depends on individual performance, managers must have more than a passing knowledge of the determinants of individual performance. This unit covers personality, perception, attitudes, motivation, job satisfaction and stress in an organizational context.

3 *Interpersonal and group processes.* Much of our time is spent interacting with others in groups, whether they are social or work groups. Our personal identity is derived, in part, from the way in which we are perceived and treated by other group members. Thus, skills in interaction and in group dynamics are vital for all managers who seek to get the best from individuals working within organizations.

The productivity resulting from effective group action makes the development of group skills one of the most essential aspects of managerial training. Furthermore, membership in productive and cohesive groups is essential to maintaining psychological health throughout a person's life.

This unit concentrates on group dynamics, leadership and conflict.

4 *Integrating mechanisms.* The integrating mechanisms within an organization largely determine how efficient, if not effective, an organization is going to be in reality. However, not all behaviours are aimed at improving the organization's performance. Power and political behaviour are significant elements of organizational life. Workers and managers use power to accomplish goals and, in many cases, to strengthen their own positions in the organization.

This unit examines integrating mechanisms from an individual, group and organizational perspective, and covers such areas as learning, communications, and power and politics.

5 *The organization.* The process by which an individual learns of the organization's expectations is through the organization's culture: the set of shared assumptions and understandings about how things really work in the organization (that is, which policies, practices and norms are really important).

To work effectively, all members of the organization must have a clear understanding of the organization's structure, its goals, and their role in relation to these. This unit considers organizational decision making, culture and design in order to determine concepts of organizational effectiveness.

6 *Change processes.* The management of change involves adapting an organization to the demands of a changing environment and modifying the actual behaviours of its members. If organization members do not change their behaviours, the organization cannot change. A manager must consider many things when undertaking organizational change, including the types of pressure being exerted on the organization to change, the kinds of resistance to change that are likely to be encountered, and those who should implement change.

This unit is specifically concerned with change from an individual, group and organizational perspective.

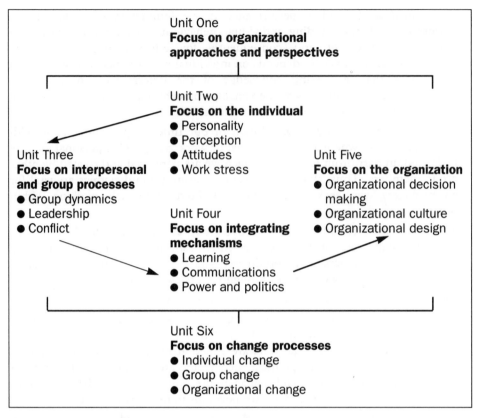

Figure 0.1 Interrelationship between the main foci identified.

The relationships among these foci as well as the key dimensions of each are illustrated in figure 0.1.

Notes

1 Gyllenhammar, *People at Work*.

2 The concept of 'effectiveness' does need other non-people attributes, from capital to land, but it is the people dimension that brings the whole thing to life. See the Introduction to the Series for a discussion on aspects of an 'effective manager', which we can transfer over in part to the effective, goal-oriented organization or collection of people working towards some common goal. Here, we will develop this concept of an 'effective organization'.

3 *Effective Labour Relations* looks at a collective perspective involving trade unions, and *Effective Personnel Management* takes on a functional/discipline approach as compared to the organization-wide perspective in this book. This text should be used as prerequisite reading before tackling the other people books of the series.

Acknowledgements

The authors and publisher would like to thank Richard Denison, Delia Goldring, Samantha Jenkins and Evelyne Lee-Barber for their advice and assistance in the development of this book. In addition, the authors express their gratitude to Maureen Anderson for her immense efforts in putting their scribbles into some sort of order.

Unit One

Focus on Organizational Behaviour Approaches and Perspectives

Learning Objectives

After completing this unit, you should be able to:

- understand the relationship between organizational behaviour and the behavioural sciences;

- understand basic behavioural science research methods;

- understand the nature of organizations;

- appreciate the range of perspectives and approaches to organizations;

- apply the generic skills.

Contents

Unit One

> ❝ All organizations are different. Frequently the implication is that there can be little in common between them and consequently no coherent description of organizations. ❞
>
> *Pugh et al.*[1]

Overview

Organizations are complex social systems which affect us all at one time or another. Understanding the impact that organizations have on us and vice versa is important at a personal level. From an organizational perspective, understanding the behaviour of people in organizations has become a key concern for managers, as the effectiveness of any organization is influenced, to a large extent, by the people it employs. Simply, organizational behaviour focuses on the behaviour of people within an organizational setting.

Many of the concepts and ideas that are used in an attempt to understand the behaviour of individuals and groups in organizations are based on knowledge gained from the behavioural sciences. (The behavioural sciences represent a systematic body of knowledge from such disciplines as sociology, psychology, economics and anthropology.) Therefore, we can say that organizational behaviour is truly interdisciplinary.

This unit focuses on the importance of organizational behaviour, the nature of the behavioural sciences and their influence in understanding organizations, as well as considering a range of organizational perspectives and approaches.

Organizational Behaviour: An Interdisciplinary Approach

Organizational behaviour is not a single discipline. It draws from a range of other disciplines in an attempt to provide an integrative approach to a complex social system – an organization. For example, psychology focuses primarily on individuals and their behaviour; sociology focuses primarily on social systems and social behaviour. The contribution of such disciplines as psychology, sociology and other behavioural sciences provides useful knowledge in the understanding of the behaviour of people

3

in work organizations, and consequently underpins the field of organizational behaviour. (The scope and value of these disciplines is summarized in Box OB1.1.)

BOX OB1.1

Organizational behaviour: scope and value

The social sciences to which organizational behaviour belongs, have been summarized as: 'all activities which are concerned systematically to investigate aspects of the relation between the individual and society'.[1] This idea of people interacting with their work environment goes to the heart of the study of organizational behaviour. The systematic vision and method of work seek 'regularities in social life' comparable to the laws of the physical sciences.

Many disciplines contribute to a study of people in work groups and in work organizations. Economists give us a rational choice between alternatives and keep us tuned in to the concept of risk in the organization and to external turbulence. Social anthropologists, with their study of pre-industrialized peoples, may focus comparative analysis of industrialized labour more sharply.

Social historians can give us a context to management:labour relationships. Political scientists add to the historians' stock of examples of power in societies. Above all, though, the subject draws on the psychologist for the analysis of the individual, the social psychologist for that of the group, and the sociologist for that of the social roles, interaction and organization of work.

Yet much of the literature of organizational behaviour seems to have been hijacked by a purely managerialist frame of reference, and the intentionally value-free assumptions of the pure social scientists have been prostituted.

Braverman notes that social scientists abandoned 'their confident beginnings as "sciences" devoted to discovery of the springs of human behaviour in order to manipulate them in the interests of management'.[2]

It is important that people are examined in their own terms as well as from the perspective of management. On objectivity[3] the purists' view may be sacrificed to some extent, but that does not necessarily mean that the study degenerates into a pure managerial manifesto. The economic and accounting visions of many managers can only work in the long term if the needs of employees and the quality of working life are considered and acted upon. The task needs people. Is this manipulation? Probably, but there are various approaches to this manipulation, and a more liberal view is followed by the application of sound principles of organizational behaviour. So there is considerable value in studying the subject as it aims to reconcile the needs of the enterprise with the needs of individuals and groups. It reinforces the point that the organization is really about a collection of people, and that human behaviour is the key factor in determining the success or failure of any organization.

Sources:
1   Lupton, *Management and the Social Sciences*
2   Braverman, *Labor and Monopoly Capitalism*. Likewise, some time ago, Albrow noted this objectivity being prejudiced by a managerialist bias. See Albrow, 'The study of organisations: objectivity or bias'
3   For an interesting debate on objectivity and the historian, which can be transferred over to our subject quite easily, see Carr, *What is History?*. An awareness of our own bias and prejudice may help us take a more objective stance

Given this heavy emphasis on the behavioural sciences, it seems pertinent at this point to look at the nature of the behavioural sciences in the context of organizational behaviour.

The Nature of the Behavioural Sciences and Organizational Behaviour

Some behavioural scientists, in their quest for objectivity, maintain that the only legitimate subject matter for 'scientific' study is the observable behaviour or overt acts of individuals. This, however, is a too narrow view for organizational behaviourists to adopt; in other words, organizational behaviour is also concerned with how individuals experience their world of work, the way they perceive their physical and social environment, and the meanings that they attribute to them. Thus, 'the fact that a goal of science in this area is to be as objective as possible should not ... mislead us into ignoring or downgrading the very real importance of subjective phenomena.'[2] It will be seen as the book progresses that, for example, such subjective phenomena play an important part in motivation, in interaction with other people, etc.

Let us now turn to the term 'science'. To what extent can behavioural science be regarded as scientific?

Certainly, if we regard a science as being a body of general laws governing a particular aspect of nature then behavioural 'science' is a misnomer. There is little or nothing to approximate to the general laws of the physical sciences. It is generally accepted that the behavioural sciences, and therefore organizational behaviour, do not have 'laws' equivalent to those of they physical sciences, but there are those who would settle for 'verifiability'. But even on this basic dimension, the behavioural scientist has problems. For information to be verified it must be gained in a form and under conditions which are 'replicable'; that is, other people should be able to 'reproduce' the same situation in which the original findings were made and undertake similar studies that result in similar findings. Such is the variability of human nature that genuine replicability is never really attainable. This means that even if a researcher is able to control every aspect of a situation, matching people with any degree of accuracy is not possible: different people will perceive and react to the same situation differently. This problem cannot be overcome simply by placing the same person in the same situation on different occasions, because 'people remember some of what happens to them, thereby making each separate experience distinctive'.[3]

This leads us to adopt an alternative view of science; that is, seeing it not so much as a collection of facts but rather as what scientists do. Such enquiry takes the form of 'systematic exploration, description and explanation'.[4] Its aims are 'understanding, prediction and control above the levels achieve by unaided common sense'.[5]

In the natural sciences, the dominant method for meeting these aims is the experiment. In its basic form, the experiment involves the researcher manipulating one aspect of the environment (the independent variable) and observing and measuring its effect on another (the dependent variable), while holding all other variables constant. However, there are many problems in attempting 'to hold all things constant' in the behavioural sciences.

Measurement is also a problem in the behavioural sciences. Many of the important variables cannot be measured in absolute or direct terms. This has been overcome to some extent by refinements in statistical analysis. The representation of data in a quantitative form makes it easier to analyse, but it does not make it any more accurate. Striving for scientific credibility has led many behavioural scientists to emulate the methods of the physical sciences. This has increasingly been criticized by behavioural scientists themselves, for example, 'in that [the first group] prescribe[s] methods which reduce the true complexity of experience by imitating the physical and natural sciences'.[6] What is needed is a greater emphasis on developing and refining methods that have their origin in the field of study, and less emphasis on adopting the methods of other sciences.

The value of the behavioural sciences to management rests not on whether the label 'science' is justified, but rather on the fact that they do represent an alternative to what has been referred to as 'the accumulated folklore, mythology and superstition that too often passes for traditional managerial wisdom'.[7]

The Use of Behavioural Science Methods

Effective management involves the ability not only to understand employee behaviour but also to make valid predictions about future behaviours. Behavioural scientists have developed a number of methods and approaches that attempt to do just that.

One method for gathering and analysing information systematically and objectively is the scientific approach. This follows essential key steps: observation, measurement and, finally, prediction. It encourages managers to study all the events that could affect an individual's performance. A thorough study is required, not just observations of isolated incidents. The scientific approach requires a systematic test of assumptions. It guards against preconceived ideas and bias by requiring as complete an assessment of the problem or issue as resources permit.

How a manager goes about adopting such an approach will vary depending on the nature of the problem or issue and the time and resources available. But ultimately, the research design adopted will determine the validity of the information obtained.

One of the fundamental aspects of research design is hypothesis testing. A hypothesis is a statement about the relationship between two or more variables. A particular occurrence of one of the factors determines the occurrence of another factor. For example, employees who are happy are more likely to be more productive.

We often make hypotheses and then investigate them to determine whether the facts support or disprove them in an informal way. Formalizing this approach is adopting an 'experimental' methodology.

There is a growing recognition that managers and others need a basic knowledge of certain research methods in order to understand the contributions and limitations of research in organizational behaviour.

The four most common types of research design are the case study, the survey, the laboratory experiment and the field experiment.

(1) *Case study*. In a case study, information is obtained from a variety of sources: documentary sources, interviews, questionnaires and observations. This method can provide great insights into complex issues. The researcher makes no attempt to manipulate variables but makes an in-depth study over a period of time. It is more of a fact-finding expedition rather than a testing method. The researcher attempts to organize what he or she has observed into some meaningful generalizations.

The case study's main limitation is that its findings cannot be generalized to other cases, and the value of the study is dependent on the interpretative skills and freedom from bias of the researcher. It does not lend itself to cause-and-effect relationships, as the researcher has virtually no control. Case studies, therefore, do not substantiate or refute hypotheses; however, they do provide clues and insights for further investigation. They are also a good source for understanding the real situation and useful for generating hypotheses which can later be tested in a more controlled manner.

(2) *Survey.* The survey method makes it possible to include a much wider range of situations in the study. In a survey, data is collected through interviews and/or questionnaires from a sample of people selected to represent the group under investigation. Using a sample is effective in terms of both time and cost. The intention of a survey is to discover how people feel or think, and not to change or influence respondents. It cannot, however, manipulate variables and study the effect on other variables. It can only establish correlations, and cannot be certain of causations.

(3) *Laboratory experiment.* The laboratory experiment attempts to reproduce the controlled conditions of the natural sciences, which allow the researcher to manipulate one variable at a time in order to establish a causal relationship between variables. A great deal of work undertaken in the laboratory deals with events that cannot be reproduced in or applied to real-life situations. Many behavioural problems in organizations cannot be isolated to permit their examination under laboratory conditions. The researcher, therefore, cannot be certain of the applicability of findings made in artificial settings differing from the world outside the laboratory.

(4) *Field experiment.* This is an attempt to apply the laboratory method to real-life situations. It attempts to overcome some of the artificiality of the laboratory experiments by carrying out the study in the organizational setting. Some variables are manipulated while others are held constant. The subjects in the field experiment normally know that they are under investigation, so the researcher adopts procedures to minimize the possibility of subjects changing their behaviour simply because they know they are being observed. Furthermore, since the researcher is operating in a natural environment, the chances are greater of uncontrolled variables influencing the results.

It is important to note that none of these research designs is better or worse than the others. In fact they are best regarded as complementary to each other, the disadvantages of one approach being counteracted when used with another. However, there is still room to improve the methodologies of the behavioural sciences. Despite this qualifier, the systematic methods of enquiry described do allow for the study of individual and social behaviour 'above levels achieved by unaided common sense'.[8]

Now tackle Activity OB1.1.

Managers observe and gather data all the time. The problem is that it is invariably ad hoc and frequently unreliable and biased. The quality of research depends on the adequacy not only of the research design but also of the data collection methods used. The researcher can collect data in a

ACTIVITY OB1.1

SCIENCE AND BEHAVIOUR

Activity code
- ✓ Self-development
- ✓ Teamwork
- ✓ Communications
- ☐ Numeracy/IT
- ✓ Decisions

Task

From the discussion to date, summarize the arguments on the following issue as an individual, or debate it as a group: 'The behavioural sciences may involve looking at the actions of people but they can never be seen as "scientific". Consequently, organizational behaviour is built on shifting sands.'

number of ways; for example, from documentary and published sources, through observation, through questioning, etc.

The following is a brief description of some methods used to collect data.

Documentary and published sources

Documentary and published sources take a variety of forms including letters, institutional records, administrative records (that is, personnel records), published and unpublished reports, and data collected from previous studies. All organizations, for example, maintain some records on their personnel (records are distinguished from data as they are produced for reasons other than aggregate study). The information is concise and quantitative. However, such sources usually describe how things ought to be done rather than how they are actually carried out.

Observation

Observation generally covers methods that do not involve direct questioning. It involves the researcher observing what is happening and noting it down at regular intervals. Observation may be obtrusive or unobtrusive, in the sense that subjects are aware or unaware that they are being observed.

ACTIVITY OB1.2

RESEARCH METHODS: DATA COLLECTION

Activity code
- ☑ Self-development
- ☐ Teamwork
- ☑ Communications
- ☐ Numeracy/IT
- ☑ Decisions

Task

Below, you will find five methods of data collection. From the discussion in the text and your own thoughts, give the merits and shortcomings of these methods of data collection.

Method	Merits	Shortcomings
Observation		
Personal interview (usually structured)		
Telephone interview		
Postal questionnaire (design is important; for example, pre-coded or free response)		
Panels (permanent 'standing' group)		

Participant observation

Participant observation is fairly similar to observation, except that the researcher actually works alongside the workers being studied.

The major difficulties with observational techniques are the extent to which observers affect the behaviour of those being observed by their presence, the so-called Hawthorne Effect, but observation can give a vivid picture of what is happening.

Questioning

Questioning procedures cover a range of information gathering which requires the participation of the respondent in providing the information directly to the researcher. It relies on the willingness of individuals to communicate.

Two common questioning techniques are interviews and questionnaires.

Interviews

Interviews can take place with people doing the job, their supervisor or their workmates. Obviously if a person is doing a job then they are in a good position to talk about it. However, this person may have problems with terms of reference; for example, knowing what is essential. Further, a person can say anything – it does not have to be true.

Questionnaires

Questionnaires are one of the most common methods of data gathering. If well constructed they can provide quantitative, standardized information which is useful in a large project. However, they are usually not sensitive enough to procure information concerning more complex problems and issues.

Now tackle Activity OB1.2.

The organizational behaviour research designs and data collection methods outlined above are similar in approach to those adopted by students when undertaking an in-company project or dissertation. Three key ways of learning about organizational behaviour from the learner's perspective are: experimental, experiential and action learning. These are outlined in Boxes OB1.2, OB1.3 and OB1.4.

BOX OB1.2

Organizational behaviour: an experimental methodology

Applied research into people in work organizations is fundamental to the whole subject of organizational behaviour. The design of the research programme can follow many different routes.[1] One useful approach is as follows.

Problem or issue
This is often the most difficult aspect. Defining the problem or issue in a workable format which is containable seems to cause problems to many students.

In general terms, most organizational phenomena can be studied, and a useful starting point is often how the actors in a particular system define 'their' problem. Yet the organizational behaviour researcher needs to be aware of the limits of such actor participation in the problem formulation stage of the research. A greater objectivity is required than that normally associated with the actors within an organization.

The problem cannot be unique or one-off, as testing and replication could not then occur. Values and attitudes need to be divorced from facts as well. For example, we can test a proposition that experiential learning leads to more rapid recall of information than passive learning; we would find it difficult to test whether experiential learning is 'better' than passive learning, as it involves people.

Context
Issues always have some wider context or backcloth. We need to ensure that the constraints and opportunities in a given scenario are noted as they impact on the problem or issue. Relevant organizational, group or individual variables should be noted at the outset.

Literature search
The narrower the definition of the issue the better, for the literature search on a more generalized topic can become a lifetime's work. Relevance is the key, and good scanning techniques must be employed.

Initial study
A brief pilot study or dry run may iron out methodological problems; for example, in questionnaire design. Instruments or devices of measurement, classification schemes, etc., can be tested at this time.

Premises and/or theories
The underlying frame of reference must be noted. If a given theory is being used, its inherent assumptions must be outlined. Premises underpinning the work must be clear and unambiguous, so that another researcher can tackle the same subject but from different premises or assumptions.

Hypothesis testing
Cases, fieldwork, laboratory work, correlation studies, comparative studies and 'controlled' experiments using quantitative and qualitative data test the initial issue or problem.[2]

Deductions and applications
The findings from the research must be extrapolated and applied via recommendations or a plan of campaign in a real situation.

Sources:
1   See Burgess, 'Research methods in the social sciences'
2   The range of actual research techniques is covered well by Mitchell in ch. 4 of *People in Organizations*

BOX OB1.3

Organizational behaviour: an experiential methodology

How do adults learn about organizational behaviour?

The Kolb[1] learning cycle tells us that learning is really a pattern of experiences based on reflection, theorizing, testing and further experiences, hence the term 'experiential'. This method of learning is particularly relevant for mature learners.

Some principles of experiential learning, which may help us to understand more about organizations and our approach to the subject, include the following:[2]

- Take account of the independent adult mind and the adult's past experiences.
- Build new experiences on to past experiences.
- A voluntary commitment to learning will make for less resentment and create an ease of learning.
- Utility and relevance must prevail for learning to be meaningful.
- Prefer an action approach to passive learning.
- Participant involvement is important, through skills and knowledge inputs.
- The individual must come to 'own' the learning, and continuous development is sought.

Sources:
1 Kolb, 'Towards an applied theory of experiential learning'
2 See A.H. Anderson, 'The learner without clothes', which accepts the importance of the learner but argues for a wider context to the whole process of learning at work

BOX OB1.4

Action learning: a method for learning about organizations

Dennis Barker, a fellow author in another volume in this series,[1] has studied the impact of action learning projects in a UK business school.[2] This links to some of the research methods examined previously and to the action orientation of management. The cases cited are illustrative of the application of action learning in organizations.

Example 1. One student was employed in a group of companies targeted to make a 100 per cent year-on-year growth for the 1990s. His company needed to find about 100 additional multi-site managers. This was in the climate of: a shrinking youth labour force; a growth in the adult labour force, especially women returning to employment and people aged 50 and over. He defined the objectives of the project as: to classify the roles of the single and multi-site managers using competences; to examine the roles of these managers in the organization of the future; and to establish the extent to which the products and services of the training departments provided a platform for developing competences. The benefits derived from this work were claimed to be that it became possible to clarify the managers' roles using job effectiveness descriptions. A manager's output could be recognized and a fairer reward and remuneration system could be offered as a result of a more objective assessment. Accreditation for prior learning and for experience or qualifications obtained at work could be developed. This could be used to develop managers and gain access to courses in order to obtain qualifications. Thus the development of recruitment and succession plans was made easier. It also became easier to restructure the organization, and the realization of the concept of a 'learning organization' became a possibility. A learning organization facilitates the learning of all its members and continually transforms itself.

Example 2. A group of companies had begun installing a computerized accounting system, and one of the company managers set herself the task of implementing the system in her unit. Although at that time she had little experience of computing, the task involved writing an updated manual, which would then be used throughout the group. In order to do this she had to examine company and group strategy, resources and training, and then identify the faults in the system.

The benefits were claimed to be that managers distributed their time spent on accounts more evenly over the month. Accounts were sent out to clients more quickly, thus improving cash flow significantly. Time was saved by not having to travel to head office, since, when the old system broke down, whole days of staff time were often lost. Disadvantages were also identified; for example, the availability of central accounting on the computer from 08.30–18.00 was not long enough. The duties of operations staff required later working of the computing operations to be available. The accuracy of the figures on the screen was questioned, and also the variances once hard copies were obtained. The system reaction time was sometimes too slow and the system was not complete. These factors have had an effect on the investment programme and future strategy.

Example 3. A move towards accident-free working was seen to be essential by the board of a group of companies, since there had been a steady increase in the number of accidents per million exposure hours. Thus one manager set himself the task of examining the opportunities and threats associated with this move.

The major issues identified were: attitudes to accident-free working showed conflict between hygiene and safety; the cost of accidents to clients and company was insignificant. The major causes of accidents were identified, and staff needed training. A programme was instigated to satisfy the following objectives: to introduce the principle of accident-free working; to introduce a training plan to decrease accidents: to set up a simple monitoring system that would measure improvement and provide a starting point, from which the company can move forward to consider further issues relating to accidents at work. A number of spin-off benefits, such as extra sales of materials and equipment, were also identified, and the company is now able to position itself as a caring and responsible employer.

Example 4. One quickly growing company servicing multi-site equipment had forecast an increase in operators from eighteen to sixty-six by 1995. The number of machines per operator would also increase, as the clients would be closer together and so travelling time would be reduced. However, according to the manager there were several problems with the company structure: unclear lines of responsibility; poor communication channels; isolation of operators – no team spirit, and co-ordination was becoming difficult.

The result of this exercise was that a new structure was developed, based on teams, and a measurement system was developed, based on field assessment, administration assessment and external feedback. Recognition for high scores on the assessment sheets was to be made in various ways, such as bonuses and prizes. The cost implications of these developments were examined and it was found that no additional costs would be involved other than those already set aside. Therefore an action plan was developed which envisaged implementing the changes in the other regional areas after the first year of operation.

Example 5. Another area manager examined the purchasing effectiveness of the units under his control. At the time, effectiveness was measured by the discount earnings, but he wanted to know what was actually happening within the units. This involved analysing the leading purchases that were bought regularly in a selection of typical units. Based on this analysis, a number of ideas were offered to improve earnings and reduce the cost of products to the units, while not trading downwards in terms of quality to the customer. These were tested over a two-month period. This exercise identified several fundamental issues, such as data collection and presentation, which had to be overcome. However, projecting forwards the discount improvement for twelve months improved the company discount earnings for five units by £12,500. When this approach is taken up by the group, savings of 1 per cent or more on purchases will be made – nearly £1.0m.

Example 6. Another manager, who was examining the operational strategies required for a new company project, was shocked when his board of directors cancelled it. This was the result of a series of environmental bombshells which exploded on the company. On taking stock of the situation, the manager decided to evaluate the original company strategy and its relevance in the light of the environmental changes that had occurred. Why was the company not able to adapt to change? To answer this question, the manager turned to Ansoff[3] in order to position the company's organization culture. He discovered that the culture of the company was to reject change, reject risk, focus on repetitive operations, not to 'rock the boat' and only to respond to a crisis. In Ansoff's terms, these were characteristics of a 'custodial' organization culture. The internal characteristics of management competence were also 'custodial'. The main focus was in production, the management systems were by policy and procedure manuals, and the management information system was largely informal. There was no structural environmental surveillance and problems were solved by trial and error as they arose. These are all characteristics of a custodial or production-oriented culture. However, the environment had become turbulent over the previous five years, and the company had not, until hit by a crisis, been able to alter its strategy. For optimum profitability, the responsiveness of the organization must match the turbulence of the firm's environment. In this case there was a strong mismatch. The manager and two colleagues asked for, and were given, the opportunity to present their findings to the board of directors, and it was not difficult to get the acceptance of the evaluation. The group of three was empowered to develop the company's strategic management capabilities and was strengthened by the addition of two of the board members. The group has since produced a number of strategic choices with both internal and external actions.

Sources:
1   See A.H. Anderson and Barker, *Effective Business Policy*
2   Cases quoted with the permission of the author. See Barker, 'Action learning in management development'
3   Ansoff, *Strategic Management*

Now tackle Activity OB1.3.

Before we progress with the varying approaches to organizational behaviour, it is important that we are clear as to what an organization is all about.

Putting the Organization into Perspective

All organizations have fundamental characteristics that can be grouped around four major questions, which provide a look at the anatomy of organizations. They are skeletal definitions that delineate the minimal outlines of what organizations are and do.

Who makes up an organization?

Organizations are social entities in which people take part and to which they react both as individuals and as part of a group.

ACTIVITY OB1.3

METHODOLOGY: ACTION AND LEARNING

Activity code
- ✓ Self-development
- ☐ Teamwork
- ✓ Communications
- ☐ Numeracy/IT
- ✓ Decisions

Task

Discuss the following topic: 'Action learning involves much activity but little learning or behavioural change. It leans too far towards an experiential methodology and abandons the rigour of the experimental process.'

Individuals do not work in isolation – this fact has an impact on their behaviour and their thinking. Individuals contribute a number of factors to the organization; for example, physical attributes, aptitudes and abilities. However, they also carry with them other factors which might, from an organization's view, impede their usefulness; for example, attitudes, personality disposition, feelings, emotions, etc. The organization, therefore, employs more than just a nervous system or a pair of hands.

The other key element in the social composition of organizations is the group. Groups consist of limited numbers of individuals who have common interactions and, to some degree, values and norms (that is, standards of behaviour).

Why do organizations exist?

Organizations exist to achieve certain goals and objectives. This orientation serves important functions:

- It focuses attention. It is a prescription of what should be done.
- It provides a source of legitimacy.
- It serves as a standard.
- It affects the structure of the organization.
- It provides clues about the organization.

Thus it can be said that organizations have an 'instrumental' nature – they are social instruments set up to do something.

How are organizations' goals and objectives achieved?

There are two major methods that are seen as essential in the process of trying to achieve goals and objectives:

■ differentiation of functions and positions;
■ rational co-ordination and direction of activities.

The consequences of differentiated functions are their impact on individual interactions. The division of labour within an organization places certain limitations on who interacts with whom. It also has an impact on the individual's attitudes. Differentiation is necessary to the organization, since without it people would not be able to achieve anything beyond what would result if they all worked as isolated individuals.

The method of rational co-ordination acts to integrate the activities or efforts of individuals in a way that makes organizational sense. In other words, intended rational co-ordination is the twin to differentiated functions – you cannot have one without the other.

When do organizations exist?

Organizations exist through time on a continuous basis. This does not necessarily mean forever, but refers to an extension of relationships and interrelated activities longer than momentarily and on more than a one-time-only basis.

See Box OB1.5 for a summary of the fundamental characteristics of organizations. Box OB1.6 presents a useful range of views on what an organization is all about.

BOX OB1.5

Organizational characteristics

Work organizations will tend to display some or all of the features outlined below.

■ They exist to perform clear goals and have established values.
■ They comprise a 'set of persons' and hence form a social system.
■ The work (task) is performed through those people or the social system.
■ The organization is in constant interaction with its external environments in a reciprocal relationship, with changes in one affecting the other.
■ Organizations attempt to alter, if not control, these external environments. Certainly they must adapt to these environments in order to survive and grow.
■ Organizations have a set of activities and roles usually based on some division of labour.
■ Organizations have communication and power structures aimed primarily at meeting the task goals.

- Individual and group needs and aspirations must be taken into account, and they may run counter to the predominant value system.
- Organizations tend to display a distinct personality or culture.
- Structures and processes are inherent in meeting the task.
- Organizations all control, motivate and co-ordinate the activity of people in meeting the task and adapting to external environments.

BOX OB1.6

What is an organization?

Robbins presents a useful range of views on what an organization is all about.[1]

Goal-oriented format	A rational approach: organizations pursue established aims.
Coalitions	A pluralistic vision: many interest groups come together and allocate resources on their (own) behalf.
Systems	An environmental interface: the organization comes to terms with its external environment and adapts accordingly.
Symbolic entity	An artificial creation: it is maintained as such to demonstrate the power, prestige, etc., of its actors.
Conflicting goal format	Pluralism: various competing interests and separate goals are forwarded.
Political entities	Built on the conflicting goal approach: the organization becomes the scene of power struggles.
Instruments of authority	Small jobs, rules and regulations constrain individual freedom. We are citizens outside work but servants within it.
Mechanisms of information processing	Decisions are required, so the information from inside and outside the organization must be retrieved, collated and edited. See Box OB5.1 on J.R. Galbraith, who pursues this approach.
Contractual relationship format	A form of reward: effort equation exists between employer and employee.
'Psychic prisons'	Organizations constrain individual initiative and freedom for their own ends. Robbins' use of the term conjures up a vision of the mind (if not body) being held captive from 9 to 5.

Source:
1 Range adapted from Robbins, *Organizational Theory*

By its very nature, an organization is a complex social system which impinges on how people behave and are managed within it.

Historically, there are a number of different perspectives and approaches to organizational behaviour.

Historical Overview of Approaches to Organizations

Writings in the field of management and organizations by both practitioners and academics have been prolific over the past hundred years. Many of these attempts to understand organizations are still relevant today as they provide useful insights about organizations.

Management and organizational approaches can be conveniently classified into five discrete schools of thought:[9]

1 structure of organizations
2 functioning of organizations
3 management of organizations
4 people in organizations
5 organizations in society

The remainder of this unit will concentrate on these five approaches in order to determine what clues they provide about organizations.

Structure of organizations

As we saw in the previous section, one of the fundamental characteristics of any organization is the necessity to make provision for continuing activities directed towards the achievement of goals and objectives. This is achieved through task allocation, supervision and co-ordination. These three factors represent the structure of the organization. The fact that these three activities can be arranged in different ways means that organizations can and do have different structures.

There are many prominent theorists who suggest that an appropriate structure is vital to the effectiveness of an organization, and structure is therefore seen as a focus of study in its own right. For example, some writers are primarily concerned with postulating a classification of the different types of organizational structure.[10] Weber outlined three different types of organization by examining authority. He described the ideal type of organization that emphasized order, system, rationality, uniformity and consistency – a bureaucracy. For most of us 'bureaucracy' is synonymous with time-consuming red tape, whereas Weber felt a bureaucracy led to equitable treatment of all employees by management. Bureaucratic organizations are impersonal and have strict rules, and Weber saw these characteristics as ensuring fairness to all workers. Gouldner went on to develop further Weber's notion of bureaucracy by suggesting that three variants of this type can be found.

Within this approach, however, there are those who are primarily concerned with the effect of technology on the organization's structure.[11] Woodward studied the relationship between production systems, technology and structure, and argued that the technology of the organization was a major determinant of structure. Burns was more concerned with the impact of changing technologies and the attempts of organizations to adjust to new situations.

Equally, there are those who emphasize the dimensions of structures rather than types[12] and others who emphasize the appropriateness of the organization's structure in relation to its environmental requirements as the basis of effectiveness.[13] (These are developed in Unit Six where we focus on the organization.)

Functioning of organizations

The functions of an organization can vary from one to another. However, attempts have been made to develop a unified analyses of functions by both managers and academics. Much of the work carried out in this area has been by actual practitioners[14] and their analyses are based on their personal insight and experience. Fayol and Barnard developed a broader theory of general management that is identified today as the classical view of organizational theory. Fayol categorized the role of management as planning, organizing, commanding employees, co-ordinating activities, and controlling performance. Barnard believed that the most important function of a manager was to promote co-operative effort towards the goals of the organization. Co-operation depends on effective communications and a balance between rewards to, and contributions by, each employee.

Another approach encompassed in this category regards organizations as functioning, open, socio-technical system.[15] The socio-technical school assumed that managers could exclude neither technology (representing organizational structure) nor work groups (reflecting human relations) when trying to understand a work system.

Management of organizations

Organizations may have different structures and may function in different ways, but it is argued that they all have to be managed. 'As long as there is management there will be a problem of how to manage better.'[16] The prominent contributors to this approach have all concentrated on the ingredients for better management.[17]

Taylor made significant contributions to management thinking and is often referred to as the 'father of scientific management'. It has been suggested that Taylor revolutionized management thinking. 'Scientific management' refers to the principles and practices that developed from the work of Taylor and his followers, characterized by their concern for efficiency and systematization in management. The application of these principles by Taylor's disciples has meant a task orientation at the expense of people, so Taylorism may be efficient but is not necessarily effective.

People in organizations

Organizations are systems of interdependent people who not only work for the organization, but *are* the organization. As such they affect the structure, functioning and management of the organization.

A famous study, the Hawthorne Experiment,[18] examined the impact of working conditions and the nature of supervision on output. The researchers speculated that something other than the physical work environment was responsible for the surprisingly improved productivity they observed among workers. By observing and interviewing employees, researchers discovered that the employees, by participating in the experiments, felt somewhat special. Their morale improved and they produced more. This influence that behavioural researchers can have on the people they study became known as the Hawthorne Effect. The attitudes and feelings of workers can significantly influence productivity.

There have been many other contributors to this approach; for example, Likert, McGregor, Herzberg, Blake and Mouton.[19] These contributions will be discussed further in the subsequent units, but suffice it to say that the primary focus of each of these perspectives has been the individual.

McGregor described two types of managers. Those who adhere to Theory X believe that workers have an inherent dislike of work, must be controlled and threatened with punishment if they are to put forth adequate effort, and prefer to avoid responsibility. Managers who believe Theory Y, on the other hand, believe that employees feel work is as natural as leisure, will exercise self-direction toward objectives to which they are committed (requiring less strict control), and can learn to seek responsibility. McGregor, together with other researchers, postulated that the assumptions managers hold affect the way they treat their employees and thus affect employees' productivity.

Some of the key managerial schools of thought thus far are outlined in Box OB1.7.

Organizations in society

Organizations do not exist or operate in a vacuum; they are social institutions. Many have tried to show how far the nature of modern organizations has changed society.[20] Two sociological perspectives are outlined in Box OB1.8.

BOX OB1.7

Managerial schools of thought: some outlines

Weber's vision

The issues of structure and leadership in a rational organization reflect the work of Weber in our area of study. His 'ideal type' forms the basis of the bureaucratic model. The organization has to survive human fickleness, and it has to pass on from generation to generation. The answer lies in the rational mechanism of office holders within a bureaucratic organization. We develop this concept later, but the main principles are as follows:

■ Rules, regulations, policies and procedures must be standardized to give uniform treatment for all and to ensure consistency.

■ Competence (not nepotism or corruption) should be the basis of holding office.

■ Spheres of competence are established by the bureaucracy so that officials can give a rational structure.

■ A hierarchy exists of these diverse spheres of competence, and office holders should be separate from owners.

■ The hierarchy emphasizes a top-down approach to control, co-ordination and communications.

■ The bureau (office) needs records, and transactions have to be in writing for both internal records and external scrutiny (pro-continuity and anti-corruption rationales).

Fayol's managerial principles

Fayol, a practical manager-cum-theorist advocated a series of guiding principles on how to manage an organization. The lines of authority and the allocation of duties permeate this approach. Unity is important:

■ There should be one plan for a group of activities.

■ There should be one boss.

■ The boss should have the authority to give orders.

■ There should be a scalar chain (hierarchy) from top to bottom.

Order and control are important:

■ Discipline is necessary to keep order.

■ The work is specialized, for economy (and for control).

■ An ordered society tends towards a centralized controlling authority.

■ The individual's needs must be subordinated to the organizational needs.

People are not forgotten:

■ Compensation should be fair.

■ A feeling of equity should prevail.

■ There should be stability of tenure, to give greater security.

■ Initiative should be stimulated by high morale or esprit de corps.

Taylorism and scientific management

The forerunners of this school can be seen in the work of both Weber and Fayol, but the scientific managers believed (and believe) in reducing work to an objective scientific process. The task dominates, but people are not ignored.

The main tenets are as follows.

■ A true science of work is possible. The knowledge of workers needs to be studied, documented, collated and written up. It is stored, and managers become the 'brain' while workers become the 'brawn'. Laws can apply.

■ Scientific selection follows on and trained workers will give better output.

■ Productivity rises through fully selected and trained people combining together with managerial brainpower.

■ People management is important. (Taylor's followers tended to absorb his task science but not his views on people.) Relationships were critical to Taylor.

A people perspective

Partly as a reaction to the task orientation of the earlier theorists, we find people being placed centre stage by the human relations school of management.

A socio-technical approach

This combines the people aspect of the human relations perspective with that of the technical or task dimension which is evident in the systems perspective. 'Technology' is important to this view.

Contingency

No one way is correct; a range of factors needs to be taken into account in organizations, from social to technical to group dynamics to individuals. The results are contingent, or dependent on a given situation or set of variables at that time.

BOX OB1.8

Sociological perspectives: some outlines

The main approaches to the sociology of organizations involves a structural or society-wide perspective, with work organizations placed in this context, and a micro, more interpretative approach.

Structural perspectives

Society has an objective reality of its own and conditions work in an organization. Control and socialization processes, from management budgets to induction training, are important to structuralists. However, they are rationally divided into functionalists and conflict theorists.

Functionalists see the work organization as a means to an end. Harmony at work is the normative expectation of this perspective, with conflict, if it exists, being seen as a 'breakdown' in the 'system'. Conflict theorists see the work organization as a mirror of the wider society, a microcosm of conflicts particularly between social classes. Indeed, the factory or office becomes the arena of this conflict within the economic system between these owning capital and those who sell their labour.

Interpretative perspectives
Objective reality is not seen to exist; society and the work organizations within it exist only through the eyes and the mouths of people who agree that they do so. The normative justification of a given society or organization can be questioned, and differing norms used to replace this justification.

Interactionists believe that ongoing negotiation and discussion can change the whole playing field, for that is itself a subjective constraint. Phenomenologists also appear in the psychological grouping, as they take a very subjective, personalized view of both society and the individual's approach to the work organization.

These interpretative perspectives can also be seen as social action theories, in which the roles of the actors rather than the institutions are very important.

There has certainly been an evolution in organizational thought in the past few decades, in that it has tended to emphasize the integration of structural and human perspectives. More recently contingency theory has added an emphasis on fitting organizational features to the work situation.

The contingency approach is based on the assumption that there is no one way of managing or organizing organizations that is best in all situations. It rejects the notion that universal principles can be applied to managing behaviour in organizations. Therefore, each situation must be analysed separately and then managed on the basis of the available information. It professes that the key to becoming a successful manager is the ability to diagnose a situation correctly. According to this approach, the nature of the organization's environment, its size, its technology, the character of its markets, its personnel and other factors do not only confront the organization with problems but simultaneously offer opportunities. Thus organizations should adapt to situations.

The basic concepts of the contingency approach are more difficult to grasp than the traditional principles of management. They do, however, help managers to develop a more thorough understanding of complex situations.

We have looked at some of the key areas relating to organizational behaviour as a behavioural science and the various approaches people have adopted in an attempt to achieve a better understanding of organizations. Here is a chance for you to act as a behavioural scientist. Read the Natural Beauty scenario in Activity OB1.4 and complete the task required. Then move on to the more philosophical Activity OB1.5.

ACTIVITY OB1.4

NATURAL BEAUTY

Activity code
- ✓ Self-development
- ✓ Teamwork
- ✓ Communications
- ☐ Numeracy/IT
- ✓ Decisions

The firm was getting bigger and bigger (see appendix for a full description). Doddie was not really strong on managerial control and he did not believe in sitting on his people.

The fragrance factory and the non-franchised shops had considerable manpower. Bob Brain, the personnel director, with his people orientation, convinced Doddie that top management were becoming more and more isolated from the shop floor. Doddie accepted this point and left Brain to organize some applied social research to get a better feel of the wants and needs of the staff, and to determine their core attitudes towards the firm.[1]

Simeon Gullible, a researcher at Pinetree Management Centre, was consulted and retained to conduct some research on the shopfloor. Simeon was interested in organizational culture, and he was impressed by the enterprise of the senior managers as well as their caring attitudes to their product portfolio. One issue seemed to be whether this enterprise and caring attitude were shared by the staff. He was given carte blanche to do his research – within cost constraints, of course.[2]

Gullible was not a social scientist[3] but he had moved into that discipline. The convert believed strongly in the scientific approach of enquiry, seeking information in an unbiased manner and reporting back on the information. At the same time his college was very much a commercial[4] institution interested in pursuing its products, such as 'customer care for all', 'quality management' and 'people skills'. Indeed it had recently started an MBA degree as well. Obviously if an opportunity arose to mention these 'products' he would at least raise them with the management of Natural Beauty.

He used his own model of an organizational system to place Natural Beauty in context. This involved discerning the history of the firm, the nature of its philosophy, its products, its marketplace, and its internal organization and people management.[5]

He preferred gathering data[6] by questionnaire and interview. Indeed, he had a standard method that he adapted for different firms. He liked the self-reporting technique, as it was action-oriented. The number of subjects tested could be quite significant, as the costs of the project were not significant to the firm.[7]

Simeon was interested in two variables in particular – the caring attitude of the staff and the dissemination of an enterprise culture throughout the firm. This led him to think first of research using a correlation coefficient. However, part of the research would still be experimental.[8]

Ideally he would have liked a control group to monitor the research. Indeed his college could provide a laboratory-type environment for an experiment where simulations could occur.[9]

He was conscious of bias[10] so when questioning people he would work to a standardized script and remain aloof from the event, passing no comment and merely noting their points.

Finally he was ready to go, convinced that his empirical research would be both valid and reliable.

Task

In the text, ten numbered points are noted. In the context of research methods for the social scientist, make a comment on each point below.

1

2

3

4

5

6

7

8

9

10

Appendix

Natural Beauty plc is a large American multinational firm specializing in beauty and skincare products. Currently it has 182 outlets with 5,000 independent door-to-door agents, covering almost every European country and North America. It is a classic example of the 'American Dream' with a Scottish flavour.

Some fifteen years ago, George (Doddie) McDonald had taken up his uncle's invitation to visit him in San Pedro, California. The uncle had left Scotland in the late 1950s as a young man and was glad to keep in touch with his native land. Doddie, a super salesman with a company selling toiletries and a range of domestic appliances from airfresheners to brushes and polish, had been working hard on his all-commission job. With no basic salary – merely 40 per cent commission on the mainstream items – he was still very successful. A dogged determination, a sound knowledge of his product range and a gift of the gab meant that his sales exceeded those of most other sales people in Scotland. Month by month his figures were quite exceptional. His sales patter became almost legendary among his predominantly female clientele. But Doddie knew that men were more gullible and he tried a less flattering approach with the man of the house – to find that they would buy even more goods than their female counterparts.

Doddie loved California. The sun, the food, the people, the style, the life were all so different from Scotland. It was hot – probably too hot for a fair-skinned, freckle-faced young Scotsman. He went to the local store and bought some special aftersun lotion for his sun-marked body. (His uncle had called him a lobster.) The cream was marvellous and the pain from the sunburn soon went. He thought nothing of it.

When talking to his aunt later, he mentioned the cream. 'Oh, that's Old Tom's cream made from lanolin and honey wax! You won't find that in Scotland.' Doddie was intrigued. If the truth be known he was probably bored as well – he was a go-getter, and the holiday, while fine in itself, was a little tame. Next day he went back to the shop, enquired about Tom and got his address. They met and Doddie found that Tom was a retired pharmacist. This was a bit of a hobby for him. Tom's sense of business or greed got the better of him. 'Look, I'm a salesman – one of the best around – let me take an agency from you and I'll sell your cream.' Tom said that the lack of sun in Scotland meant that there would be no market there! Both laughed. 'I'll take over the sales of this cream, the foundation cream and the cleanser cream for my territory back home, and we'll take it from there.'

When he returned home, the skincare products were seen as a natural adjunct to his other lines. The new products took off. One or two women decided to join him in selling the creams to their friends. Doddie was not concentrating most of his time on these products. He needed more agents and he got them. His 'party plan' approach was working. He needed more saturation and door-to-door agents were appointed. Old Tom was amazed at the success. After some wheeling and dealing Doddie, who was financially very secure by now, bought Tom out. Doddie now owned the formula but Tom would have a percentage cut and was asked to develop more products.

Doddie could spot a main chance and he knew it. He knew about door-to-door selling and he excelled at it. The costs of the material were quite high, owing to the transportation charge from the States. If he could keep the American name but manufacture it in the UK, costs would fall and this could be passed on, in part, to the consumer.

A fragrance factory came up for sale near Banchory in Aberdeenshire. Traditionally the factory had been involved with toilet water and perfumed soaps for a middle-of-the-road market. Neither cheap nor dear, the products had depended on 'own-brand' retail outlets. When a large order for a national retail outlet had been lost, so was the company.

Doddie moved in for the kill. Expertise in the industry, a small sales team, a production facility, a warehousing and distribution network and R & D in toiletries all fell into his hands. Old Tom came over for six months to work with the R & D people.

The firm grew stronger and stronger with Doddie, Tom and a newcomer in business policy called Dennis Marsden. Dennis joined the company from a large pharmaceutical firm, with a lot of expertise in toiletries, over-the-counter (OTC) medicines such as cough syrup, and headquarters marketing planning for a large franchise concern. Doddie 'inherited' the personnel director of the old fragrance company, Bob Brain, a strong believer in welfare policies as being the crux of effective management.

The financial specialist was head-hunted from a large multinational company in the food sector. She had a lot of experience in finding capital projects and a reputation for delivering the goods. Her name was Liz Montgomery, and she was an American by birth.

The product range continued to expand. It included:

- hair shampoo – coconut oil, primrose oil and Danzinc, a zinc pyrithione anti-dandruff agent;
- hair conditioner – protein glycerine, hair conditioner and Dodgel, a unisex hair gel;
- skin cleansing lotion – witch hazel with avocado oil for skin treatment and vitamin E. The beeswax formula for sun treatment continued to sell and was being used as a type of cleansing cream as well;
- skin moisturizer – a lemon and glycerine compound and wheatgerm/vitamin E anti-wrinkle formulation.

A new range of cosmetics, from blushers to foundation creams to nail varnish, was also being quite aggressively marketed. The fragrances of the old Scottish factory had been suitably and exotically updated to produce sophisticated perfume oils for the skin.

Wherever possible, natural elements were used in production and no animal testing was allowed in the product development. The market had also been segmented into men/women, babies, teenage girls, mature women and the older woman range. Essentially this involved different packaging rather than material differences between the ranges.

ACTIVITY OB1.5

ORGANIZATIONAL BEHAVIOUR: FRAMES OF REFERENCE

Activity code
☑ Self-development
☐ Teamwork
☑ Communications
☐ Numeracy/IT
☑ Decisions

Task

1 Review Boxes OB1.7 and OB1.8.

2 Relate the following frames of reference to a work organization of your choice and determine which, if any, mirror that organizational reality. Give a rationale for your response. The references are:

- Weber's vision
- Taylorism
- a people perspective
- a socio-technical approach
- contingency
- structural perspectives
- interpretative perspectives

Notes

1 Pugh et al., *Writers in Organizations*.
2 Porter et al., *Behavior in Organizations*.
3 Smith, 'Behaviors, results and organizational effectiveness'.
4 Sills, *The Volunteers*.
5 Allport, 'Historical background'.
6 Gross, *Organizations and their Managing*.
7 Gellerman, *Behavioral Science in Management*.
8 Allport, 'Historical background'.
9 Pugh et al., *Writers in Organizations*.
10 Weber, *The Theory of Social and Economic Organizations*; Gouldner, *Patterns of Industrial Bureaucracy*.
11 Woodward, *Industrial Organizations*; Burns, 'Industry in a new age'.
12 Pugh and Hickson, *Organizational Structure in its Context*.
13 Lawrence and Lorsch, *Organization and Environment*.
14 Fayol, *General and Industrial Management*; Barnard, *Functions of the Executive*.
15 Trist, 'Socio-technical perspective'.

16 Pugh et al., *Writers in Organizations*.

17 Taylor, *Principles of Scientific Management*; Drucker, *Practice of Management*.

18 Mayo, *Human Problems of an Industrial Civilization;* and Dickson, *Management and the Worker*.

19 Likert, *New Patterns of Management*; McGregor, *The Human Side of Enterprise*; Herzberg, *Work and the Nature of Man*; Blake and Mouton, *The New Managerial Grid*.

20 Burnham, *The Managerial Revolution*; Whyte, *The Organization Man*; J.K. Galbraith, *The Affluent Society*.

Unit Two

Focus on The Individual

Learning Objectives

After completing this unit you should be able to:

- understand the concept of individual differences;
- appreciate the complexity of personality, perception and attitudes and their effect on individual behaviour;
- understand three organizationally related factors affecting individual behaviour: motivation, job satisfaction and stress;
- apply the generic skills.

Contents

Overview

Personality

- ▶ Personality and the individual
- ▶ Personality and behaviour
- ▶ Back to basics: how do we measure personality?

Perception

- ▶ Perception and the individual
- ▶ The perceptual process

  Selective noticing

  Organizing what is noticed

  Interpreting what is organized

  Responding to perceptions
- ▶ Perception of others

  Characteristics of the person perceived

  Characteristics of the perceiver

  Characteristics of the situation
- ▶ Perceptual errors

Attitudes

- ▶ Attitudes and the individual
- ▶ Functions of attitudes
- ▶ Attitudes and behaviour

Motivation

- ▶ Defining motivation
- ▶ The importance of motivation

► Signs of motivation

► Basic considerations in motivation

► Approaches to motivation

  Content theories of motivation

  Process theories of motivation

► Why do people work?

Job Satisfaction

► Sources of job satisfaction

► Job satisfaction and behaviour

Work Stress

► Whom does stress affect?

► Managing stress

Unit Two

" An organization employs more than just a nervous system or a
   pair of hands. "

Anon

Overview

In an ideal world, two people doing the same job under the same
conditions would be as effective as one another. In the real world,
however, some employees are more effective than others. The reason for
such variations in behaviour can often be explained in terms of **individual
differences**; that is, the characteristics that distinguish one individual from
another.

Sometimes choosing a person with not quite the 'right' characteristics to
do a job, be they personality, intelligence or attitude, can have disastrous
results; for example, lost customers, minor accidents, frequent absences, or
damaged equipment. In some organizations the costs of ineffective
employees mount indefinitely, because the organization lacks the
mechanism, or the will, to identify them and develop or dispense with their
services.

Why people are different is a question which management ask
themselves. Managers, therefore, need to be aware of and appreciate
individual differences in order to understand the reason why people behave
the way they do in complex environments such as organizations.[1]

It is important to note, however, that employee behaviour is not just a
question of individual characteristics but involves a complex interaction
between an individual and his or her work environment. This unit,
therefore, focuses on a number of major individual characteristics which
affect individual behaviour, such as personality, perception, attitudes,
motivation, job satisfaction and work stress, in the context of the working
environment.

Personality

Personality and the individual

Personality is considered to be one of the key individual characteristics
when selecting the right person for a job. Companies are increasingly using

various means of assessing personality in order to ensure that they are getting the right person. However, there is no universally accepted definition of personality, despite the attempts of psychologists. Definitions include: 'that which permits a prediction of what a person will do in a given situation';[2] 'one's habits and usual style, but also ... abilities to play roles';[3] and 'the dynamic organization within the individual of those psychophysical systems that determine his unique adjustment to his environment'.[4] A key idea in the literature is that personality represents personal characteristics that lead to consistent patterns of behaviour.

Personality and behaviour

Do personal characteristics have a consistent impact on individual patterns of behaviour? Behavioural science research suggests that there are a number of personal characteristics that are closely connected to individual behaviour;[5] for example, self-esteem, locus of control, introversion/extraversion, authoritarianism and dogmatism. Each of these is pertinent to understanding organizational behaviour.

- *Self-esteem* refers to how an individual assesses his or her worth. This self-evaluation is largely influenced by the situation, past experience (successes and failures) and how others perceive the individual. Those with low self-esteem are likely to take more note of the opinions of others and to set lower goals for themselves, while those with high self-esteem are less likely to be influenced by others' opinions and to set higher goals for themselves. In other words, self-esteem is positively related to efforts to accomplish set goals. (A recent study showed that individuals with high self-esteem placed more value on attaining performance goals than did employees having low self-esteem.)[6]

- *Locus of control* refers to the extent to which individuals believe that they can control events affecting them. Those having a high internal locus of control (belief that the events in their lives are primarily the result of their own behaviours) have better control over their own behaviour, are more active politically and socially, and seek information about their situations more than those with a high external locus of control (belief that the events in their lives are primarily determined by external factors). Those with a high internal locus of control are more likely to try to influence others that be influenced. They are more achievement-oriented.

- *Introversion/extraversion.* We use the terms 'introvert' and 'extravert' in everyday language to describe a person's social adjustment: introverts tend to be shy, timid people, while extraverts are outgoing. The terms have similar meanings when used to refer to a personality dimension. Introversion is a tendency to be inwardly directed and to have a greater affinity with abstract ideas and personal feelings. Extraversion is an orientation of the mind toward other people, events and objects. (For the theoretical background, refer to Jung and Eysenck.)[7]

  Most people fall between the two extremes. As might be expected, extraverts are well represented in managerial occupations. Research even suggests that some extraversion is important in managerial success.[8] However, extreme extraversion or extreme introversion can affect an individual's effectiveness in an organization.

An important implication of the introversion/extraversion personality dimension for organizational behaviour is its relationship with task performance in different environments. There is some evidence to suggest that introverts perform more effectively in an environment where there is little sensory stimulation, while extraverts are more effective in an environment with greater sensory stimulation – more people, noise, change, and so on. Thus, the stereotype of the extreme introvert working best alone in a quiet office and the extreme extravert in a noisy office with many people may be well founded.

■ *Authoritarianism and dogmatism.* The characteristics of the authoritarian personality are a high regard for traditional values, obeying recognized authority, being concerned with power and rejecting subjective feelings. The characteristics of the dogmatic personality, on the other hand, refers to the strength of a person's beliefs. The highly dogmatic individual perceives his or her environment as threatening, regards legitimate authority as absolute and measures others on the basis of their compliance with accepted authority. In other words, the highly dogmatic individual is closed-minded and the undogmatic person is open-minded.

As the preceding section has demonstrated, personality has important implications for organizational behaviour. The challenge for managers is to understand the crucial role played by personality in explaining individual behaviour at work rather than trying to change or control employee personality.

Back to basics: how do we measure personality?

There are a number of tests and techniques which attempt to measure personality, and each is based on one of three main theories or approaches to personality. For a brief description of the basic assumptions of these, see Box OB2.1. Psychoanalysis relies on dreams and free associations; motive and need theories favour projective tests; trait theory accepts questionnaires and inventories; behaviourists prefer behavioural measures, such as work samples. In practice, distinctions are blurred; questionnaires are used to test all types of personality theory, even psychoanalysis.

Some of the benefits and limitations of each of these instruments of measurement are briefly discussed below:

■ *Observation.* Observing a live situation has obvious benefits; however, managers normally only observe a limited, edited performance, lasting between the thirty minutes of a typical interview and the three days of an assessment centre. Moreover, observation cannot elicit the thoughts and feelings of a potential employee.

■ *Situational tests.* Waiting for behaviour to occur 'naturally' is very time-consuming; the situational test saves time by contriving an occasion for significant behaviour to occur.

BOX OB2.1

Theories and approaches to personality

Trait approaches

These attempt to isolate and describe the basic properties of the individual that direct behaviour. Two examples of these approaches are the classic and the 'modern' biochemical theories.

The classic biochemical theories date back 2,000 years. Emotional equilibrium was then thought to be dependent on the appropriate balance among four fluids (humours) within the body. The four humours identified were:

- sanguine (blood)
- choleric (yellow bile)
- melancholic (black bile)
- phlegmatic (phlegm)

Personality was dependent on whichever fluid was dominant. For example, individuals with an excess of blood had a sanguine personality – they were sociable, outgoing, talkative, lively, etc. If, on the other hand, they were choleric (excess of yellow bile), they were touchy, restless, aggressive, changeable and excitable. (The various characteristics for each of these can be seen in figure 2.1.)

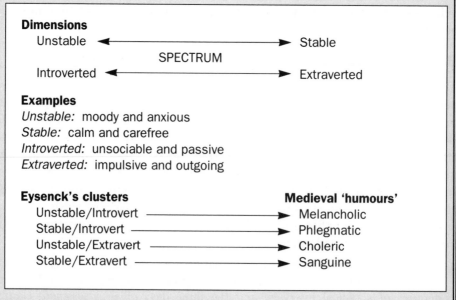

Dimensions

Unstable ⟵⟶ Stable

SPECTRUM

Introverted ⟵⟶ Extraverted

Examples

Unstable: moody and anxious
Stable: calm and carefree
Introverted: unsociable and passive
Extraverted: impulsive and outgoing

Eysenck's clusters	**Medieval 'humours'**
Unstable/Introvert ⟶	Melancholic
Stable/Introvert ⟶	Phlegmatic
Unstable/Extravert ⟶	Choleric
Stable/Extravert ⟶	Sanguine

Figure 2.1 Eysenck's typology of personality.

Source: Adapted from Eysenck, *Dimensions of Personality.*

Eysenck[1] 'modernized' the classic biochemical theories. The individual temperaments or humours were described by a small number of different 'types'. Eysenck's personality trait theory proposed two basic dimensions:

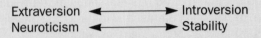

Figure 2.1 examines the dimensions, with examples, and relates them to the medieval concept of 'humours'. Few individuals fit them completely. Most people fall somewhere in between.

According to Eysenck, personality is rooted in biology. It is not inherited directly; rather, an individual inherits a particular type of nervous system which predisposes him or her to develop in a particular direction. The final shape of an individual's personality is determined by the interaction between his or her biological disposition and the environmental influences that he or she encounters in life.

Social theories

Trait theories focus on personal determinants and assume consistency in different situations. Social theories, by contrast, emphasize the importance of environmental or situational determinants of behaviour.

Individual differences in behaviour are a result, to a large extent, of differences in the kinds of learning experience encountered in the course of growing up. The reinforcement that controls the expression of learned behaviour may be:

- direct – through tangible rewards, social approval or disapproval, or alleviation of adverse conditions;
- vicarious – through observation of someone receiving a reward or punishment for behaviour similar to one's own;
- self-administered – through evaluating one's own performance with self-praise and reproach.

Psychoanalytic theories

The basic assumption of the psychoanalytical approach is that unconscious motives direct behaviour. Freud's[2] personality structure consists of three interrelated systems: the id, the ego and the superego. Each system has its own functions and it is the interaction of the three that governs behaviour.

The *id* is said to be the most primitive part of personality, present in newborn infants, from which the ego and superego later develop. It contains basic biological impulses or drives such as the need to eat, drink, eliminate wastes, avoid pain and gain sexual pleasure. The id seeks immediate gratification of these impulses and works on the *pleasure principle*; that is, to avoid pain and seek pleasure regardless of external circumstances.

The *ego* recognizes that impulses cannot always be immediately gratified. It develops and learns to consider the demands of reality. The ego thus works on the *reality principle*: the gratification of impulses must be delayed until the appropriate environmental conditions are found. The ego mediates between the demands of the id, the realities of the world, and the demands of the superego.

The *superego* is the internalized representation of the values and morals of society taught to us by our parents and others. Essentially, it is our conscience; it judges whether an act is 'right' or 'wrong'.

In summary, the id seeks pleasure, the ego tests reality and the superego strives for perfection. These three systems interact, and it is this interaction that determines our behaviour, according to the psychoanalytic approach.

Sources:
1   Eysenck, *The Structure of Human Personality*
2   Freud, *The Ego and the Id*

- *Questionnaire or inventory.* Observation is time-consuming, so short cuts need to be taken in order to gather more information more quickly. One short cut is the questionnaire or inventory; instead of watching the person to see if he or she is nervous about talking to strangers, one asks, 'Do you tend to be nervous when talking to strangers?'. Questionnaires are very economical and questions can tap thoughts and feelings as well as behaviour: for example, 'Do you often long for excitement?', 'Are you troubled by unusual thoughts?'.

An example of a personality inventory is the Minnesota Multiphasic Personality Inventory (MMPI) – the first major multi-score inventory, dating from the late 1930s. MMPI asks 550 questions and measures nine psychiatric syndromes. MMPI can be used for screening, but is rather long and offends some people by asking too many intrusive questions. The 16PF measures sixteen personality 'source traits', derived from factor analysis. The 16PF is very popular in the UK, partly because tradition allows non-psychologist managers to be trained to use it (it is also used by 38 per cent of UK occupational psychologists).

- *Ratings and checklists.* The second short cut is to ask someone who knows the individual well to describe him or her: references, rating and checklists.

- *Projective tests.* People react when being observed, and may not tell the truth about themselves or others; projective tests are supposed to by-pass individuals' defences, and measure personality despite themselves. Projective tests assume that everything people do, say, write, think, paint or even dream reflects their personality.

The classic example of a projective test is the Rorschach Inkblot Test, where subjects describe what they see in a set of inkblots. Another is the Thematic Apperception Test (TAT), where a set of pictures is carefully chosen for both their suggestive content and their vagueness. The individual describes what led up to the event shown in the picture, what is happening, what the characters are thinking and feeling, and what the outcome will be. The individual 'projects' into the story his or her own dominant drives, emotions, sentiments, complexes and conflict.

See Box OB2.2.

BOX OB2.2

Examples of personality tests

The sixteen personality factor test (16PF) was first designed by Raymond B. Cattell and its first edition appeared in 1949. It is still going strong.

The test is based on factors or dimensions of personality which are seen to be differentiated from one another. A range of factors include: warm-heartedness, intelligence, calmness, assertiveness, cheerfulness, conscientiousness, social boldness, sensitivity, suspiciousness, imaginativeness, shrewdness, self-confidence, radicalism, self-sufficiency, self-control and tenseness. Profiles can be derived by working through a six-page booklet based on three choice questions throughout.

The factors are arguably 'traits' and the trait approach to personality may be debated; the factors measure temperament rather than, say, motivation to act. For selection and training models of expectation are also required as to what profile constitutes a 'successful' candidate; this can be time-consuming, involving a longitudinal study, validity co-efficients and an analysis of overall performance.

Yet the studies of the 16PF to date seem to illustrate that the test has some benefit, although, according to Handyside, it is not 'a magic elixir'.[1]

Source:
1   See Handyside, 'The 16PF'

Measuring personality is a complex process, and personality tests are certainly different from the ones found in women's magazines. However, the validity of such tests has been disappointing, as they proved to have no more predictive validity than the interview, although they do have the advantage of being cost effective and standardized.

Now tackle Activity OB2.1.

In the section after next, we continue to explore individual differences. Here we focus on the important process of perception.

Perception

Perception and the individual

Perception is understanding the world in which we live. We behave on the basis of what we perceive reality to be, not necessarily on the basis of what reality actually is. Simply, we receive information, we assemble it and interpret it into a meaningful experience unique to ourselves. We, in other words, paint a picture of the 'real' world that expresses our own personal

ACTIVITY OB2.1

THE LONDON BREWING COMPANY

Activity code
☑ Self-development
☑ Teamwork
☑ Communications
☑ Numeracy/IT
☑ Decisions

Task

AApma has just completed a search for the London Brewing Company. Your task is to make a 'paper decision' on the candidates (alternatively the candidate profiles can be used for role playing and an 'action decision' can be made).

Below, the person and job specifications are outlined and sketches of the main contenders given. Assume that all the candidates are interested in the job and that any geographical difficulties will be resolved. Payment, terms and conditions are not problems to London Brewing. The job is based in the southern region of the company.

The person

Ideally the right person should:

1 have a degree in organization behaviour, psychology, sociology or personnel management;
2 be a good all-rounder in personnel management;
3 have considerable experience in commercial organizations;
4 have practical knowledge of organizations and development;
5 possess 'presence';
6 be quick thinking and good at listening;
7 be able to get the point over without causing conflict;
8 be mature, able, stable and disciplined in work and in private life.

The company realizes that this specification may be difficult to reach, but it is looking for the candidate who comes closest.

The job

The title is 'organization and development manager responsible to the regional personnel director'. The southern region of London Brewing is involved with brewing, warehousing, distributing and marketing beers, ales, wines and spirits. It employs 500 people and the headquarters is in Hampshire.

The job involves training, development, organizational reviews and effective performance management. The firm is looking for an objective 'in-house' consultant who will not be a 'line' personnel person. Planning and resourcing may also be added to this role in time. It is a good training ground for potential personnel directors.

The candidates
Bill Boothy: After initial recruitment experience as a consultant with a firm in the Midlands, he moved into engineering in machine tools as a senior personnel officer. He completed his professional qualification at that time. He moved on to become training assessor with a training board in this sector. Since that time he has had considerable exposure to many cultures and firms as an advisor in both organization and development.

He is a tall fellow who was slightly aloof at interview. He says that he enjoys working with people. Examples of critical incidents at work showed him to be a little impulsive but a good decision maker. He is a good spokesperson who argues well.

His domestic arrangements seem to be problematic.

Personality profile	Low (1–2)	Average (3–4)	High (5–6)
Energy and initiative		4	
Aggression and assertiveness			6
Diplomacy and Tact	2		
Flexibility and adaptability to change		4	
Determination			5
Manipulation of people	2		
Getting things done through the group			5
Impressing superiors		4	
Selling self and ideas			5
Confidence level and poise		3	

Martin Mulberry: A degree in social studies from a middling university and a postgraduate diploma in training gives him good core knowledge of the area.

His experience has been that of a generalist personnel person with the same multinational firm for the last seven years. He has moved up slowly but surely. He has exposure to food distribution, which is similar to drink distribution.

He is a smallish person, slightly on edge, and makes darting, almost suspicious sideways glances. His jerking body movements seem to display a nervous disposition. Examples of critical incidents at work showed him to be a solid decision maker who is prepared to 'get and go'. He would dominate group activity. He is single but has had a steady relationship with a married woman for four years.

Personality profile	Low (1–2)	Average (3–4)	High (5–6)
Energy and initiative			6
Aggression and assertiveness			6
Diplomacy and Tact		3	
Flexibility and adaptability to change		4	
Determination		4	
Manipulation of people		3	
Getting things done through the group			6
Impressing superiors	2		
Selling self and ideas		4	
Confidence level and poise	1		

Susan Smith: Born in Florida to British parents, she has part-American education and part-British. She has a masters degree in labour relations from an American institution. Her past personnel experience has been in education services and in hotel and catering. Currently she is employed as a research analyst with the Trevingstoke Institute of Human Relations. She has considerable exposure to both organizations and development.

She is slightly overweight and comes over as a little bossy, if not self-opinionated. At interview she seemed to be somewhat disorganized at the outset, but she settled down and the rest of the discussion reflected her able mind. She is a little domineering and could be a better listener. She argues well – but takes no prisoners in discussion. Domestically she says that everything is well; on probing, it appears that she has a strained relationship with her partner.

Personality profile	Low (1–2)	Average (3–4)	High (5–6)
Energy and initiative		4	
Aggression and assertiveness			6
Diplomacy and Tact	1		
Flexibility and adaptability to change	2		
Determination			6
Manipulation of people		3	
Getting things done through the group	2		
Impressing superiors		3	
Selling self and ideas	2		
Confidence level and poise			5

Terry Thompson: he is currently an academic at a West London college. He has had a technical education at a technical college and laughingly said at interview his colleagues called him 'Tec Terry'. He holds a masters degree from this institution. He has written one book on a relevant subject.

His past industrial life was in the motor and engineering sectors as a generalist personnel person. His current work is research-based and he would like to return to Industry.

'Tec Terry' is an affable fellow. He will get on with most people. He seems to work like a Trojan and this may compensate for a lack of brilliance. Yet the specification does not call for an intellectual, and Mr Thompson fits that bill.

Examples of critical incidents at work showed him to be a good, if deliberate, decision maker. He has four children and is married to a fellow lecturer.

Personality profile	Low (1–2)	Average (3–4)	High (5–6)
Energy and initiative			6
Aggression and assertiveness	2		
Diplomacy and Tact		4	
Flexibility and adaptability to change		3	
Determination			6
Manipulation of people		3	
Getting things done through the group			6
Impressing superiors			5
Selling self and ideas	2		
Confidence level and poise		3	

view. Therefore, no two people paint exactly the same picture. In a very real sense, each of us lives in our own world.

Recognizing the differences between the perceptual world and the real world is important in understanding organizational behaviour. The manager who is aware of this difference makes decisions with greater care and does not make complex and important decisions based on sketchy evidence.

Our behaviour is influenced by environmental as well as endogenous factors; in other words, we learn and retain what we have learnt. Thus, there is an interaction between maturational and experiential factors in determining our behaviour. The importance of the environment in determining behaviour lies in its significance for us. When stimuli are misinterpreted, they will influence our behaviour on the basis of this significance rather than of their 'true' nature.

So we can say that perception, or perceiving, refers to the process whereby sensory stimulation is translated into organized experiences. That experience, or percept, is the joint product of the stimulation and of the process itself. See Box OB2.3 for the distinction between sensing and perceiving. The controversial debate of whether perception is a learnt phenomenon or an innate one is beyond the scope of this book, but for a brief overview see Box OB2.4.

BOX OB2.3

Sensing and perceiving

Many philosophers and psychologists have accepted the fundamental distinction between sensing and perceiving (or between sensations and percepts). To demonstrate empirically that sensing and perceiving are indeed different, however, is quite another matter. It is often said, for example, that sensations are simple and percepts are complex. Clearly, any attempt to identify and categorize the factors in each grouping would be purely arbitrary and, therefore, cannot be subjected to empirical test.

Another commonly offered basis for distinction is the notion that perceiving is subject to the influence of learning while sensing is not. It might be said that the sensations generated by a particular stimulus will essentially be the same from one time to the next (barring fatigue or other temporary changes in sensitivity), while the resulting percepts may vary considerably, depending on what has been learned between one occasion and the next.

The above definitional criteria all relate to the properties of experience; that is, they are psychological. An alternative way of distinguishing between sensing and perceiving that has been widely accepted is physiological–anatomical rather than psychological. In this case, sensations are identified with neural events occurring immediately beyond the sense organ, whereas percepts are identified with activity further 'upstream' in the nervous system, at the level of the brain. This assignment of anatomical locations to sensory and perceptual processes seems consistent with psychological criteria. That is, the complexity and variability of percepts (both a product of learning) are attributed to the potential physiological modification inherent in the vastly complex neural circuitry of the brain.

BOX OB2.4

Perception: nature or nurture?

The organization apparent in percepts has been attributed by some to learning, as being built up through the arbitrary associations of elements that have repeatedly occurred together in a person's experience. Other theorists, particularly Gestaltists, stress the view that perceptual organization is physiologically inborn, being inherent in innate aspects of brain functioning rather than depending on a synthesizing process of learning to combine simpler elements into more complex, integrated wholes.

One way of resolving such theoretical disputes would be to deprive people from birth of all visual sensory experience, and hence of all opportunity for visual perceptual learning. Then, when normal sensory function was restored, they would need to be tested to determine what perceptual functions, if any, were intact.

Experiments have been carried out on people who have been blind from birth due to cataracts (clouded lenses in the eye). After removal of their cataracts, such newly sighted people were found to be normally sensitive to changes in intensity of illumination and to colour. Though they were able initially to tell when a figure was present, they could not at first discriminate one simple shape from another, nor could they remember the shape of a just-exposed object. This deficiency extended to such socially important stimuli as people's faces. Only after a long period of experience – several months – did such seemingly primitive visual performances as discriminating a square from a triangle come easily. Until then, they had to count the corners of the object to achieve accurate discrimination.

In other words, research suggests that certain factors in the perceptual process are innate while others are learned through experience.

The perceptual process

Perception is the process by which we select, organize and interpret environmental stimuli to provide meaningful experiences for us. Perception includes an awareness of world events, people, objects, situations and so on – and involves searching for, obtaining and processing information about that world.[9]

The key words in the definition of perception are *selection, organization* and *interpretation*. Figure 2.2 summarizes the basic elements in the perceptual process from the initial observation to the final response.

We experience our environment through an active process: we receive environmental stimuli through our senses (sight, hearing, smell, taste, touch); we selectively notice different aspects of our environment; we appraise what we see in terms of our past experiences; and we evaluate what we experience in terms of our own needs and values. Since our needs and past experience often differ markedly from those of others, it is not surprising to learn that our perceptions of the environment and each other do as well.

To make sense of our environment, we face two perceptual tasks:

1 selecting what to pay attention to and what to ignore;
2 interpreting those factors we intend to pay attention to, and making sense of them in the context of our own experience.

There are a number of stages which we go through in perceiving our environment.

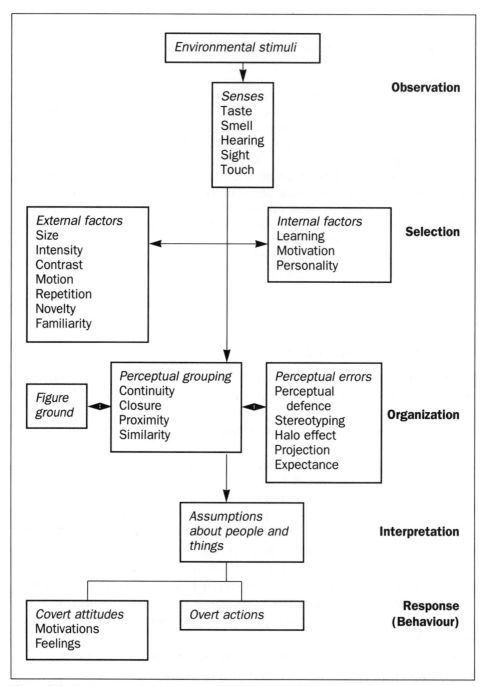

Figure 2.2 Basic elements in the perceptual process.

Selective noticing

Our environment provides many more stimuli than we are cognitively able to handle. Which aspects we notice depends partly on the nature of the stimuli themselves and partly on our previous experience.

Stimuli which are highly distinctive within the usual environmental context are more likely to be noticed than are stimuli which do not 'stick out' in some unusual way. Refer to Activity OB2.2; some feedback is given in Box OB2.5.

ACTIVITY OB2.2

PERCEPTION: EXTERNAL FACTORS AND SELECTIVE NOTICING

Activity code
- ✓ Self-development
- ☐ Teamwork
- ☐ Communications
- ☐ Numeracy/IT
- ✓ Decisions

External factors of perception are features or characteristics that influence whether the stimuli will be noticed. We have noted six characteristics.

Task
Outline your perception of these:

1 size
2 intensity
3 contrasts
4 motion
5 repetition
6 novelty and familiarity

BOX OB2.5

External factors affecting selective noticing

External factors of perception are characteristics that influence whether the stimuli will be noticed. Some examples of these external factors may be stated as *principles* of perception:

1 *Size* – the larger an external factor is, the more likely it is to be perceived.
2 *Intensity* – the more intense an external factor, the more likely it is to be perceived (bright lights, loud noises, etc.). In addition, even the language in a memo can

reflect the intensity principle. A memo that reads 'Please stop by my office at your convenience' will not fill you with the sense of urgency that you would get from a memo that reads 'Report to my office immediately!'.

3 *Contrast* – external factors that stand out against the background or that are not what people expect are the most likely to be perceived. In addition, the contrast of objects with others or with their background may influence how they are perceived.

4 *Motion* – a moving stimulus is more likely to be perceived than a stationary one.

5 *Repetition* – a repeated factor is more likely to be perceived than a single one. Marketing managers use this principle in trying to get the attention of prospective customers. An advertisement may repeat key ideas, and the advertisement itself may be repeated many times for greater effectiveness.

6 *Novelty and familiarity* – either a familiar or a novel factor in the environment can attract attention, depending on circumstances. For example, people in a busy London high street would quickly notice an elephant walking down the street, but you are most likely to perceive the face of a close friend among a room full of strangers.

A combination of these or other similar factors may be operating at any time to affect perception. They, in combination with certain internal factors of the person doing the perceiving, determine whether any particular stimulus is more or less likely to be noticed.

Thereafter, we should consider prior learning, personality and motivation as important facets of determining what we notice. Refer to Activity OB2.3, and *then* to the feedback given in Box OB2.6.

ACTIVITY OB2.3

PERCEPTION: INTERNAL FACTORS AND SELECTIVE NOTICING

Activity code
- ✓ Self-development
- ☐ Teamwork
- ☐ Communications
- ☐ Numeracy/IT
- ✓ Decisions

Perceptual selection is inherent within the perceiver. We have identified three characteristics.

Task
Outline your perception of these three:

1 personality   2 learning   3 motivation

BOX OB2.6

Internal factors affecting selective noticing

Internal factors of perception are aspects of the perceiver that influence perceptual selection. Some of the more important internal factors include personality, learning and motivation.

The internal factors of perception, particularly learning, are important in developing perceptual sets. A perceptual set is an expectation of a perception based on past experience with the same or similar stimuli. The powerful role that personality, learning and motivation play in perception manifests itself in many ways.

Personality

This has an interesting relationship to perception. Personality is shaped, in part, by perceptions; in turn, personality affects what and how we perceive. Personality appears to affect strongly how an individual perceives other people – the process of 'person perception', which we will discuss shortly.

Learning

Perception is strongly influenced by past experiences and what was learned from those experiences. For example, an estate agent, an architect and a manager are all walking towards a tall office block. These three individuals may notice distinctly different things about the building. The estate agent may first perceive the general condition of the building and the surrounding area, factors that would influence the building's price and saleability. The architect may first notice the architectural style and the construction materials used in the building. The manager may be more concerned with the functionality of the building. Each employee pays attention to different aspects of the same general stimulus because of their background and training.

Motivation

This also plays an important role in determining what a person perceives. A person's most urgent needs and desires at any particular time can influence what he or she perceives. For example, an employee whose firm has just announced the pending lay-off of five thousand workers is more sensitive to job advertisements than an employee at another firm whose job is not threatened.

In general, people perceive things that promise to help satisfy their needs and that they have found rewarding in the past.

Organizing what is noticed

We then organize the stimuli selected into meaningful and recognizable patterns. It is still not precisely clear how we do this, but certain principles in perceptual organization, such as figure–ground and perceptual grouping, have been established as important. See Box OB2.7 for a brief outline of these two principles.

BOX OB2.7

Principles of perceptual organization

The *figure–ground principle* refers to the ability to distinguish 'figure' (dominant features) from 'ground' (surrounding or competing stimuli). We tend to perceive the factor that we are most attentive to as standing out in a background. For example, in a noisy cafeteria, we are able to hold a meaningful conversation with a colleague because we are able to distinguish the sound and sight of that person (figure) from the sight and sound of other people (ground). Although the entire scene is perceived, we only respond to the most relevant ones to us. If we responded to all, nothing meaningful would result.

Perceptual grouping is the tendency to form individual stimuli into a meaningful pattern by such means as continuity, closure, proximity or similarity:

■ *Continuity* is the tendency to perceive objects as continuous patterns. It is often a useful organizing principle, but it may also have negative aspects. For example, the tendency to perceive continuous patterns may result in an inability to perceive uniqueness and detect change.

■ *Closure* is the tendency to complete an object so that it is perceived as a constant, overall form. It is the ability to perceive a whole object, even though only part of the object is evident.

■ *Proximity:* a group of objects may be perceived as related because of their nearness to each other. Often employees working together in a department are perceived as a team or unit because of their physical proximity.

■ *Similarity:* the more alike objects are, the greater the tendency to perceive them as a common group.

These principles and, in general, the ways individuals organize their perceptions to make sense of the world are not something that managers and organizations can safely ignore.

Interpreting what is organized

Even if a stimulus is noticed there is no guarantee that it will be perceived accurately. The meaning we attach to any given stimulus is very much dependent on our needs, values and expectations: we often distort stimuli to match our needs and values.

Responding to perceptions

There are many events which take place within the environment which we simply take note of and store away for future reference. There are stimuli, however, which need additional 'processing' after perception. These stimuli are the ones which require an action or behaviour to follow. When we perceive a stimulus that requires us to do something, then we assess how acceptable that message is to us. In other words, we weigh up the advantages and disadvantages of adopting such behaviour. Based on this assessment, we either act on the request, reject it, or modify or redefine it until it becomes acceptable.

Perception of others

Of particular interest in organizational behaviour is person or social perception. Person perception refers to the act of attributing characteristics or traits to other people. It follows the same principles as object perception – that is, *observation, selection, organization, interpretation* and *response* – but the element being perceived in the environment is another human being. The factors influencing person perception are, in a general sense, the same as those that influence perceptual selection; that is, both external and internal factors affect person perception. However, it is particularly useful to categorize factors that influence how a person perceives another as:

- characteristics of the person perceived;
- characteristics of the perceiver;
- characteristics of the situation or context within which the perception takes place.

Characteristics of the person perceived

You meet people for the first time and within a few minutes of talking to them you have made judgements about them. Our first impressions are based on scanty information. It is said that the first information we receive has the greatest impact on our overall impressions – this is referred to as the *'primacy effect'*.

What actually causes the primacy effect is still a matter of some controversy, but the hypothesis is that we pay more attention to initial information received when we are first trying to form some judgement about a person; after having formed an initial impression, we pay less attention to subsequent information.[10] There is evidence also that when subsequent information contradicts earlier information, people tend to regard the first impression as representing the 'true' person. Therefore, we can say, that the primacy effect is important in situations like job interviews. However, *'recency effects'* play a more important role in lasting relationships, where subsequent information helps us correct any ill-informed impressions we may have made.

Interpersonal perception is influenced by a number of factors, such as:

- *physical appearance* – for example those dressed in business suits are generally thought to be professionals while those in work clothes are thought to be lower-level employees;

- *verbal communication* – the way we use language provides clues about our culture and education;

- *overt expressive behaviour* – for example, facial expressions (people who smile constantly are often thought to have positive attitudes) and body language, which expresses inner feelings subconsciously through physical actions (looking someone straight in the eye as opposed to looking at the floor);

- ascribed attitudes such as *status* – people attribute different motives to those they believe to be high or low in status, even though they may behave in the same way; for example, high-status people are seen as having more control over their behaviour and to be more self-confident and competent than low-status people;

- *occupations* – for example, describing people as salespeople or as accountants conjures up different images.

In perceiving someone else, we process a variety of cues: facial expressions, general appearance, skin colour, posture, age, gender, voice quality, personality traits, behaviours, and so on. At best, the way that people group characteristics and traits helps them to organize their perceptions to understand their world better.

Characteristics of the perceiver
How we perceive another person is, to some extent, determined by our own personality and attitudes. For example, accurate perception of a person from a completely different culture to ours can be difficult. This is often due to the fact that we perceive others on the basis of our own cultural experiences, attitudes and values.

Characteristics of the situation
There are a number of characteristics relating to the situation or setting which influence how one person perceives another. One is the *social context*: a friendly, co-operative environment tends to create more trust.[11] Another is the *organizational role*: a study of executives from the accounting, sales and production departments were each asked to identify a major problem that a new company director might face. The findings were that the executives were influenced by the departments in which they work; in other words, the sales executives answered from a sales perspective, the accounting executives from an accounting perspective, and so on.[12]

Perceptual errors

The perceptual process can result in errors in judgement and understanding in a number of ways. We will explore in a little more detail the accuracy of judgement in person perception. In addition, we will discuss five of the most common types of perceptual errors: perceptual defence, stereotyping, the halo effect, projection, and expectancy effects.

How accurate are we in our perceptions of others? This is an important question in organizational behaviour. For example, inaccurate judgements of a prospective employee at an interview could result in the appointment of an inappropriate person. The more common interview errors include:

- *Similarity error.* Interviewers are positively drawn toward applicants who are similar to them (for example, in background, interests or hobbies) and negatively biased against those who are not.
- *Contrast error.* There is a tendency to compare applicants rather than applying objective criteria.
- *Overweighting of negative information.* Interviewers may overreact to negative information as though looking for an excuse to disqualify an applicant.
- *First impression error.* The primacy effect discussed earlier may affect the employment decision. It is said that the first four minutes of an interview are the most important.

Accuracy is a vital issue in understanding behaviour, and we can learn to make more accurate judgements in person perception by simply being aware of the potential biases that are involved in the perceptual process:

- *Perceptual defence* is the tendency for people to protect themselves against ideas, objects or situations that are threatening.
- *Stereotyping* is the tendency to assign attributes to someone solely on the basis of a category in which that person has been placed. Most of us have learned that stereotypes can be misleading. They often have no basis in fact, and sometimes they are formed to rationalize our prejudices, but the process of stereotyping has a purpose. It is a necessary one. It is simply not possible to deal with every person as if he or she were unique or as if we knew nothing about him or her until all the data has been accumulated.
- *The halo effect* is the process by which the perceiver evaluates all dimensions of another person based solely on one impression, either favourable or unfavourable. A 'halo' blinds the perceiver to other attributes that should be evaluated in attaining a complete, accurate impression of the other person. A manager may single out one trait and use it as the basis for all other performance measures. For example, an excellent attendance record may produce judgements of high productivity, quality work and industriousness – whether they are accurate or not.
- *Projection* is the tendency for people to see their own traits in other people. That is, they project their own feelings, tendencies or motives into their judgement of

others. This may be especially true for undesirable traits that perceivers possess but fail to recognize in themselves.

■ *Expectancy effects* in the perceptual process are the extent to which prior expectations bias the way that events, objects and people are actually perceived.

Fortunately, through training and experience, we can learn to judge or perceive others with greater accuracy.

Attitudes represent another type of individual difference that affects behaviour in organizations. An individual's attitudes are a result of a person's background and life experiences. As with personality development, significant people (parents, friends, group members) strongly influence attitude formation.

Before we move on to attitudes, tackle Activity OB2.4.

ACTIVITY OB2.4

PERCEPTION

Activity code
✓ Self-development
☐ Teamwork
☐ Communications
☐ Numeracy/IT
✓ Decisions

This activity consolidates your understanding of people perception.

Task
In a work or leisure context, define the concept and give examples of each of the following. Do not consult the text at this stage.

Concept	Definition	Example
Primacy effect		
Recency effect		
Perceptual defence		
Similarity error		
Stereotyping		
Halo effect		
Projection		
Expectancy effects		

Attitudes

Attitudes and the individual

The study of attitudes can be said to cover the full range of human behaviour and experience. We develop attitudes towards whatever we experience: people, religion, politics, etc. Therefore, we can say that attitudes are 'relatively lasting feelings, beliefs and behaviour tendencies directed towards specific persons, groups, ideas, issues or objects'.[13] They are means of classifying objects or events and of reacting to them with some degree of consistency. While attitudes logically are hypothetical constructs (that is, they are inferred but not objectively observable), they are manifested in conscious experience, verbal reports, behaviour and physiological symptoms.

Some insight is offered by social psychologists, who often describe an attitude in terms of three components:

1 an *affective* component, or the feelings, sentiments, moods and emotions about some person, idea, event or object;

2 a *cognitive* component, or the beliefs, opinions, knowledge or information held by the individual;

3 a *behavioural* component, or the intention and predisposition to act.

Thus the informational content of any attitude is cognitive. For example, in our attitude towards an ethnic group, the cognitive aspect embraces the stereotyped beliefs (valid or misinformed) we may hold about the group's ability, appearance, etc. Our feelings of like or dislike about the group represents the affective aspect of the attitude, which most epitomizes the evaluative nature of attitudes. Our tendency to exhibit overt behaviour toward the group is behavioural.

As a rule, favourable attitudes are characterized by positive directions for all three attributes; unfavourable attitudes tend to involve the reverse. These components of an attitude do not exist or function separately. An attitude is based on the interrelationship of a person's feelings, cognitions and behavioural tendencies with regard to something – another person or group, an event, an idea and so on.

Functions of attitudes

Attitudes have instrumental, noetic and expressive functions. Each of these contributes to the wellbeing of an individual:

■ *Instrumental function* – attitudes as means to other ends. In seeking social acceptance an individual may show a hostile attitude toward some minority group held in low esteem by neighbours, or may take up golf to enter a desired social group. Attitudes thus function as facilitators for achieving goals, retrospectively on the basis of past pleasant experiences or in prospective anticipation of future reward. To the extent that our attitudes serve as a means to an end, the instrumental function intensifies from its perceived effectiveness in goal attainment.

■ *Noetic function* – attitudes as a way of thinking and understanding. Attitudes have the same cognitive role in everyday life as theories have in our broader philosophical or scientific understanding. Our experiences are so diverse and the range of available responses is so extensive that the simplifications inherent in attitudes are urgent if we are to avoid chaos. If we did not systematically associate classes of objects and events with consistent sets of responses, life would be an uninterrupted sequence of strange new problems. Despite potential errors, generalizations such as those embodied in attitudes permit the only feasible approach to rational activity.

■ *Expressive functions* – attitudes as a means for emotional release. The expressive aspect of attitudes is held to relieve psychological pressure as if it were some sort of safety valve. Attitudes are useful tension reducers in their own right. The gratification of tension release through expressive attitudes is epitomized in such phrases as 'it's really nice to be in love' or 'the person you love to hate'. In their expressive function, attitudes provide a number of alternatives to overt action. It is held that, if we can release hostile tensions through relatively safe attitudinal activity (i.e. fantasy or daydreaming), we do not have to act them out with aggressive behaviour. Thus attitudes can be said to be substitutes for action.

Attitudes and behaviour

We often think of attitudes as a simple concept, clearly related to individual behaviour. In reality, attitudes and their effects on behaviour can be extremely complex.

To what extent do attitudes predict or cause behaviour? For many years, it was thought that our behaviour was consistent with our attitudes. While there is little doubt that some attitudes are related to behaviour, it is now widely accepted that a simple, direct link between attitudes and behaviour does not exist. A model of the attitude–behaviour relationship has been developed by Ajzen and Fishbein.[14] In their behavioural intentions model, they suggest that behaviour is more predictable (and understandable) if we focus on a person's specific intentions to behave in a certain way rather than solely on their attitudes towards that behaviour. Intentions depend on both attitudes and norms regarding the behaviour. Norms are rules of behaviour, or proper ways of acting, which have been accepted as appropriate by members of a group or society. Norms thus represent 'social pressures' to perform or not to perform the behaviour in question.

Box OB2.8 outlines the principal approaches to changing attitudes with a view to changing behaviour. After reading this, attempt Activity OB2.5.

BOX OB2.8

Attitudes

An attitude can be seen as 'an enduring system of positive or negative evaluations, feelings and tendencies towards action'.[1] It has a thinking or *cognitive element* which can manifest itself in a *belief system*. An *emotional* element may reinforce the cognitive aspect, and an *action or behaviour* may follow from the cognitive-emotional aspects.

The formation and the change of attitudes are both popular fields of study for organizational behaviour (OB) people. Attitudinal change and structuring are often seen as key determinants in influencing people's behaviour.

The ethics of trying to manipulate people's attitudes apart, the OB theorists tend to fall into two camps over this changing of attitudes. The first sees an almost linear progression: change the beliefs and/or emotions and the resultant behaviour is altered. The second approach concerns the concept of *cognitive dissonance* and is advocated by Festinger.[2] His view is that a change in beliefs follows on from the change in behaviour. His theory of cognitive dissonance underpins this approach. According to this, and basically, if we voluntarily act in a way that is different from what we believe, cognitive dissonance will occur. Doubts, anxieties and self-questioning may follow, and we attempt to get rid of these or at least to reduce them. One way to do this is for our beliefs to alter so that they come in line with our actions. This could well be at the level of the unconscious, and so it is difficult for us to be aware of any fundamental shift.

To Festinger the key to attitude change is free will. If compliance or force of any kind comes from others this cognitive dissonance will not occur. Perhaps when there is no obvious or clear-cut rationale behind our behaviour, cognitive dissonance will occur.

Yet we can take Festinger's views further. If the belief system is rigid, with some ideological slant, perhaps a shortfall between this belief and everyday events will lead to such dissonance or anxiety that the action itself may change rather than the belief system. For example, if you are a radical person of the left and you hold a position in say, operations management dealing with making people redundant, the belief and action may not tally. The action could be justified or rationalized as saving the work of the majority, and the belief system thus modified to be in line with the action. However, the actions may not be acceptable to the belief system (unchanging over a matter or principle), in which case the action must stop (new job, transfer, not doing it thoroughly, etc.)

The dynamic between thought, belief, emotion and action may be less clear than we think.

Sources:
1 Krech et al., *Elements of Psychology*
2 Festinger, *Theory of Cognitive Dissonance*

ACTIVITY OB2.5

ATTITUDE CHANGE

Activity code
- ✓ Self-development
- ✓ Teamwork
- ☐ Communications
- ☐ Numeracy/IT
- ✓ Decisions

Task

Below are two scenarios. Give a view on the possibility of attitude change in each.

1 Phil Smith, the newly appointed line manager, had interviewed the two most suitable 'internal' candidates according to the pre-selection criteria. He was very pleased with both candidates. Both were highly qualified, had the right mix of experience and came over as pleasant people with whom he could work well. The problem was that there was only one job. He had to select one. Smith picked Tom Ewing after his boss had said to him that the selection was purely down to him.

   Will his attitude towards the rejected candidate, Mary Blackhorse, now alter? What do you expect his attitude to be towards Ewing?

2 'The number of female senior academics in this teaching hospital is very low indeed' said Ms Oram, the administrator.

   Professor Bill Johnson agreed: 'It's not so much that they are not qualified for the posts, but discrimination by men is rampant out there.' Ms Oram said, 'We need to tackle this now. Attitudes can change and will change and the behaviour of these men must alter. How do we do it, Bill?'

   'To be honest, I don't know', said Bill. 'We've tried training, awareness sessions and women-only developmental teams. We need to hit them over the head with legislation. We could call them into a seminar on equal rights, and use the law as the final arbiter if they don't change after the seminar.'

   Is an attitude change in the men possible in this situation? If so, how?

In organizational behaviour, perhaps the attitudes that are of greatest interest are the general attitudes toward work: motivation and job satisfaction.

Motivation

All too often, managers place the blame for organizational problems firmly on lack of motivation on the part of their employees (see Box OB2.9). Researchers studying organizational behaviour also recognize the importance of motivation as a determinant of effective performance and

---

BOX OB2.9

Motivation

Too many of my players have no instinct or love for this club. They don't see playing for Liverpool as the pinnacle of their careers. They are only interested in getting another move or another lump of money, and that is totally unacceptable.

A successful football career used to be about winning things, but today it is about how much money you end up with. You can have players with all the ability in the world but, when they go out not wanting to run around and fight for the ball as much as other teams, then you are going to lose.

Graham Souness, former manager of Liverpool FC,
Guardian, 15 January 1993

---

have invested a lot of effort in trying to understand and explain the causes and consequence of motivation.

A great deal of research has been aimed at trying to develop answers to motivational questions. We begin by trying to define the term motivation and then turn our attention to the various attempts at understanding it.

Defining motivation

Although it is generally accepted that motivation is a critical factor in determining behaviour within organizations, there is less agreement on what it actually means and how it should be defined.

There is thus no single, widely accepted definition of the concept, but there are a number of common themes which pervade most attempts. In general, motivation has to do with three broad areas with respect to an individual's behaviour:

1 direction – what someone is trying to do;

2 effort – how hard someone is trying;

3 persistence – how long someone continues trying.

Human behaviour is complex and often individuals do not know the true reason for their behaviour. Because of this complexity, individuals are in many instances unpredictable.

Different forms of behaviour are sometimes similarly motivated; for example, one may try to acquire prestige through clothing, through one's job, by getting married, by staying single, etc. The converse is also true: different motives may result in one form of behaviour.

The importance of motivation

Motivation is vital in any job if people are to give their best to it. Assuming that employees are given the opportunity for good performance and have the necessary skills, effectiveness depends on their motivation.

Motivation represents the forces acting on or within a person to behave in a specific, goal-directed manner. The specific work motives of employees affect their performance at work. One job of management is to channel employee motivation effectively towards achieving organizational goals.

There may not be much agreement about what motivates workers, but there is agreement that the organizational and work settings must allow three activities to occur:

1 People must be attracted not only to join the organization but also to remain in it.

2 People must perform the task for which they were employed.

3 People must go beyond routine performance and become creative and innovative in their work.

Thus, for an organization to be effective, it must tackle the motivational problems involved in stimulating people's desires to be members of the organization and to be productive workers.

How do managers know when an employee is motivated or not?

Signs of motivation

The attitudes and behaviour of employees very often reflect motivation or lack of it. Examples of the signs of motivation are:

■ high performance and results being consistently achieved;

■ the energy, enthusiasm and determination to succeed;

■ co-operation in overcoming problems;

■ the willingness of individuals to accept responsibility;

■ willingness to accommodate necessary change.

Conversely, employees who are demotivated or who lack motivation often display:

■ apathy and indifference to the job;

■ a poor record of time keeping and high absenteeism;

■ an exaggeration of the effect of or difficulties encountered in problems, disputes and grievances;

■ a lack of co-operation in dealing with problems or difficulties;

■ unjustified resistance to change.

Managers generally complain about employees' lack of motivation. However, managers have some responsibility for such an attitude.

Repetitive, monotonous and uninteresting jobs can be made more acceptable if managers understand the motivational process.

Basic considerations in motivation

A basic motivational principle states that people's performance is based on their level of ability and motivation. According to this, no task can be performed successfully unless the person who is to carry it out has the ability to do so. Ability relates to the person's talent for performing goal-related tasks. Regardless of how talented an individual is, however, his or her abilities alone are not sufficient to attain a high level of performance. The person must also desire to achieve that performance level. When managers discuss motivation, they are concerned with

■ what drives behaviour;
■ what direction behaviour takes;
■ how to maintain it.

The motivational process begins with identifying a person's needs. Needs are deficiencies that a person experiences at a particular time. These deficiencies may be psychological (such as the need for recognition), physiological (such as the need for water, air or food) or social (such as the need for friendship). Needs act as energizers that make a person more susceptible to motivational efforts, because needs create tensions which the individual wishes to reduce.

Motivation is goal-directed. A goal is a specific result the individual wants to achieve.[15] An employee's goals may be viewed as forces that attract the individual; moreover, accomplishing desirable goals can significantly reduce need deficiencies. Some employees have a strong desire for advancement – an expectation, for instance, that working long hours will lead to a promotion. Such needs, desires and expectations create tensions within these employees, making them uncomfortable. Believing that some specific behaviours can overcome this feeling, these employees act. They direct their behaviours toward the goal of reducing this state of tension. Initiation of behaviour sets up cues that feed information back to them on the impact of their behaviour. For example, employees who seek to advance may try to work on major problems facing their organization in hopes of gaining more visibility with senior managers, as well as influence in attaining the organization's goals. If they receive promotions and raises, the company is sending signals (feedback) to them that their need for advancement and their behaviours are appropriate. Once the employees receive either rewards or punishments, they reassess their needs.

The general model of the motivational process is simple and straightforward. In the real world, however, the process is not so clear cut. The first complication is that motivators can only be inferred; they cannot be seen. The second centres on the dynamic nature of needs. At any one time, everyone has many needs, desires and expectations. Not only do these factors change, but they may also conflict with each other. Employees who put in extra hours at work to fulfil their needs for accomplishment may find that these extra hours conflict directly with needs for affiliation and their desire to be with their families.

A third complication is the considerable differences in the way people select certain motives over others and in the energy with which people pursue these motives.

Approaches to motivation

There is no shortage of motivation theories and managerial tactics that attempt to motivate employees.[16] However, they can be categorized into *content theories* and *process theories*.

Content theories of motivation

The content theories of motivation attempt to explain the factors that energize and direct behaviour; that is, the things that motivate people. Four important content theorists are:

1 Maslow – hierarchy of needs theory[17]
2 Alderfer – ERG theory[18]
3 McClelland – achievement motivation theory[19]
4 Herzberg – two-factor theory[20]

See Box OB2.10 for a brief outline of the content theories.

BOX OB2.10

Content theories of motivation

Maslow's hierarchy of needs
Maslow developed a general theory of human motivation which has been applied to the work setting by others. It is probably the best-known theory of motivation in this context. He proposed five classes of human needs which are hierarchically ordered:

1 *physiological* – the need for food, drink, warmth etc.: survival factors;
2 *safety* – the need for physical and psychological safety; in other words, a predictable and non-threatening environment;
3 *social* – the need to feel a sense of attachment to another person or group;
4 *self-esteem* – the need to feel valued and respected by the self and significant other people;
5 *self-actualization* – the need to fulfil one's potential, develop one's capacities and express them.

Maslow's theory assumes that individual needs affect behaviour in accordance with two principles:

1 The *deficit principle:* a satisfied need is not a motivator of behaviour. People act to satisfy 'deprived' needs; that is to say, the needs for which a satisfaction 'deficit' exists.

2 The *progression principle:* the five need categories exist in a strictly ordered hierarchy of prepotency (the power to come before) from the most basic (physiological) to the highest (self-actualization). A need from any one level only becomes activated once the next lower need has been satisfied.

Review of research evidence and criticism identified a number of serious flaws in this theory.[1]

Alderfer's ERG theory

Alderfer modified Maslow's theory of motivation and proposed a model reducing the need categories to three:

1 *existence* or basic survival needs;

2 *relatedness,* involving social interaction and respect or recognition from others;

3 *growth,* involving self-fulfilment, autonomy and success.

This has been better received than Maslow's theory,[2] but it is argued that, like Maslow's, its vagueness makes it difficult to verify.[3]

McClelland's need achievement theory

McClelland identified three basic needs that people develop and acquire from their culture:

1 need for *achievement* (N.Ach);

2 need for *affiliation* (N.Aff);

3 need for *power* (N.Pow);

The theory proposes that each of us will be, at different times, influenced by N.Ach, N.Aff or N.Pow, and that the strength of that need will vary with the situation. Each of us is likely to have developed a dominant bias towards one of these needs, on the basis of socialization and past experiences. People high in N.Ach are said to seek situations where they have personal responsibility for solving problems, where it is easy to tell how well you are doing, and where the goals are moderately challenging. There is evidence to suggest that this need is associated with relative success in entrepreneurial activities.[4] However, later work suggested that high N.Ach is rarely associated with good general management, especially in large organizations – people like this are primarily interested in their own achievement.[5] In the same study, it was found that successful managers (in the USA) had high N.Pow and low N.Aff.

Herzberg's two-factor theory

In the original study,[6] 200 US engineers and accountants were asked to describe times when they felt either particularly satisfied or particularly dissatisfied with their jobs. Analysis of these accounts revealed a pattern suggesting that different sets of factors were involved in being satisfied and being dissatisfied. In short, it was concluded that:

- There are two types of factor: *motivators or satisfiers,* which, when present, result in motivation or satisfaction with the job; and *hygiene factors or dissatisfiers,* which are a source of dissatisfaction.
- The motivators are: achievement, recognition, the work itself, responsibility, advancement and personal growth. These are all intrinsic to the job.
- The hygiene factors are: company policy and administration, supervision, interpersonal relations, money, status and security. These are all extrinsic to the job.
- Motivators have little or no impact on dissatisfaction; hygiene factors have little or no effect on feeling motivated or satisfied. Two separate factors are argued to influence motivation to work and satisfaction with it.

The theory has been particularly strongly criticized because of the research methods used (critical incident technique),[7] the restricted sample,[8] and the fact that other research has failed to support it.[9]

However, the model has remained popular among practising managers, essentially because it is clear and seems to provide practical solutions to problems of motivation and dissatisfaction.

Sources:

1   Wahba and Bridwell, 'Maslow reconsidered'; Salancik and Pfeffer, 'Examination of need satisfaction models of job attitudes'; Rauschenberger et al., 'Test of need hierarchy concept'
2   See for example Wanous and Zwany, 'Cross-sectional test of the need hierarchy theory'; Rauschenberger et al., 'Test of need hierarchy concept'
3   Staw et al., 'Dispositional approach to job attitudes'
4   McClelland and Winter, *Motivating Economic Achievement*
5   McClelland and Boyatzis, 'Need for close relationships and the manager's job'
6   Herzberg et al., *The Motivation to Work*
7   Kanfer, 'Motivation theory in industrial and organizational psychology'
8   Dunnette et al., 'Factors contributing to job dissatisfaction'
9   House and Wigdor, 'Herzberg's dual-factor theory of motivation and job satisfaction'

What do these content theories have in common?

They all emphasize the basic motivational concepts of needs, achievement motivation, and hygiene motivators. Maslow's hierarchy of needs serves as the basis for the ERG theory. Therefore, there are some important similarities between the two: self-actualization and esteem needs make up growth needs; social needs are similar to relatedness needs; and safety and physiological needs are the building blocks of existence needs in ERG theory. A major difference between these two theories, however, is that Maslow's offers a static needs hierarchy whose pinnacle is fulfilment, whereas the ERG theory presents a flexible, three-needs system.

Herzberg's two-factor theory draws on both of the needs theories. That is, if hygiene factors are present, relatedness and existence needs (ERG theory) are not likely to be frustrated. Motivator factors focus on the job itself and the opportunity for people to satisfy their own higher-order or growth needs (ERG theory). Need achievement theory does not recognize lower-order needs: the need for affiliation can be satisfied if a person meets hygiene factors on the job; if the job itself is challenging and provides an opportunity for a person to make meaningful decisions, it is motivating. These conditions go a long way toward satisfying the need for achievement.

At the heart of the debate revolving around the needs and wants of employees is the choice between interesting work and good money. Box OB2.11 highlights the conflicting views of workers and managers.

BOX OB2.11

Interesting work v. good money

Which do workers want: interesting work or good wages?

The answer to this question is 'It depends who you ask.' Of 1,000 employees who were asked 'Why do you work?',[1] most answered 'interesting work'. If this is the answer, then all that is necessary is to make all work interesting. Then we will have happy, productive employees who come to work on time and do not resign.

Unfortunately, not all jobs can be made interesting. More importantly, what is interesting to one person may not be interesting to someone else. Also, not everyone wants an interesting, challenging job.[2]

If immediate supervisors or managers are able to recognize the differences between their employees, then perhaps they can make sure that everyone is in a job he or she finds interesting. However, when managers were asked what they thought their employees wanted from their jobs, the supervisors claimed that their workers' highest performance was not for interesting work but for good wages.

If we accept what managers believe as being true, then all we have to do is ensure that we pay good wages to all our employees. Good wages are probably easier to offer than interesting work, but employees say that salary alone does not rank extremely highly on their list of preferences.

So we are now faced with differing opinions: employees state they prefer interesting jobs while managers say their employees prefer good wages. Three surveys were carried out over a period of forty years to determine employee and management rankings of motivation items. Employees' rankings shifted from good money to more interesting work over the period. Why was this? One of the reasons is the change in the economic, social and political context in which employees worked – these conditions were very different in 1986 from those in 1946. By 1986 there had been forty years of relative prosperity and a rise in the standard of living. It is not surprising that what workers wanted from their job had changed.

On the other hand, managers' rankings remained remarkably static – that is, employees prefer good wages. Their collective perception of factors that motivate employees had not changed and, more importantly, a comparison of rankings shows that managers had an 'inaccurate' perception of what motivates employees.

Why this disparity? Possible answers are:

■ Perhaps managers believe that employees find 'money' socially undesirable as a reason for working, and are therefore paying lip service to more socially acceptable factors, such as 'interesting work'.

■ Managers choose rewards for which they are less responsible – for example, pay levels are normally determined by organizational policies and not by individual managers. So managers can 'pass the buck' when it comes to assigning blame for poor levels of employee motivation.

These explanations are largely untested, but a third possible reason is 'self-referencing', where managers offer rewards or behave towards workers in ways that would motivate themselves. McClelland[3] found that managers are usually high achievers who are interested in concrete measures (money reflects how well they have done). For managers, money is a quantifiable way of keeping score. Despite a vast amount of behavioural research into what motivates people, management self-referencing seems to be as much a problem today as it was forty years ago – a sad commentary on the implementation of research results in the workplace.

Sources:
1 Kovach, 'What motivates employees?'
2 Goldthorpe et al., *Affluent Worker*
3 McClelland, *Achieving Society*

The content theories provide managers with an understanding of the particular work-related factors that start the motivational process. These theories, however, promote little understanding of why people choose a particular behaviour to accomplish task-related goals. This aspect of choice is the major focus of process theories of motivation.

Process theories of motivation

Process theories attempt to describe and analyse how the personal factors (content theories) interact and influence each other to produce certain kinds of behaviour. Two important contributions are:

1 expectancy theory

2 equity theory

See Box OB2.12 for an outline of these two prominent process theories.

BOX OB2.12

Process theories of motivation

Expectancy theory

Expectancy theory was developed by Vroom[1] and extended by Porter and Lawler.[2] Its major components are:

- *Outcome* – a result of an action, such as better performance, or greater fatigue, resulting from putting more effort into a task; and/or results that such outcomes themselves may produce, such as better pay, promotion, stress. (These two forms of outcome are often referred to as first-level and second-level outcomes respectively.)
- *Valence* – the amount of satisfaction an individual anticipates receiving from a particular outcome; how attractive the outcome is. This could vary from 'highly attractive' (for example, increased pay) through 'indifferent' to 'highly unattractive' (for example, dismissal).
- *Instrumentality* – an individual's subjective belief that the likelihood (perceived probability) that second-level outcomes will follow from first-level outcomes (for example, belief about how likely increased pay or promotion are as the result of improved performance).
- *Expectancy* – the individual's subjective belief about the likelihood (perceived probability) that a particular action will be followed by particular outcomes (for example, belief about how likely it is that improved performance will actually result from increased effort).

Vroom's model is expressed in mathematical terms, but in essence argues that the force on a person to act in a particular way is a function of multiplying together valence, expectancy and instrumentality.

The implications of this for managers who want to ensure that their employees are motivated to perform are that managers need to ensure that employees:

- see themselves as possessing the necessary skills and abilities to do their job (expectancy);
- believe that if they perform their jobs well they will be rewarded (instrumentality);
- find the rewards offered for successful performance attractive (valence).

There are problems with such an approach.[3] Some studies suggest that people do not necessarily distinguish expectancy from instrumentality, that better prediction can be made by adding (as opposed to multiplying) valence and instrumentality or expectancy, that the theory works poorly where any of the outcomes has a negative valence (are viewed as undesirable),[4] etc.

This is a theory that concentrates on process, pays little attention to why people value or do not value particular outcomes, and invokes no concept of underlying need.

Equity theory

The central theme of equity theory is that people are motivated to get what they consider a fair return for their efforts, rather than to get as much as they can. It suggests that there is a need for equity (fairness) in one's relations with others, that inequity is painful, and that people are motivated to reduce it.

Adams,[5] a prominent theorist in this area, states that equity theory has three components:

1 *Inputs* – anything the individual regards as an investment in the work situation worthy of some return; for example, education, training, experience, effort, etc.
2 *Outcomes* – anything the individual regards as a return from the organization; for example, pay, fringe benefits, pleasant working conditions, etc.
3 *Comparison other* – some other person or group with whom individuals compare themselves in arriving at judgements concerning equity.

The theory proposes that individuals are influenced by the ratio of what they see as their outcomes to what they see as their inputs. Each input and outcome is weighted by its importance to the individual. This ratio is compared with what is perceived to exist for the comparison other. If the two are equivalent then the situation is said to be 'equitable', a pleasant state generating no changes in behaviour or attitudes. If the comparison other's ratio is higher, the situation is one of under-reward inequity, which is unpleasant, and the person is motivated to reduce it. The greater the inequity, the greater the distress and the more the person is motivated to reduce it.

The bulk of research in this area has been carried out through laboratory experiments as opposed to field experiments, so there is some difficulty in generalizing the findings to the real world. However, reviews of research[6] suggest that on the whole the predictions of the theory are well supported.

Equity theory is widely used by managers and compensation specialists to set pay scales for jobs.[7]

Sources:
1 Vroom, *Work and Motivation*
2 Porter and Lawler, *Managerial Attitudes and Performance*
3 Schwab et al., 'Between-subjects expectancy theory research'; Kanfer, 'Motivation theory in industrial and organizational psychology'
4 Leon, 'Role of positive and negative outcomes'
5 Adams, 'Inequity in social exchange'
6 Goodman and Friedman, 'Examination of Adams' theory of equity'; Vecchio, 'Individual-differences interpretation'; Miles et al., 'Equity sensitive construct'
7 Greenberg, 'Cognitive reevaluation of outcomes'

What do process theories have in common? The expectancy and equity theories emphasize different aspects of motivation. Expectancy theory assumes employees are rational and evaluate how much the reward means to them before they perform their jobs. How well employees perform their jobs will thus depend in part on what they believe is expected of them. Once their manager communicates these expectations, then employees assign probabilities that their efforts will lead to desired first-level outcomes (performance, quality of work, absenteeism, etc.) These outcomes are linked to valued rewards (for example, high pay or job security) that they desire from their jobs. It is the manager's job to make the desired rewards attainable to employees by clearly linking rewards and performance.

In contrast to expectancy theory, where employees make internal judgements of the value of rewards, equity theory assumes that what is equitable is determined by employees comparing themselves to similar others. According to equity theory, people are motivated to retreat from inequitable situations and are attracted to remain on the job and perform at high levels in equitable situations. Because equity theory deals with perceptions of fairness among employees, it is reasonable to expect that they react to inequitable situations in different ways.

Both theories emphasize the future role of rewards and an individual's decision-making processes. These theories suggest that managers concerned about improving employee performance should actively create proper work environments, match employees to jobs, and establish clear performance-reward systems. Motivation for high performance will not exist unless managers recognize such performance when it occurs and reward it.

Expectancy and equity theories emphasize different aspects of motivation. Equity theory suggest that people are motivated by comparing their own situation with that of others who are in the same or a similar situation, while expectancy theory is more internally orientated.

Over the years a growing number of behavioural scientists have carried out investigations into what motivates people. It would be wrong to ignore this accumulated knowledge, but equally wrong to pretend that each viewpoint holds the key to solving our problems of motivating people. The results and findings of some, however, do give an insight of practical significance which can be helpful to managers' understanding.

Why do people work?

Psychologists and management experts have sought the answer to this question for many years. If a company knows why some employees come to work on time, stay with the company and are productive and useful, then it might be able to ensure that all employees behave in such a way.

Whether for a professional or a manual worker, it is not exceptional in a full working life to expend around 100,000 hours of physical and mental effort. The fact that this effort is concentrated into a period in the human lifecycle when the individual is most physically and mentally able gives this figure even greater significance. Further, though the length of the standard working week has tended to decrease over time, the length of the standard working week, including overtime, had declined relatively little since the 1930s. So the importance of work in the lives of most individuals in our society is apparent.

A major error in industry has been the oversimplification of the concept of motivation. Too often, since Taylor's[21] time, it has been assumed that the primary reason that people work is to make money. People in industry are just as complex as people in any other phase of life, and any attempt to reduce their behaviour to a single system of motivation must result in artificiality and narrowness.

A classic study carried out in the USA on samples of both manual and white-collar workers concluded that, for most people, work is more than merely a means of providing an income:

> For most men, having a job serves other functions than the one of earning a living. In fact, even if they had enough money to support themselves, they would still want to work. Working gives them a feeling of being united into the larger society, of having something to do, of having a purpose in life.[22]

The researchers, Morse and Weiss, saw this conclusion as being consistent with the feelings of isolation and dislocation frequently experienced by the unemployed and also the retired, even when the latter have an adequate income. Studies of unemployment in Britain[23] have reinforced the claim that those unable to work can experience severe psychological deprivations, with detrimental effects for their personal relationships both within and outside the family.

Part of Morse and Weiss's research focused on the question, 'If by some chance you inherited enough money to live comfortably without working, do you think you would work anyway or not?' Eighty per cent of respondents claimed that they would continue working and two-thirds of those who gave positive reasons for their decisions did so for such factors as job interest, job satisfaction, maintaining self-respect, etc. The remaining one third gave negative reasons, such as 'I would otherwise feel bored and isolated', 'I would feel lost', 'I would not know what to do with my time', etc. Morse and Weisse claimed that one reason why such people may want to work is that, although they may not find their work intrinsically rewarding, they have few alternative ideas for making use of their energy.

The percentage of respondents who said they would opt to give up work increased quite markedly with age; perhaps this is not surprising, given that older workers may have already begun to adjust to the idea of a life outside the workplace. The kind of work held by respondents did not generally influence attitudes on wanting to continue working. The only exception to this was among unskilled workers, only about 50 per cent of whom said they would continue working.

When asking how satisfied they were with their current job, 80 per cent claimed to be either 'satisfied' or 'very satisfied'. However, this should not be taken as an indication that their jobs were intrinsically interesting and stimulating. Morse and Weiss in fact stated: 'This finding suggests that most individuals accommodate themselves to their chances and possibilities in life and in general do not maintain, as conscious aspirations, chances and opportunities not within their scope to realise.'

Another, but not unrelated, suggestion as to why workers occupying relatively unrewarding jobs tend to claim high or fairly high levels of job satisfaction has been commented upon by Goldthorpe et al.[24] They point out that numerous studies have revealed that workers, when asked how they like their jobs, tend to report favourably even in cases where they obviously experience severe deprivations in performing them. However, they argue it is difficult for a worker to admit that he or she dislikes his or her job without 'thereby threatening his [or her] self respect'. People's work tends to have an important influence on their image of themselves, and to say that they find their job unacceptable can be tantamount to saying they find themselves unacceptable.

Morse and Weiss found that many respondents who claimed fairly high levels of satisfaction said that, if they inherited enough money to live comfortably without working, they would continue to work but change their jobs. Hence it appeared that commitment to their current jobs was weaker than to their work in general. This was particularly true for manual worker respondents, only 34 per cent of whom said they would continue in their current line of work (this compares with 61 per cent of white-collar respondents). Many of those in manual occupations expressed an interest in self-employment, though they were often unsure often as to what sort of business this would be. The appeal of self-employment appeared to lie in the prestige and autonomy to be gained without the necessity for additional formal education and training.

In a final summary of the meaning of work for the people they studied, Morse and Weiss stated that:

> To the typical man in a middle-class occupation, working means having a purpose, gaining a sense of accomplishment, expressing himself. He feels that not working would leave him aimless and without opportunities to create. To the typical man in a working-class occupation working means having something to do. He feels that not working would leave him no adequate outlet for physical activity; he would just be sitting or lying around.

In the western world, work has long been considered a central life interest.[25] Indeed, Weber has claimed that the capitalist system itself rests on the moral and religious justification that the Reformation gave to work. However, Dubin's research indicates that the kind of commitment to work required to make it a central life interest is often absent among industrial workers, and that it is the family and non-work life which is more frequently the area of central life interest. Dubin found among the workers he studied that only 24 per cent identified work as their main areas of life interest; the remainder tended to see other areas of life interest – outside the workplace – as being more important to them. Further, only 9 per cent claimed the workplace as their most meaningful source of informal human associations. The rest attached more meaning and importance to the family and other non-work contacts as sources of preferred informal social relationships.

The majority of workers studied regarded work as mandatory, and some form of social interaction within the workplace was preferred. However, for the most part, these social contacts were not highly valued, and did not result in primary social relationships. Participation in the workplace was seen as being economically necessary but not important as a source of meaningful social experience. Nevertheless, in 63 per cent of cases, work was identified by respondents as their main focus of attachment in their organizational and technical environment. Dubin makes the interesting suggestion on the overall significance of work that:

> The characteristics of industrial work that are alleged to be disturbing of the individual (monotony, repetitiveness, mechanistic nature, and over specialisation) are the very features that make obvious to its participants the nature of symbiotic or technological interdependence. In short, industrial work may be functional for the society because it sharply etches for the individual some awareness of the division of labour and its resultant interdependence.

The ideas examined thus far, those of Morse and Weiss and of Dubin, indicate that the relationship between the individual and work is often of a rather complex nature. While the degree of attachment to work may be high in the sense that work-life is regarded as both necessary and important, commitment to work is often lower when work fails to measure up to the emotional significance of other areas of life.

In a wide-ranging survey on work orientations and satisfactions,[26] it has been shown that levels of job satisfaction are closely related to position in the industrial hierarchy. The most satisfied are professionals and senior managers and the least satisfied are manual workers, especially those employed in mass production.

We may assume that job satisfaction is positively correlated with the degree to which the individual makes work a central life interest. Blauner makes the point that the most senior occupational roles in industry confer on the individual high personal status. In such roles the individual has considerable autonomy and control over others, both of which make a positive contribution to the individual's identity, and are also clearly linked with the individual's central life interest. Confirmation of this point is provided by Parker,[27] who reports that individuals in senior occupational roles rarely make a sharp distinction between work and leisure.

The gradual reduction in the length of the standard working week has led many people to talk of the coming 'crisis of leisure'. However, perhaps such concern is premature: 'Faced with the choice of leisure time or more income, a good many British workers still choose more income from overtime, a second job, or do-it-yourself activities, which are hardly leisure.'[28] In a similar vein, Sillitoe has written: 'The striking point ... is how little the actual working week has shortened since the 1930s. What has happened is that although the "basic" or negotiated working week has come down considerably, people have preferred to work as long as before but at overtime rates.'[29]

ACTIVITY OB2.6

MANAGEMENT AND MOTIVATION

Activity code
☑ Self-development
☑ Teamwork
☐ Communications
☐ Numeracy/IT
☑ Decisions

Managerial motivational strategies must start with the needs of people. If these needs can be met, the chances are that the individual or group will be more motivated. The task here is to determine what managerial motivational policies can be related to these needs in order to maximize the contribution of the individual.

If we pull together the main elements of motivational theory there are certainly some common denominators. The needs of people can be grouped under:

■ Basic needs
■ People and relationship needs
■ Self-growth needs

Needs	Proposed motivational strategies
Basic needs – these will involve meeting physiological, safety and security aspects.	
People and relationship needs – companionship, affiliation to groups, power, status and perhaps competition may be involved.	
Self-growth needs – being competent and able to achieve a task through to self-fulfilment.	

Motivational skills can be developed, but it is necessary for the motivator to translate these into everyday leadership action, which will in turn bring about the required results and, ultimately, the accomplishment of the task. See Activity OB2.6.

A closely linked subject to motivation is job satisfaction.

Job Satisfaction

In recent years a great deal of attention has been devoted to the study of job satisfaction. Locke[30] refers to 3,350 publications in the ten years preceding his seminal work on the topic. There is general consensus in the literature on the definition of overall job satisfaction. Evans, for example, defines it as 'a general affective orientation to all aspects of the job',[31] and Kalleberg as 'an overall affective orientation on the part of the individual towards work roles which they are presently occupying'.[32] In the most general sense, job satisfaction is 'a pleasurable or positive emotional state resulting from the appraisal of one's job or job experiences'.[33] This positive assessment or feeling is said to occur when work is in harmony with the individual's needs and values. Job dissatisfaction is seen to occur when there is a discrepancy between the individual's values and the capacity of the job to satisfy the needs associated with those values.

Sources of job satisfaction

Job satisfaction is sometimes regarded as a single concept; that is, a person is either satisfied with their job or not. However, it is best considered as a collection of related job attitudes that can be divided into a variety of job aspects. For example, a popular measure of job satisfaction – the Job Descriptive Index – measures satisfaction in terms of five specific aspects of a person's job: pay, promotion, supervision, work itself, and co-workers.[34] An employee can obviously be satisfied with some aspects of the job and, at the same time, dissatisfied with others.

Sources of job satisfaction and job dissatisfaction vary from person to person. Sources thought to be important include: challenge of the job, degree of interest that the work holds, extent of physical activity, working conditions, rewards, and the nature of co-workers.

The effects of various work factors on job satisfaction are show in Box OB2.13. An implication of these work factors is that job satisfaction should perhaps be considered primarily as an outcome of an individual's work experience. Thus, high levels of dissatisfaction might indicate to managers that problems exist with physical working conditions, the organization's reward structure, role conflict or clarity, and so on. However, workers may bring with them to work negative (or positive) attitudes from their personal and/or social lives, and these may strongly colour their supposed job satisfaction.

BOX OB2.13

Effects of various work factors on job satisfaction

Work Factors	Effects
Work itself	
Challenge	Mentally challenging work that the individual can successfully accomplish is satisfying.
Physical demands	Tiring work is dissatisfying.
Personal interest	Personally interesting work is satisfying.
Reward structure	Rewards that are equitable and that provide accurate feedback for performance are satisfying.
Working conditions	
Physical	Satisfaction depends on the match between working conditions and physical needs.
Goal attainment	Working conditions that promote goal attainment are satisfying.
Self	High self-esteem is conducive to job satisfaction
Others in organization	Individuals will be satisfied with supervisors, co-workers or subordinates who help them attain rewards. Also, individuals will be more satisfied with colleagues who see things the same way they do.
Organization and Management	Individuals will be satisfied with organizations that have policies and procedures designed to help them attain rewards. Individuals will be dissatisfied with conflicting roles and/or ambiguous roles imposed by the organization.
Fringe benefits	Such benefits do not have a strong influence on job satisfaction for most workers.

Source: Adapted from Landy, *Psychology of Work Behaviour*

Job satisfaction and behaviour

Of particular interest to managers and organizations are the possible relationships between job satisfaction and various job behaviours and other work outcomes. For example, a commonly held view is that job satisfaction leads to better performance ('a satisfied worker is a more productive worker'). Yet numerous studies have shown that a simple link between job attitudes and job performance often does not exist.[35]

Although job satisfaction does not lead directly to good performance, employee job satisfaction is very important for organizations for a number of other reasons:

- It can be a diagnostic tool, identifying potential problem areas.
- There is a link between job satisfaction and absenteeism, turnover, physical and mental health.[36]

Vroom[37] reviewed the major research studies up to the mid-sixties and attempted to categorize them in terms of which job behaviours were correlated with job satisfaction. Specifically, he grouped them into studies of turnover, absenteeism, accidents and job performance.

- *Satisfaction and turnover:* The seven studies reviewed indicated a negative relationship: the higher workers' satisfaction the less likely they were to leave the job.
- *Satisfaction and absenteeism:* Of the ten studies reviewed, four tended to support the notion of a negative relationship between the amount of job satisfaction and the degree of work absenteeism. However three studies did not support this premise, and the remaining three indicated that the magnitude of an absenteeism–satisfaction correlation was a function of the type of absenteeism measure used and the gender of the worker.
- *Satisfaction and accidents:* Two studies were reviewed, one of which found a substantial negative relationship and the other none at all.
- *Satisfaction and job performance:* The available evidence seems to suggest that no such relationship exists. This was first brought dramatically into focus by Brayfield and Crockett,[38] who examined all available research relating job satisfaction to job performance and concluded that there was virtually no evidence of any relationship between these two variables. This, of course, is a finding critical of those who support the general human relations notion that a satisfied worker is a more productive worker. Vroom,[39] and Schwab and Cummings[40] updated the work of Brayfield and Crockett, and there seems little doubt that there is at best only a small relationship existing between these variables.

Therefore, the evidence suggests that the traditional human relations school of thought that a 'satisfied worker is a more productive worker' is not supported. However, job satisfaction does have important implications for other job-related behaviours, such as turnover, absenteeism and accidents, which in turn can have serious repercussions on the effectiveness of organizations.

Another serious concern for organizational effectiveness is the impact of stress on individual effectiveness. The costs of stress are high, estimated at as much as £30 million for an organization employing over 2000. Clearly, the diagnosis and reduction of stress can contribute significantly to increased individual and organizational effectiveness.

Work Stress

In the USA, Britain and many other European countries, about half the deaths each year, for both men and women, are due to cardiovascular diseases. The factors associated with a high risk of heart disease include cigarette smoking, high blood pressure, high cholesterol and blood sugar levels, and excess body weight. However, a number of studies have indicated that social and psychological factors may account for much of the risk,[41] and this has promoted research into factors in the work situation that may increase susceptibility to heart disease. Among the factors that have been shown to influence such susceptibility are dissatisfaction at work[42] and occupational stress.

In recent years, the term 'stress' has been used widely and with varying meanings. Stress involves an interaction of person and environment; something happens 'out there' which presents a person with a demand, a constraint or an opportunity for behaviour. From a definitional standpoint, the extent to which that demand is 'stressful' depends on several things; from an empirical standpoint, it depends on even more variables. For example, the demand must be perceived by the 'stressee'; it must be interpreted in relation to his or her ability to meet the demand, circumvent, remove or live with the constraint, or effectively use the opportunity; and the 'stressee' must perceive the potential consequences of successfully coping with (that is, altering) the demand (constraint, opportunity) as more desirable than the expected consequences of leaving the situation unaltered. So there is 'potential for stress when an environmental situation is perceived as presenting a demand which threatens to exceed the person's capabilities and resources for meeting it, under conditions where they expect a substantial differential in the rewards and costs from meeting the demand versus not meeting it'.[43]

Lazarus defined stress as referring 'to a broad class of problems differentiated from other problem areas because it deals with any demands which tax the system, whatever it is, a physiological system, a social system, or a psychological system, and the response of that system'.[44]

He goes on to argue that the 'reaction depends on how the person interprets or appraises (consciously or unconsciously) the significance of a harmful, threatening or challenging event'. In essence, therefore, stress is thought to occur from a misfit between the individual and his or her environment: an imbalance in the context of an organism–environment transaction.

Stress, in itself, is not abnormal – nobody lives wholly free from it. And indeed, stress may be a spur to doing something positive about a situation. For example, the executive who watches a younger manager climb up the promotion ladder may increase his or her own efficiency, or the student may study harder when faced with an exam.

It is clear that far from all individuals who are exposed to the same work conditions develop abnormalities of either a physical or a psychological character – most seem to manage reasonably well. It is only when stress is irrational, unproductive and persistent that it may be a symptom of psychological and physiological illness.

The causes of stress are many and, indeed, interactive, and there are a large number of environmental sources of work stress:

- characteristics of the job itself;
- role of the person in the organization;
- interpersonal relationships at work;
- career development pressures;
- climate and structure of the organization;
- problems associated with the interface between the organization and the outside world, etc.

See Box OB2.14 for potential 'cluster' sources of stress.

BOX OB2.14

Stressed out

Stress is seen as an adaption and adjustment to pressures, both from outside and from within the individual. Stress tends to be a very individual thing, but it has been suggested that it can occur in various 'clusters'.[1]

Cluster	Examples
Personal relationships	Relationships with colleagues, impersonal treatment, constant client complaints and poor communications.
Contractual	Shifts, anti-social hours, job insecurity and unfair promotion procedures.
Job	Conflicting roles, too much or too little work, lack of control, too much or too little supervision and machine-paced work.
Environmental	From overcrowding to noisy conditions, from temperature to smoking.

An in-depth example of an employer organization attempting to confront stress-related problems[2] is provided by a UK brewing company. A scheme to help employees (the Employee Assistance Programme) was launched with an initial expenditure of some £20 per employee (£500,000). In conjunction with an occupational counselling service, the firm set up a scheme called 'Person to Person'. Now a counsellor is available on a one-to-one basis round the clock. The scheme seems to have been well supported by management and staff.

Sources:
1   See Capel and Gurnsey, *Managing Stress*
2   See Counselling and welfarist discussion in A.H. Anderson, *Effective Personnel Management*

Stress can be caused by too much or too little work, time pressures and deadlines, too many decisions to take, fatigue from physical strains of the work environment, etc. The most-researched factors relating to the job itself are working conditions and work overload. See Box OB2.15.

BOX OB2.15

Sources of work stress

Sources of stress at work	Individual characteristics	Symptoms of ill-health	Type of ill-health
Work overload Pressure Role ambiguity Role conflict Thwarted ambition Lack of job security Poor working relationships Office politics, etc.	Anxiety Level of neuroticism	Blood pressure Cholesterol Job dissatisfaction Smoking Drinking, etc.	Heart disease Mental ill-health

Sources of stress outside the organization
Family
Financial difficulties, etc.

Source: Adapted from Cooper and Marshall, 'Occupational sources of stress'

Kornhauser[45] found that poor mental health was directly related to unpleasant working conditions, the necessity to work fast and expend a great deal of physical effort, and to excessive and inconvenient hours. French and Caplan[46] differentiated between quantitative (too much to do) and qualitative (too difficult) overload. (Quantitative overload is strongly linked to cigarette smoking, an important risk factor for heart disease. Those with more phone calls and meetings were found to smoke significantly more than those with fewer such engagements.) They suggest that both quantitative and qualitative overload may produce at least nine different symptoms of psychological and physical strain:

1 job dissatisfaction
2 job tension
3 lower self-esteem
4 feelings of being under threat
5 embarrassment
6 high cholesterol levels
7 increased heart rate
8 skin complaints
9 more smoking

The role an individual has in the organization is another major source of work stress. Most research in this area has concentrated on role conflict and role ambiguity. The former exists when the individual in a particular work role is torn by conflicting job demands or troubled by having to undertake tasks which he or she does not want to do. Kahn et al.[47] found that those who suffered from role conflict had lower job satisfaction and high levels of job-related tension. Role ambiguity, on the other hand, exists when an individual has inadequate information about his or her work role. Kahn et al. found that those who suffered from role ambiguity experienced lower job satisfaction, higher job-related tension, greater futility and lower self-confidence. These were also correlated with indicators of physiological strain, such as increased blood pressure and pulse rate.

Responsibility is another potential stressor and the evidence seems to suggest that there is a need to distinguish between responsibility for people and responsibility for 'things'. Wardwell et al.[48] found that heart disease was more likely to be associated with stresses derived from responsibility for people than for things (since it involves more interaction with others, etc). French and Caplan found that this was significantly related to heavy smoking, high blood pressure and high cholesterol levels.

The nature of an individual's relationships with his or her boss, subordinates and colleagues is a significant factor for individual and organizational health – good relationships are central.[49]

Other factors contributing to stress are career development pressures, (such as lack of job security, fear of redundancy, obsolescence or early retirement), status incongruity (over- or under-promotion), and frustration at having reached one's career ceiling. The organization's structure and climate can threaten an individual's freedom, autonomy and identity, which can all pose additional pressures. Extra-organizational sources of stress should not be ignored either: for example family problems,[50] life crises,[51] financial difficulties, conflict of personal beliefs with those of the organization, conflict of organization with family demands, etc.

Whom does stress affect?

Stress is frequently considered to be an occupational hazard of managers and executives, and some research supports this view. However, in one of the major studies in this area (a large-scale investigation of the incidence of coronary heart disease among managers and workers), it was not found to be the case.[52] In fact, the results showed that managers and executives experienced fewer coronary incidents than did foremen and workers. In addition, it was found that there was no relationship between career mobility and job success and the incidence of heart disease. The conclusion was that the findings provided no evidence that people who had high levels of responsibility or who had been promoted rapidly, frequently or recently, or who were transferred to new departments or to new companies, had any added risk of heart disease.

Furthermore, it was found that those who entered the organization with a college degree experienced fewer coronary incidents at all ages, in all geographical areas and in all departments than those who did not. Hinkle et al. interpreted these differences in coronary attack rate related to education level in terms of the probably better biological make-up of the highly educated group, which was thought to be related to, but not necessarily the result of, differences in the social and economic background from which they originated. (See Box OB2.16, which illustrates the relationship between biographical features, characteristics of work situation and stress.) From this study, it appears that managers and executives are somewhat less likely to experience heart attacks than are workers, although such findings should be treated with caution.

Managing stress

To be effective, organizational members must recognize when to increase and decrease stress. The key to managing stress constructively is first to recognize its energizing or destructive effects. Managers can encourage productive stress by helping employees to build challenge into their work and to assume responsibility and autonomy.

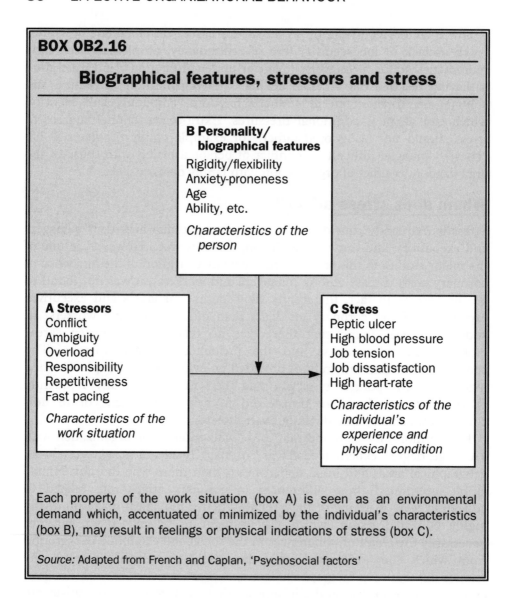

BOX OB2.16

Biographical features, stressors and stress

**B Personality/
    biographical features**

Rigidity/flexibility
Anxiety-proneness
Age
Ability, etc.

*Characteristics of the
    person*

A Stressors
Conflict
Ambiguity
Overload
Responsibility
Repetitiveness
Fast pacing

*Characteristics of the
    work situation*

C Stress
Peptic ulcer
High blood pressure
Job tension
Job dissatisfaction
High heart-rate

*Characteristics of the
    individual's
    experience and
    physical condition*

Each property of the work situation (box A) is seen as an environmental demand which, accentuated or minimized by the individual's characteristics (box B), may result in feelings or physical indications of stress (box C).

Source: Adapted from French and Caplan, 'Psychosocial factors'

Managers can also help individuals cope with dysfunctional stress by counselling the employee and directing them to an appropriate health or counselling service, but perhaps more importantly by changing or removing the stressors. Jobs can be redesigned to reduce role overload, role ambiguity and even boredom. See Activity OB2.7.

We have looked at a variety of individual differences, such as personality, perception and attitudes, as well as three organizationally specific individual differences: motivation, job satisfaction and stress. Let us now focus on interpersonal and group processes.

ACTIVITY OB2.7

PYRAMID PSYCHOLOGY

Activity code
☑ Self-development
☐ Teamwork
☐ Communications
☐ Numeracy/IT
☑ Decisions

The idea of a pyramid's meticulous craftmanship, of the physical and mental mobilization of resources needed to build the edifice, of its status as a monument to human achievement and as a thing of beauty, and of Maslow's vision of self-fulfilment at the apex of the pyramid or hierarchy of needs, were all behind the naming of the firm. It had been started eight years ago by two occupational psychologists, Kurt Stinger and Marie Anders. Both had qualified from a prestigious university and had practised abroad, Stinger in Frankfurt and Anders in California. The British view of occupational psychology seemed less 'developed'.

They had met up again at the annual dinner of their old university. Anders was writing and Stinger was in the process of being offered a senior lecturing position at a university in the north of England which had a strong presence in the field of occupational counselling and stress management. Anders shared many of these interests with Stinger. To cut a long story short, they had formed a partnership at a prestigious Cambridge address (Anders had carried out her doctorate there) and had prospered over the years – not that either of them had gone into the partnership solely for money.

Of course there were many occupational psychologists about, but most were in the land of psychometric testing and personality measurement for selection while others focused on training. The large business schools had stress specialists, other consultants existed and there were various stress, meditation, positive health units and relaxation centres dotted around the country. Few firms combined the counselling skills of Pyramid with its stress management techniques and tools. Pyramid did not believe in 'packages': they took to their work a humanistic philosophy based on the approach of Rogers,[1] and a professionalism that most senior clients readily absorbed and believed in.

Their clients were predominantly corporate. Some individuals at the executive level would pop in to see them on a regular basis for a chat but this was an extra. Their bread and butter came from large corporations which had identified an efficiency or productivity problem with individuals or with staff in general. If it was an individual problem the counselling tended to occur in Cambridge; if it was a group matter, the counselling would occur off-site at a nearby hotel. They would not counsel people at the place of work itself. With a charge rate of £900 per day, inclusive of state taxes, and a busy schedule, Pyramid kept growing.

Clients became more demanding and there did not seem to be any time between assignments. They had estimated a 60 per cent work rate over the 230 working days in the year but this last year it had come nearer 90 per cent. Dr Anders had commented, 'If this goes on we'll both be in need of stress counselling.' Stinger agreed. It was decided that they would recruit 'stress consultants', who could be not only professional counsellors but also good sales and marketing people, as both Anders and Stinger wished to focus on their research and the occupational psychology side rather than build up the business. 'While we are looking for these people, perhaps we should employ a marketing professional from an established consultancy firm', suggested Dr Stinger. 'He or she can co-ordinate all of the sales and marketing while you and I concentrate on our psychological research.'

The consultant was in the process of writing up her notes on Bill Moy, a busy advertising executive who had come to see her because he was increasingly suffering pressure at work.

Some conflicts had arisen as Bill had been asked (or told) to do a campaign on abortion which had been against his personal views. The workload was beginning to become even more excessive and he never had time to give the job 100 per cent of his effort. He was always floating from one task to another, and he had difficulty getting information out of the research people. This led to time pressures in an already hectic lifestyle, and his partner was tiring of his long hours at the office.

He was responsible to Phil Smart, the advertising director for the whole agency, who was never in the office. He believed that clients were best served by going to them. This caused fresh pressures on Moy, as he often did not know what Smart was doing. At the personal level, he found Smart an interesting, if not charming, person – though somewhat unpredictable.

The consultant found that a video of clients helped recall and saved her taking voluminous notes. The video was made with the client's permission. She watched the video tape of Moy's interview, looking for symptoms of stress.

Moy looked physically tired and slightly overweight, and was a little breathless in his speech. He had some difficulty concentrating on one topic, hopping from one subject to another. He said at the interview that he was conscious of the possibility of making errors, although these errors had not actually manifested themselves. His time pressures resulted in somewhat hasty decisions.

Emotionally he was tense and drained. He had started off quite nervously, for it had been an effort to come here in the first place. His partner's influence had been apparent in steering him into this office. She had become increasingly worried about his behaviour – excessive drinking, being unable to unwind, poor sleeping habits and the lack of normal intercourse.

Clearly the man was in a mess. The first thing to do was to recognize the problems of stress, and he had done this as the meeting progressed. A stress plan was needed.

Task
Construct a stress plan for Moy.

Source:
1   See A.H. Anderson, *Effective Personnel Management*, Unit Four, where these views are developed

Notes
1 Weiss and Alder, 'Personality and organizational behavior'.
2 Cattell, *Scientific Analysis of Personality.*
3 Cronbach, 'The two disciplines of scientific psychology'.
4 Allport, *Theories of Perception and the Concept of Structure.*
5 Digman, 'Personality structure: emergence of the five factor model'.
6 Hollenbeck and Brief, 'The effects of individual differences and goal origins on goal setting and performance'.
7 Jung, *Psychological Types*; Eysenck, 'Development of a theory'.
8 Stodgill, 'Personal factors associated with leadership'.
9 Simon, 'Invariants of human behavior'.
10 B.F. Anderson, *Cognitive Psychology.*
11 Cherrington, *Organizational Behaviour.*
12 Dearborn and Simon, 'Selective perception'.
13 Olson and Zanna, 'Attitudes and beliefs'.
14 Ajzen and Fishbein, *Understanding Attitudes and Predicting Social Behavior.*
15 Locke and Latham, *A Theory of Goal Setting and Task Performance.*
16 Steers and Porter, *Motivation and Work Behavior.*
17 Maslow, *Motivation and Personality.*
18 Alderfer, *Existence, Relatedness and Growth.*
19 McClelland, *The Achieving Society.*
20 Herzberg, *Work and the Nature of Man.*
21 Taylor, *The Principles of Scientific Management.*
22 Morse and Weiss, 'The function and meaning of work and the job'.
23 Wedderburn, 'Economic aspect of ageing'.
24 Goldthorpe et al., *The Affluent Worker.*
25 Dubin, 'Work in modern society'.
26 Blauner, *Alienation and Freedom.*
27 Parker, *Future of Work and Leisure.*
28 Ibid.
29 Sillitoe, *Britain in Figures.*
30 Locke, 'Nature and causes of job satisfaction'.
31 Evans, 'Conceptual and operational problems'.
32 Kalleberg, 'Work values and job rewards'.

33 Locke, 'Nature and causes of job satisfaction'.
34 Smith et al., *Measurement of Satisfaction in Work and Retirement.*
35 Iaffaldano and Muchinsky, 'Job satisfaction and job performance'.
36 Schneider, 'Organizational behavior'.
37 Vroom, *Work and Motivation.*
38 Brayfield and Crockett, 'Employee attitudes and performance'.
39 Vroom, *Work and Motivation.*
40 Schwab and Cummings, 'Employee performance and satisfaction with work roles'.
41 French and Caplan, 'Psychosocial factors'
42 Sales and House, 'Job dissatisfaction as a possible risk factor'.
43 McGrath, 'Stress and behavior in organizations'.
44 Lazarus, *Psychological Stress and the Coping Process.*
45 Kornhauser, *Mental Health of the Industrial Worker.*
46 French and Caplan, 'Psychosocial factors'.
47 Kahn et al., *Organizational Stress.*
48 Wardwell et al., 'Stress and coronary disease in three field studies'.
49 Argyris, *Integrating the Individual*; Cooper and Marshall, 'Occupational sources of stress'.
50 Pahl and Pahl, *Managers and their Wives.*
51 Cooper and Marshall, 'Occupational sources of stress'.
52 Hinkle et al., 'Occupation, education and coronary heart disease'.

Unit Three

Focus on Interpersonal and Group Processes

Learning Objectives

After completing this unit, you should be able to:

- explain the meaning, nature and development of groups;
- appreciate the importance of groups for effective organizations;
- explain the relationship between leadership and management;
- outline different approaches to leadership;
- appreciate the varying views of conflict;
- identify the levels and stages of conflict;
- apply the generic skills.

Contents

Overview

Group Dynamics

▶ Defining groups

▶ The group and individual performance

▶ Framework for analysing groups

▶ Group development and effectiveness

Forming

Storming

Norming

Performing

Adjourning

Leadership

▶ Defining leadership

▶ Leadership and management

▶ Approaches to leadership

Trait approach

Behavioural leadership theories

Situational leadership theories

Conflict

▶ Defining conflict

▶ Views of conflict

Positive view

Negative view

'Balanced' view

► Levels of conflict

   Intrapersonal conflict

   Interpersonal conflict

   Intragroup conflict

   Intergroup conflict

   Intraorganizational conflict

   Interorganizational conflict

► Stages of conflict

► Conflict management

Unit Three

Overview

Much of our time is spent interacting with others in groups, whether they are social or work groups. Our personal identity is derived from the way in which we are perceived and treated by other group members.

Groups can alter our outlook on life and influence our behaviour in an organizational setting. Organizational behaviour is more than simply the combined behaviours of individuals. It is not their outcomes but rather a much more complex phenomenon, a very important part of which is the group.

The productivity and other factors resulting from effective group action make the development of group skills one of the most important aspects of managerial training. Furthermore, membership in productive and cohesive groups is essential to our psychological wellbeing. Thus, understanding how groups develop and their dynamics is vital for all managers who seek to get the best from individuals working in organizations.

The focus of this unit is an examination of a number of dimensions which affect interpersonal and group behaviour, using the broad concepts of group dynamics, leadership and conflict.

Group Dynamics

It has often been said that, on the one hand, 'Two heads are better than one', 'The more the merrier', while on the other hand, 'Too many cooks spoil the broth' and 'A camel is a horse put together by a committee.' What is the truth about groups? Are they as important as many say they are?

We all belong to groups, some that we enjoy and others that we do not. Whatever our own personal feelings about them, groups have become an increasingly important fact of organizational life. It can be said that to work in organizations today is to work in groups. To be responsible, as a manager, for getting things done means recognizing the need to work through and in groups. (On average, managers spend 50 per cent of their working day in one sort of group or another, and for senior managers this can rise to 80 per cent.)

What is it about groups that make organizations increasingly rely on them? Fundamentally, the complex nature of organizational activity makes it virtually impossible for individuals to cope at a satisfactory level. There is a clear requirement for people to operate in groups, in order for them to combine their knowledge and abilities to solve complex problems. It has been suggested that groups are used to perform many formal organizational functions:[2]

- distribution of work, etc.
- management and control of work
- problem solving and decision making
- information processing
- information and idea collection
- testing and ratifying decisions
- co-ordination and liaison
- increased commitment and involvement
- negotiation or conflict resolution
- inquest or inquiry into past

Furthermore, the growth of group activities in organizations relates to the belief that organizations should be managed in an essentially participative manner (see the section on organizational culture in Unit Five). Involvement of staff may not only influence their feelings of satisfaction, but also help to ensure that implementation goes more smoothly than might be the case where little or no participation takes place. Therefore, we can say that groups are also instrumental to the individual. For example, they offer:

- organizationally related gain – assisting in getting the job done;
- contact with others (that is, work groups), which Warr and Wall suggest 'is essential as a stimulus to mental activity or behaviour';[3]
- social comparison – comparing our beliefs;
- the establishment or testing of a sense of self-identity;
- a sense of security and influence over our environment;
- the instrumentality of the group (motivation).

The implications for managers responsible for achieving results through managing groups are clear. They have a responsibility to their organizations and their staff to develop their knowledge and understanding of groups; to work and develop the skills needed to encourage groups to become more effective; and finally, to develop their own group participation skills, enabling them to function effectively as group members, as well as group leaders.

Defining groups

A wide range of definitions has been expounded, yet no universally accepted definition has emerged. It is, however, generally accepted that most definitions fall along a continuum from the 'group mind' to the 'individuals' view.

```
┌─────────────────────────────────────────────────────────────────┐
│  Group mind – where the group is seen as an entity in its own right │
└─────────────────────────────────────────────────────────────────┘
                                 ↕
┌─────────────────────────────────────────────────────────────────┐
│  Groups are real – they exist in the perceptions of members; subjectively │
│  real, therefore, they can influence behaviour, but the individual remains │
│                    the prime focus of study                       │
└─────────────────────────────────────────────────────────────────┘
                                 ↕
┌─────────────────────────────────────────────────────────────────┐
│  There is no study of groups which is not a study of individuals  │
└─────────────────────────────────────────────────────────────────┘
```

Two widely used definitions, which fall somewhere in the middle of the continuum, are:

> *Two or more employees who interact with each other in such a manner that the behaviour and/or performance of a member is influenced by the behaviour and/or performance of other members.*[4]

> *Any number of people who interact with one another, are psychologically aware of one another and perceive themselves to be a group.*[5]

Defining groups has been tackled from a number of perspectives, the primary focus being, for example: *perception* (where members must perceive their relationship to others);[6] *organization* (where the group has a set of norms that regulates the performance of the group and its members);[7] *motivation* (as a means of satisfying needs);[8] *interaction* (where interdependence is the core to groupness).[9]

Each of these perspectives is important, since each points to a key factor relating to groups. Furthermore, we can say that if a group exists in an organization, its members:

- are motivated to join;
- perceive the group as a unified unit of interacting people;
- contribute to group processes;
- reach agreements or disagreements through interaction.

Different types of groups emerge within organizations – namely, formal and informal groups – for various reasons:[10] needs, proximity, attraction, goals and economics.

Formal groups are deliberately created to carry out some specific task. Examples are project teams, audit teams, committees and boards. Their structure, rules and membership are likely to be explicitly stated by the organization. A command group is the most common type of permanent formal group. This is reflected in the organization chart – the group is made up of subordinates who report directly to a given supervisor, while a temporary task group works together to complete a particular task or project, but its members do not necessarily report to the same supervisor.

Informal groups, on the other hand, arise spontaneously through friendship or common interest. Examples are ad hoc meetings, discussions and cliques. They evolve naturally, membership is voluntary and changes, and members have mutual objectives which are not necessarily related to those of the organization. There are three common types of informal work group: horizontal cliques (with members of similar rank in the same work area); vertical cliques (with members from different hierarchical levels in the same department); and random cliques (with members from various departments, locations and hierarchical levels). They can be permanent or temporary. They can be a most effective device for blocking and obstructing new ideas, or the best way of putting them into practice.

The group and individual performance

The presence of others seems to have a significant effect on an individual's performance – whether it is enhancing or inhibiting.[11] Therefore, others have an arousing effect on us either to behave or perform 'better' or 'worse'.

Whether to use groups or to pool individuals together to work depends on the situation. Here are some of the facts relating to groups.

Groups often take longer to complete a task than individuals would working alone. This tends to be the case when we talk in terms of time spent in completing a task – an important consideration for managers. But 'the evidence ... strongly supports the conclusion that groups produce more and better solutions to problems than individuals.'[12] However, experts may do better on their own than a group of less competent people.

On the whole, there is likely to be more information available in a group, there is a greater chance for errors and mistakes to be recognized and corrected, and groups can be creative. However, group membership can inhibit us, and restrict our creativity. We may adopt the same approach to the problem as the group in order not to appear difficult or different. But groups tend to continue to produce ideas indefinitely whereas we as individuals would run dry eventually.

Given that groups have received such attention in organizations, it is important that we look at them in more detail.

Framework for analysing groups

Although every group is different, possessing its own unique attributes and dynamics, all groups tend to display similar patterns of evolution. The group phenomenon can be understood in terms of the interaction of three groups of variables:

1 formation variables – the way the group is composed, the context within which it is operating;

2 development variables – factors emerging from the interaction of members in a given situation;

3 effectiveness variables – the extent to which the group does adequately fulfil organizational and individual functions.

Now tackle Activity OB3.1.

ACTIVITY OB3.1

A GROUP FRAMEWORK

Activity code
✓ Self-development
✓ Teamwork
✓ Communications
☐ Numeracy/IT
✓ Decisions

Task
In a team (if possible), consider the three groups of variables discussed in the text: formation, development and effectiveness. Brainstorm and derive examples of what your group feels would make up a useful diagnostic tool in examining the framework of a work group.

Variable	Examples
Formation	
Development	
Effectiveness	

Group development and effectiveness

Some groups appear to go through a five-stage developmental sequence: forming, storming, norming, performing and adjourning.[13] Managers need to understand the developmental stages of groups, as each one can play an important role in effectiveness. It is, however, important to note that all groups do not necessarily progress through these stages in the same way. For example, time pressures from a superior could accelerate or alter the development of the group.[14] Yet group performance may be enhanced by this sequence.

Forming

This constitutes the initial formation of the group and the bringing together of a number of individuals. In the forming stage, members focus their efforts on defining goals and developing procedures for performing their task. This also involves getting to know each other and understanding leadership and other member roles. In this stage, individual members might: keep feelings to themselves until they know the situation; act more secure than they actually feel; experience confusion and uncertainty about what is expected of them; be nice and polite, or at least certainly not hostile; and try to ascertain the personal benefits relative to the personal costs of being involved in the group.[15]

The context or environment can directly affect the behaviours and effectiveness of a group. This context includes the conditions and factors outside the group that it cannot directly control. These might include technology, physical working conditions, management practices, formal rules, and organizational rewards and punishments.[16]

Goals influence the effectiveness and efficiency of individuals, groups and organizations, each of which has multiple goals. Obviously, individual and organizational goals are likely to influence the types of group goal and actual group behaviour in pursuit of these goals. Group goals are the end states desired for the group as a whole, not just those desired by each individual member.[17]

Both compatible and conflicting goals may exist within and between individuals, groups and organizations. The pursuit of only task-related or people-related goals can in the long run reduce effectiveness, increase conflicts and result in the break-up of the group.[18] The influence of goals on group behaviours and effectiveness becomes even more complex when the possible compatibilities and conflicts between individual member goals, group goals and organizational goals are considered.

Effective group size can range from two members to a normal upper limit of sixteen. Twelve is about the largest size that enables each member to react and interact easily with each of the other group members.[19]

Some of the effects of group size are shown in table 3.1. Members of groups of seven or less interact differently from members in groups of thirteen to sixteen.

Table 3.1 Effects of group size

Dimension	2–7 members	8–12 members	13–16 members
Leadership			
Demands on leader	Low	Moderate	High
Differences between leader and members	Low	Low to moderate	Moderate to high
Direction by leader	Low	Low to moderate	Moderate to high
Members			
Tolerance of direction from leader	Low to high	Moderate to high	High
Domination of group interaction by a few members	Low	Moderate to high	High
Inhibition in participation by ordinary members	Low	Moderate	High
Group process			
Formalization of rules and procedures	Low	Low to moderate	Moderate to high
Time required for reaching judgement decisions	Low to moderate	Moderate	Moderate to high
Tendency for subgroups to form within group	Low	Moderate to high	High

Source: Adapted from Hellriegel et al., *Organizational Behaviour.*

Storming

There is normally some anxiety in groups as members try to create an impression, to test each other and to establish their own personal identity. This often leads to conflict and hostility. The storming stage is very important – the group needs to work through this conflict. During it, competition over the leadership role and conflict over goals are dominant. The key is to manage conflict at this stage, not to suppress or withdraw from it. The group cannot effectively evolve into the third stage if the leader and the members go to either extreme: suppressing conflict would probably create resentment, which would last long after members' attempts to express their differences and emotions; withdrawal could cause the group to fail more quickly.

Norming

As conflict starts to be controlled, members of groups will establish guidelines and standards and develop their own norms of acceptable behaviours. Information is shared, different opinions are accepted and positive attempts are made to reach mutually agreeable decisions on the group's goals. This is also the stage during which the group sets the rules by which it will operate. Co-operation within the group is a dominant theme. A sense of shared responsibility for the group develops.

Group norms play a large role in determining whether the group will be productive or not, and managers can play a major role in setting and changing these. Understanding how norms develop and why they are enforced helps managers diagnose better the underlying tensions and problems in groups.

The extent to which members of a group like each other and want to remain members of the group is referred to as *cohesiveness*. Differences in cohesiveness are apparent in sports teams, work groups and even families. Cohesiveness, as a concept, is important for understanding groups in organizations, as is the recognition of the impact of groups on performance.[20] The degree of cohesiveness can have positive or negative effects depending on how group goals match up with those of the formal organization. It is derived from a number of factors:

- *Interaction* – that is, the amount of contact between group members. The more time spent together, the greater the cohesion.
- *Shared goals* – agreeing on the purpose and direction of group activities serves to bind the group together. This increases as co-operation and democratic setting of goals mean that group members can share in the success when meeting goals.
- *Similarity of attitudes and values* – birds of a feather flock together: the group socially validates members' beliefs.

If cohesiveness is high and the group accepts and agrees organizational goals, then group behaviour will probably be positive from the organization's perspective. However, if the group is highly cohesive but has goals which are not congruent with the organization's, group behaviour probably will be negative from the organization's perspective.

If a group is low in cohesiveness and has no affinity with organizational goals, the results will be negative. Behaviour will be more on an individual basis than on a group one. It is, however, possible to have a group low in cohesiveness where goals agree with the organization's. Here results will be positive, although more on an individual than a group basis.

The evidence suggests that group cohesiveness increases group effectiveness, but not in the ways most managers suspect. The greater the cohesion the higher morale is (that is, members enjoy and value work as something pleasant, the climate is relaxed and less tense, and there is less absenteeism, turnover and conflict). The effect on productivity, on the other hand, is not as clear cut. Among members of a work group, cohesiveness decreases variability in productivity, but it does not necessarily increase productivity as a whole. Whether this happens depends on the group norms.

Norms are rules and patterns of behaviour that are accepted and expected by members of a group.[21] In general, norms define the kinds of behaviour that group members believe are necessary to help the group reach its goals. Porter et al.[22] identified three salient characteristics of norms:

- Norms apply only to behaviour, not to private thoughts and feelings.
- Norms are generally developed only for behaviours which are viewed as important by most group members.
- While groups might give the greatest approval to a certain type of behaviour, for most group norms there is a range of acceptable behaviour.

Norms develop gradually and informally. Most norms develop in one of five ways: individuals carry over past situations and bring certain expectations with them; the first behaviour pattern that emerges in the group often sets group expectations – primacy; critical incidents set the precedent; explicit statements are made by supervisors or co-workers; or the group consciously decides. These norms are likely to be strongly enforced if they: ensure group success or survival; reflect the preferences of supervisors or other powerful group members; simplify or make predictable what behaviour is expected of group members; reinforce specific individual members' roles; and help the group avoid embarrassing interpersonal problems.

Studies of small groups in organizations have emphasized the importance of emergent, or informal, leadership in accomplishing goals. Virtually all other factors affecting group behaviours and effectiveness (such as size, member composition and roles, norms, goals and the context) are greatly influenced by an effective group leader. For example, the effective group leader often assumes a key role in the relations between the group and external groups or individuals, and probably influences the selection of new group members. Even when the group participates in the selection process, the group leader often screens potential members, thereby limiting the number and range of alternatives.

We have only touched on the behaviours and qualities of effective group leaders here. These are discussed in more detail in the next section.

Performing
Only after progressing successfully through the previous stages will the group create the structure and cohesiveness to work effectively as a team. The roles of individual members are accepted and understood. The members usually understand when they should work independently and when they should help each other. Some groups continue to learn and develop from their experiences and new inputs, and these groups will

---

BOX OB3.1

Mature groups

'Maturity' is the culmination of the ageing process of the group. In many ways the mature phase is about effective group working, tolerance of others, sound communications and working accommodations on the task in hand.

Bennis and Shepard suggest this mature phase is characterized by:

- Conflict is task-based and not over 'socio-emotional' issues.
- Differences are accepted and group conformity is not an objective.
- Decisions are not forced, and come about through rational discussion.
- Group processes and interactions are known by the members of the group.

Source: Adapted from Bennis and Shepard, 'A theory of group development'

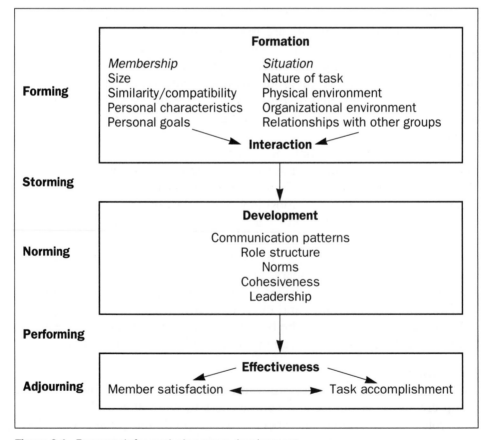

Figure 3.1 Framework for analysing group development.

improve their efficiency and effectiveness. Other groups – especially those that developed norms not fully supportive of efficiency and effectiveness – may perform only at the level needed for their survival. A minimally adequate level of performance may be caused by excessive self-oriented behaviours by group members, the development of norms that inhibit task effectiveness and efficiency, poor group leadership, or other factors.[23]

At this stage, it can be said that the group has 'matured'. It is at this point that the group becomes effective. See Box OB3.1.

Adjourning

Some groups, such as a project team created to investigate and report on a specific problem within three months, have a defined date for adjournment. Other groups, such as executive committees, may go on indefinitely. Figure 3.1 summarizes this whole process.

The roles allocated or given in a group and the behaviour of the actors can impact on team effectiveness. Box OB3.2 discusses effective team roles and the associated behavioural pattern in meetings. Once you have read this, undertake Activity OB3.2.

BOX OB3.2

Effective team roles and associated behavioural patterns in meetings: a proposal

Belbin's[1] work on individual roles in building an effective team is well established, as is Rackham and Morgan's[2] work on behavioural patterns that make for a constructive dialogue with others. Here we fuse aspects of both to give a *proposal* on the effective group team and its behavioural patterns.

Let us recap first on Belbin's material. The *company worker*, with his or her dutiful approach, is an asset to the calm, controlled *chair*. The highly strung yet dynamic *shaper* may not gel with the *plant* or the serious-minded individual. The *resource investigator*, with his or her exploratory perspective, is tempered by the *monitor/evaluator's* prudent commentary. The *team worker*, although a little indecisive, is helped along to the finishing post by the *completer*, who is painstakingly conscientious.

To Rackman the actual behavioural pattern displayed was important. The range includes: proposing or suggesting; building or developing; supporting; disagreeing; defending or attacking; blocking and/or stating difficulties; opening up in a non-defensive manner; testing and understanding; seeking information; giving information; shutting out or excluding people, and bringing people into the debate or discussion. Some of these behaviours are 'positive' and others are 'negative'.

The proposal is to limit Belbin's roles to:

- the *chair*;
- an *innovator* or ideas person (more than one may be required, depending on the degree of brainstorming);
- *specialists*, who in effect can help to give input and answer technical questions and so rotate the chair;
- *team task workers* – a large group that focuses on the issues at hand;
- *team people workers* – another large group that, while not ignoring the issues, focuses on the socio-emotional maintenance of the group.

This team should also focus on a range of positive behavioural patterns, helping to produce positive behavioural roles.

Role	Behavioural pattern
The chair	*Proposing* – putting forward new ideas and suggestions. These may, however be better left to others unless there is some stalemate; if he or she constantly proposes issues the chair will become quite autocratic.
	Bringing in – this is a key role of the chair. By scanning the group he or she can anticipate dissent, withdrawal etc., and involve people in the debate.
	Testing and understanding – seeking a clear, unambiguous feedback on an item ensures that potentially good ideas are not lost and can be stored.
	Summarizing – the chair has a key role in restricting contributions, particularly before the meeting or team moves away from one idea.
Innovator(s)	*Proposals* should emanate from this (these) person(s), who can also *build* on the contributions of any group member, as creativity and a different angle on an issue are the hallmarks of the innovator's contribution. All members have the right to disagree, and the innovator may have to face such *disagreement* from the group without adopting a defensively aggressive posture. He or she should be able to offer an *'open' behavioural pattern*.
Specialists	They have a role in *proposing and building* on the ideas of less specialist people if applicable to their subject. They can offer to *disagree* on the basis of their sapiential knowledge. They can question others (specialist and non-specialist) to *clarify issues* and to *seek more information*. As experts their key function is to *give objective information* to all on their specialist area.

Role	Behavioural pattern
Team members	They can be divided into two camps, in a sense; but, aspiring to the ideal, we can fuse the *task needs* of the meeting with the *socio-maintenance needs* of the group *in the same people*. The social side involves genuinely supporting others, building on the ideas of others, and employing an 'open' approach to events. The task side can be seen in proposing or building, disagreeing on a point of principle rather than for its own sake, and both giving and particularly seeking information in a non-edited, open fashion.

Sources:

1 Adapted from Belbin, *Management Teams*
2 Adapted from Rackham and Morgan, *Behavior Analysis in Training*

ACTIVITY OB3.2

THE TEAM MEETING

Activity code
☑ Self-development
☑ Teamwork
☑ Communications
☑ Numeracy/IT
☑ Decisions

Task

Using the classification scheme(s) in Box OB3.2, and the grids at the end of this activity, classify the team roles of the actors in each speech in the scenario that follows, and then note the behavioural categories being used by each person in his or her comments.

Summarize the positive nature of their comments and their overall roles.

Bill, Phil, Joe, Andreas and Sue all sat down for the weekly session. It was Friday and Tom, the boss, seemed to forget that the others had a home to go to. The time was getting on and the meeting had just begun, at 4.33 according to Sue's watch.

1 *Bill:*   I'm glad that we are all here. I've no agenda – no need of course, ha ha – we've been here for some time, all of us, and we know the score.

2 *Sue:* ['Yes', she thought, 'you consult by telling us and then try to sell it to us.']

3 *Joe:* Before we start on the non-agenda, I would like to raise an issue.

4 *Sue:* No, let's stick to the non-agenda. It's Friday and my husband and I are going out to dinner tonight and we don't all drive like you, Joe, at 100 miles per hour.

5 *Phil:* Let's get on with it, Bill.

6 *Andreas:* No, why should we? This is supposed to be a free and open discussion and I don't see much evidence of Joe getting a say.

7 *Phil:* Bill's right – the agenda is always the same – let's do it now and stop all this bickering.

8 *Bill:* Well, it can surely wait [turning to Joe], can't it?

9 *Joe:* Well, it concerns procedure, really, rather than substance. Now if we had a rotating speaker on the key items, such as market research data or sales forecasts or whatever, we could start the session with hard facts.

10 *Sue:* Yes, it would cut all this waffle. I agree.

11 *Phil:* No, Bill's the chair. He must agree.

12 *Sue:* If Bill told you to jump out of the window, Phil, you'd probably do it.

13 *Bill:* That's enough of that.

14 *Andreas:* This meeting is going nowhere. Why don't we have a rotating weekly chair? We're almost all equals according to grade, after all.

15 *Joe:* Yes, that's a good idea.

16 *Sue:* Anything, but can we move on?

17 *Bill:* Well, on the first proposal, specialists are a good idea but I am the chair.

18 *Phil:* Of course you are, Bill, and we all appreciate that.

19 *Sue:* What! More crawling, Phil? What is it – a new car or a bigger office this time?

20 *Phil:* I'm getting a little tired of you.

21 *Andreas:* We're all very tired of you as well.

22 *Joe:* We need a strong chair on some issues.

23 *Andreas:* What issues?

24 *Joe:*   Well, I specialize in the design area, so when R&D is on the main agenda I should chair it. When pure statistics on the market are to be discussed, Sue should lead.

25 *Sue:*   What about Phil, then? What's he going to lead on? He doesn't specialize in anything – apart from sycophancy.

26 *Phil:*   You quarrelsome old bat. Your figures are suspect every week. You moan and groan about your health or your dinner parties. Your contribution is zero.

27 *Bill:*   This meeting is getting out of hand. Sue, stop it.

28 *Sue:*   Don't tell him, of course. Don't upset your friendship, for goodness' sake. Look, we are the marketeers here. It's our creativity that keeps the thing going. All of us – including sycophants – are important.

29 *Phil:*   I'm not a sycophant. But Bill is the boss – he should have the final say.

30 *Andreas:* No one doubts that …

31 *Joe:*   But we should have an input as well – according to our specialization.

32 *Phil:*   Bill should decide.

33 *Bill:*   Mm. You're right of course, Phil, but the others – that is, Joe – may have a point.

34 *Sue:*   OK, we need an agenda. From that agenda we can determine who will be the chair.

35 *Bill:*   I'm the chair.

36 *Phil:*   Of course he is, and I'm his deputy.

37 *Andreas:* Deputy! First we've heard of this – another unadvertised job, methinks.

38 *Bill:*   Well, acting only when I'm on vacation.

39 *Sue:*   Yes, acting is just about right for him. The word '*poseur*' does spring to mind when we think of him.

40 *Joe:*   Appearance management is important, of course.

41 *Andreas:* We should have a vote on who is to be deputy, and as we are all on the same level it should be rotated.

42 *Joe:*   Yes. Just like the chair. What do you think, Sue?

43 *Sue:*   I agree. Andreas?

44 *Andreas:* I agree.

45 *Joe:*   It's carried by three to two, then.

46 *Bill:*   We go by the chair's decision.

47 *Joe:*   Only if the vote is evenly split, and we're three to two. Next week I suggest Andreas leads on his area, then Sue the following week and so on. [Sue and Andreas agree.]

48 *Bill:*   What about this session?

49 *Sue:*   It's too late now. I'm off.

The meeting disintegrated.

	Team role	Behavioural categories type	Positive/negative
1			
2			
3			
4			
5			
6			
7			
8			
9			
10			
11			
12			
13			
14			
15			
16			
17			
18			
19			
20			
21			

	Team role	Behavioural categories type	Positive/negative
22			
23			
24			
25			
26			
27			
28			
29			
30			
31			
32			
33			
34			
35			
36			
37			
38			
39			
40			
41			
42			
43			
44			
45			
46			
47			
48			
49			

Leadership

Leadership has always been, and probably always will be, important in organizations. The need for managerial leadership and the difficulty of providing it have grown considerably because of the increasing complexity of our world.

It could be said that the success or failure of any organization depends, to a greater or lesser extent, on the quality of its leaders. Thus it is not surprising that organizations engage in extensive searches for new methods of selecting and developing their managers and executives, and for making the best use of their leadership abilities once they are on the job.

What does it take to be a good leader, and what is the most effective leadership style? Many research studies concerning leadership have been undertaken to provide greater insight into these questions. However, none has yet produced a definitive list of traits or qualities that are consistently related to effective leadership. The only conclusion we can draw from these studies is that there is no one most effective leadership style. What we do know is that effective leadership style is absolutely essential to the survival and overall growth of every organization.

In this section, we first define leadership and examine the relationship between leadership and management. Then we examine the nature of effective leadership and discuss three perspectives that have been used to define effective leadership: trait, behavioural, and situational.

Defining leadership

There is no universally accepted definition of leadership, but most would agree that there are two common denominators in the majority of definitions:

1 Leadership is a group phenomenon.

2 It is an influence process; that is to say, intentional influence is exerted by the leader over followers.

Leadership is 'the behaviour of an individual when he/she is directing the activities of a group toward a shared goal'.[24] It is 'interpersonal influence, exercised in a situation, and directed, through the communication process, toward the attainment of a specified goal or goals'.[25]

In other words, leadership involves one person (the leader) consciously trying to get other people (the followers) to do something that the leader wants them to do. Therefore we can say that leadership is the process whereby one person influences other members towards a goal.[26]

Leadership and management

Not all employees or managers exercise leadership. Many employees are good managers but not leaders. So what is the difference between a manager and a leader?

A manager is a person who directs the work of employees and is responsible for results.[27] Effective managers bring a degree of order and consistency to their staff. Leadership, by contrast, is about coping with change. Let us explore the differences more closely.

Managers manage complexity through *planning and budgeting* (setting goals, establishing steps to achieve goals and then allocating resources to achieve them). By contrast, leading starts with setting a *direction* or *vision* of what the future might look like, and then developing strategies for producing changes needed to achieve that direction or vision.

Effective managers achieve their goals by *organizing and staffing* – creating an organizational structure and sets of jobs for accomplishing the plan's requirements, staffing the jobs with qualified employees, communicating the goals and devising systems to monitor progress. Leaders try to *align employees* who share their vision. They create teams who understand and share their vision.

Finally, managers ensure that employees reach goals by *controlling* their behaviours; that is, they monitor results by means of reports and meetings and note deviations from the goal. Effective leadership requires *motivating and inspiring* teams of employees. It taps their needs, values and emotions.

To summarize, while some managers are leaders, others are not. Each role, manager and leader, requires different behaviours.

Approaches to leadership

Historically, research on leadership effectiveness has been dominated by the trait v. situational controversy for over thirty years. There were those who searched for a definitive set of traits which would differentiate between effective and ineffective leaders, while others attempted to understand the characteristics of situations which created effective leaders. Neither the trait nor the situational approach resulted in a major advance in understanding the nature of effective leadership. The result of all this research was the revelation that effective leadership probably represents some interaction between the characteristics of the leader himself or herself and the characteristics of the situation in which leadership takes place.

Let us look at some of the many approaches to leadership in more detail.

Trait approach

The trait approach emphasizes the personal characteristics of leaders, which differentiate a 'good' from a 'bad' leader. There is no consideration given to the circumstances or the situation in which leadership occurs.

This has a common-sense appeal because it conforms to popular opinion that there are those who are 'born' leaders. What traits do you feel contribute to being a leader? See Activity OB3.3.

ACTIVITY OB3.3

LEADERSHIP TRAITS

Activity code
- ✓ Self-development
- ✓ Teamwork
- ☐ Communications
- ☐ Numeracy/IT
- ✓ Decisions

Task
As an individual or a group, list the traits or attributes that you or the group feel characterize a 'good' leader. These traits or personal characteristics can describe a tank commander or a business leader.

Traits

Psychological research does not support the trait approach. The most consistent finding from more than fifty years of studies on the trait approach is that there does not seem to be a universal set of traits that distinguishes good from poor leaders. Stogdill[28] carried out a review of leadership literature between 1949 and 1974. He found evidence to show that certain personality traits, abilities and social skills were commonly possessed by good leaders. See Box OB3.3.

Successful leaders are assumed to possess more or less of certain traits than are unsuccessful ones. Considerable research has been conducted to compare the traits of effective and ineffective leaders. Aggressiveness, ambition, decisiveness, dominance, initiative, intelligence, physical characteristics (attractiveness, height, weight), self-assurance and other characteristics were studied to determine if they were related to effective leadership.

BOX OB3.3

Characteristics of a good leader

Personality traits
- Adaptability
- Adjustment (normality)
- Aggressiveness and assertiveness
- Dominance
- Emotional balance and control
- Independence (nonconformity)
- Originality and creativity
- Personal integrity (ethical conduct)
- Self-confidence

Abilities
- Intelligence
- Judgement and decisiveness
- Knowledge
- Fluency of speech

Social skills
- Ability to enlist co-operation
- Administrative ability
- Co-operativeness
- Popularity and prestige
- Sociability
- Social participation
- Tact and diplomacy

Source: Adapted from Feldman and Arnold, *Managing Individual and Group Behavior in Organizations*

Perhaps the underlying assumption of some trait research has been that leaders are born not made; that is, the 'Great Man' theory. Although research has demonstrated that this is not the case, some people still believe that there are certain inborn or acquired traits that make a person a good leader.

Research has clearly not shown that physical traits can distinguish effective from ineffective leaders. However, the trait approach to the study of leadership is not dead: Ghiselli[29] conducted research in an effort to identify personality and motivational traits related to effective leadership. Still, in spite of the contributions of trait researchers, the trait approach to the study of leadership effectiveness has left many questions unanswered. This has led to a continuing search for an appropriate leadership style.

A major limitation of trait theory is that traits associated with leadership in one situation do not predict leadership in another.[30] In addition, there is a definitional problem on agreeing upon traits; there is difficulty in trying to measure traits; and as a method it does not provide much insight into the basic dynamics of the leadership process.

These criticisms do not imply that the trait approach is without value: a great deal of useful and important information has been gained using it. Although traits cannot fully explain effective leadership, we should take into account the personal traits and skills of leaders.

Behavioural leadership theories

Dissatisfaction with the trait approach has caused most leadership researchers to focus attention on how leaders should behave, as opposed to the traits or characteristics they should possess.

The behavioural approach is straightforward in its philosophy. It states that the best way to study and to define leadership is in terms of what leaders *do* rather than in terms of what leaders *are*. Thus one is concerned with leader *behaviours* rather than leader *characteristics*. Attempts were made to find ways of describing patterns of leader behaviour, and the relationships between various patterns of behaviour and subordinate satisfaction and performance.

In the late 1940s and 1950s, research aimed at understanding leadership and leadership effectiveness emerged, this time focusing not on the personal traits of leaders *per se* but instead on the behavioural styles which characterized their leadership activities: for example, authoritarian v. democratic, task-oriented v. socio-emotional, employee-centred v. production-centred, etc.

Research evidence has accumulated which investigates the relationships between various leadership styles and individual or group effectiveness. One series of organizational studies,[31] for example, indicated that more effective leaders tend to:

- differentiate their role from that of the employees;
- spend substantial time in supervisory functions but not closely supervising employee activities;
- be concerned with the employee rather than the task or organization.

Lewin et al.[32] examined the impact of leadership style in the *University of Iowa studies*. They conducted a controlled experiment in which they observed the impact of three separate leadership styles – autocratic, democratic and laissez-faire – on the behaviour of adolescent boys.

The basic difference in the three styles was the location of the decision-making function in the group. Authoritarian leaders made decisions for their groups and communicated those decisions to group members. Democratic leaders allowed the group to make decisions that would affect their activities; the leader merely helped the group arrive at a decision point. Laissez-faire leaders limited their interaction with group members to answering questions and providing materials when requested.

Data was gathered on the behavioural reactions of group members to each of the three leadership styles. The implications of this research were that group members preferred democratic to autocratic leaders, and conflict between members of the group was reported to be higher in autocratic and laissez-faire groups than in democratic groups. The productivity of the groups with democratic leaders was higher when unsupervised than either the autocratic or laissez-faire groups.

The findings of the Iowa studies generally supported the effectiveness of a democratic leadership style. However, the sample used (twenty boys) limits the findings, and broader applicability is questionable.

The key concern of the *Ohio State leadership studies* was the leader's behaviour in directing the efforts of others towards group goals. Two distinct dimensions of leader behaviour were identified: *initiating structure* (establishing structures geared to goal achievement) and *consideration* (establishing relationships with subordinates characterized by mutual trust, respect and consideration of employees' feelings). A manager can be high in both consideration and initiating structure, low in both, or high in one and low in the other. Although the Ohio State model describes two important elements of leadership behaviour, it does not suggest that there is one most effective combination that will meet the needs of all situations. Rather, the combination, or appropriate level, of initiating structure and consideration is determined by the *demands of the situation*.

Unfortunately, research[33] fails to support any of the effects associated with given behavioural styles of leaders.

The *University of Michigan studies* were concerned with managers with an employee orientation and a production orientation. These produced similar results to those of the Ohio State studies.[34] Differences in high-productivity and low-productivity work groups were related to differences in supervisors. It was found that highly productive supervisors spent more time planning departmental work and supervising their employees and less time working alongside and performing the same task, and that they tended to be employee-oriented.[35]

Blake and Mouton's[36] *Managerial Grid* is a two-dimensional matrix that shows concern for people on the vertical axis and concern for production on the horizontal axis. The two dimensions of the 9 × 9 grid are 'concern for people' and 'concern for production'. A score of 1 indicates a low concern and a score of 9 shows a high concern. The grid depicts five major leadership styles, each of which represents a degree of concern for 'people' and 'production'.

- *1,1: 'impoverished management'* – the manager has little concern for either people or production.

- *9,1: 'authority–obedience'* – the manager stresses operating efficiently through controls in situations where human elements cannot interfere.

- *1,9: 'country club management'* – the manager is thoughtful, comfortable and friendly, and has little concern for output.

- *5,5: 'organization man management'* – the manager attempts to balance and trade off concern for work in exchange for a satisfactory level of morale; he or she is a compromiser.

- *9,9: 'team management'* – the manager seeks high output through committed people, achieved through mutual trust, respect and a realization of interdependence

According to Blake and Mouton, the first four styles are not the most effective. They say that the 9,9 position of maximum concern for both output and people – the team management approach – is the leadership style that will most effectively result in improved performance, lower employee turnover and absenteeism, and greater employee satisfaction. Job enrichment and subordinate participation in managerial decision making contribute to this 9,9 style, where both the organization and its members are accorded maximum and equal concern. The Managerial Grid concept has been introduced to many managers and has influenced management philosophies and practices.

Most of the research which has been carried out on leader behavioural styles has been descriptive. A *normative approach to leadership style* was proposed by Vroom and Yetton.[37] The behavioural style variable they were concerned with was the way leaders involve their subordinates in organizational decision processes. This ranged from no involvement to total collaboration in reaching decisions. The model takes into account the characteristics of the organization and task, and it is these which determine, to a large extent, the leadership styles adopted. Vroom and Yetton identify five possible behavioural styles:

- *A1:* The leader makes the decision using available information.

- *A2:* The leader obtains information from subordinates and then makes the decision. Subordinates are not involved in the decision-making process.

- *C1:* The leader consults individual subordinates without bringing them together as a group. Then the leader makes the decision – which may or may not reflect the individuals' contributions.

- *C2:* The leader consults subordinates collectively, then makes the decision – which may or may not reflect subordinates' contributions.

- *G2:* The leader consults with subordinates as a group. Decisions are made through a joint process.

Vroom and Yetton also identified three criteria of effective decision making in organizations (the objective quality of the decision; the time required to make it, and the degree to which the decision will be acceptable to subordinates) as well as various attributes of the decision-making situation. These are illustrated in a flowchart which outlines the most rational decision-making style for a leader to follow in any particular situation.

This approach can be useful in diagnosing the existing styles of leaders in organizations and as an effective tool for managers, to enable them to be flexible and adaptive in their relationships with subordinates. The model clearly states what leaders should do in various organizational circumstances, rather than attempting to summarize what leaders actually do and noting the impact of these actions.

Situational leadership theories

Contingency or situational models assert that no single way of behaving works in all situations; appropriate behaviour depends on the circumstances at a given time. The development of contingency theories was a response to the failure of earlier, more universalist theories to explain or predict effective behaviour.

House's[38] *path goal theory of leadership* is based on the assumption that managers can influence employees' performance by highlighting how their behaviour directly affects their receiving rewards. In other words, a manager's behaviour can contribute to employee satisfaction. According to the path goal approach, effective job performance results if the manager clearly defines the job, provides training for the employee, assists the employee in performing the job effectively, and rewards the employee for effective performance.

According to House, effective leadership facilitates the accomplishment of a particular goal by clarifying the path to that goal. The following four distinct leadership behaviours are associated with the path goal approach:

1 *Directive:* the manager tells the subordinate what to do and when to do it (no employee participation in decision making).
2 *Supportive:* the manager is friendly with, and shows interest in, employees.
3 *Participative:* the manager seeks suggestions and involves employees in decision making.
4 *Achievement-oriented:* the manager establishes challenging goals and demonstrates confidence in employees in achieving these.

Following the path goal theory, a manager may use all four of the behaviours for four different situations.

Research findings show that employees who perform routine or monotonous jobs claim higher job satisfaction when their leader uses a supportive (as opposed to directive) leadership style.[39] On the other hand, the research suggests that employees who have loose and unstructured jobs are more productive and satisfied when their leader uses a more directive style.

Fiedler[40] stated that the most effective leadership style depends on the nature of the situation. (See Box OB3.4.) According to Fiedler, leaders can only be effective if their personality style is appropriate to a given set of situational variables. Personality style is measured by the *least-preferred co-worker* (LPC) scale.

Fiedler developed a LPC scale to measure two basic styles he identified:

1 those mainly concerned with doing the job (task-oriented);

2 those mainly concerned with developing interpersonal relations (people-oriented).

Research has suggested that low-LPC leaders emphasize the completion of tasks above all else. High-LPC leaders emphasize good interpersonal relationships not influenced by task accomplishment.[41]

Fiedler argued that a correlation exists between LPC score and type of leadership. Low LPC reflects task-oriented leadership because the leader is unable to ignore adverse behaviours of subordinates if these are likely to affect the completion of a task; high LPC reflects a people-oriented leadership style because the leader is able to ignore adverse behaviours in order to maintain a strong relationship, irrespective of its effect on the task.

BOX OB3.4

Leadership: 'It depends ...'

Fiedler is a contingency theorist.[1] For him, leadership has no fixed traits or pure functions and there is not necessarily one 'best' style; it *depends upon*, or is *contingent on*, the leader, his or her group of followers, and the nature of the situation in which the leader finds himself or herself.

The *relationship between leader and group* can be seen by 'psychologically distant managers' (PDMs) who keep their distance from the work group, and by other managers who are nearer the group – 'psychologically close managers' (PCMs).

The PDMs are formal, are reserved in their relationships, and prefer general consultation rather than informal discussion with staff. Good human relations, informality and a preference for people rather than the task will be indicative of the PCMs.

The *situation* is also very important. It can be either favourable or unfavourable (the polar opposite) to the leader. A favourable situation means:

■ the leader has the power to reward or punish;

■ the tasks of the group are clear and well defined;

■ the leader is liked and trusted by the work group.

According to Fiedler, the PDM's approach, which is more structured, works best when the situation is very favourable or very unfavourable. The middle ground – moderately favourable to the leader – means that a PCM's approach is required. This is more supportive of the group.

But we cannot keep changing formal leaders according to the situation, so a style flexibility (flex) is required. You need to be aware of your own preference and way of working, but to be prepared to analyse the situation and change your approach consequently, according to this perspective. Of course, you could always attempt to change the situation.

To summarize:

Leader's situation	Leader's style
Very unfavourable Very favourable ⟶	Task (PDM)
Moderately favourable ⟶	People (PCM)

So this leader/group effectiveness vision is really about the amount of *control and influence* that a leader has in a given situation.

Clearly we need to be able to analyse a favourable or unfavourable situation, as well as our style.

The method of determining style is called the *LPC* or least-preferred co-worker. It aims to show a predisposition to act in a certain way at the workplace. We are asked to think of one person with whom we work or have worked in the past with whom we had the most difficulty getting a job done. This person is called the least preferred co-worker (LPC). There is a scale of 1–8 on many variables, from 'gloomy' to 'cheerful' and from 'tense' to 'relaxed'.

A high score (64+) means that you are a high LPC person. This means that you are relationship-oriented. If you describe your LPC in more negative terms (under 58), you tend to be more task-motivated, prepared to do the job irrespective of other, poorer co-workers. The middling band (58–63) seem to be 'mixed' in their ideal approach.

So we should end up with a view of our ideal style towards people. Whether the co-worker style can transfer to our leadership style (above co-workers and peers) may be more debatable.

If we accept Fiedler's views, we must do the following:

■ determine our approach to the task;
■ determine our approach to the people;
■ be prepared to try and vary this ideal style;
■ analyse the situation;
■ look to the degree of control possible in the situation;
■ match our style to the situation or change the situation to our style.

Source:
1 See Fiedler et al., *Improving Leadership Effectiveness*

Fiedler identified three features of any circumstances that determine whether high-LPC (people-oriented) or low-LPC (task-oriented) managers are more likely to be effective:

1 the relationship between the leader and the followers (the better the relationship the more favourable the situation is for the leader);

2 how structured the task is (the more structured the more favourable the situation is for the leader – for monitoring);

3 position power – the amount of power that the leader has from his or her position; for example, a manager has more power than a secretary. The more power the leader has the more favourable the situation.

A basic assumption of the theory is that personality cannot really be changed, and therefore leaders in the 'wrong' kind of situation will not be effective. If anything is to change, it will tend to be the situation, although some would argue some onus lies on the leader as well.

Supporting evidence for this theory is mixed, but it is generally accepted that it has made an important contribution to the field. It attempts to identify precisely what it is that makes some leaders effective and others not effective by classifying situations as well as taking account of leader characteristics. Thus you cannot expect to always succeed as a leader just because you seem to have all the requisite personal qualities: you must also take into account the situation you find yourself in.

Theories are interesting and useful because they help to make us aware of the range of approaches available to us as potentially good leaders, but some of them may seem rather abstract. The main task of a manager is to get employees to perform to the best of their ability. So the study of leadership is critical in trying to understand how the leader comes to have influence over the followers.

Activity OB3.4 requires you to analyse leadership ability from several perspectives.

Conflict

The presence of incompatible goals, thoughts or emotions within or between individuals or groups leads to confrontation. Therefore we can say that conflict may be the result of incongruent or incompatible relationships between people.[42] Conflict occurs when:

- mutually exclusive goals or values exist in fact, or are perceived to exist, by the groups involved;

- interaction is characterized by behaviour designed to defeat, reduce or suppress the opponent, or to gain a mutually designated victory;

- the groups face each other with mutually opposing actions and counteractions;

- each group attempts to create a favoured position vis-à-vis the other.[43]

ACTIVITY OB3.4

THE SMALL ENGINEERING COMPANY

Activity code
- ✓ Self-development
- ✓ Teamwork
- ☐ Communications
- ☐ Numeracy/IT
- ✓ Decisions

It was decided to appoint a manager to free Clark from operational chores so that he could link with Jones to give more of a strategic overview of the firm and where it could be going, as both wanted to expand and capital was available to finance this expansion. The name 'Small' was that of the founder, and no longer reflected the size of the firm.

The new manager was Des Collins. His background was not strictly in this type of engineering but he had worked in some solid establishments. He hoped to join the directors in their expansion programme. The prospects of promotion and more bonus would be welcomed by him.

Collins was tidy-minded. One of his first tasks was to sort out the paper mess that he had inherited from Clark, who had been good with people but never a bureaucrat. Des was not a bureaucrat either, but he certainly loved paperwork. He was a very clear-minded man who set himself goals and usually met them. He like to 'run a tight ship' and, as in all firms, 'slack' appeared from time to time.

Clark had been quite informal with the staff; indeed, he used to whistle when he went on his rounds so that he would not catch people idle. His whistling was a well-known warning among the staff. He was popular with most of the employees.

The newcomer was different. His style meant formal Friday afternoon meetings of each 'head' of 'department'. Actually 'departments' did not really exist, but Collins created them. He tended to get embroiled in labour relations issues through his outspoken remarks and by adopting a purely managerialist frame of reference. He found trade unions a nuisance, and he made this evident.

He believed that managers were there to lead. He would determine what would be done at what time and by whom. Elaborate work schedules, duty rosters and day-off rotas were provided on his computer. He tended to be somewhat secretive when discussing issues with staff, preferring to tell them one step at a time and constantly referring back to the managers' meeting with the directors. He believed uncertainty did not help group relations, so this justified his approach. He liked to see people on a one-to-one basis wherever possible, shunning any collective discussions with the union representatives. In this way he could allocate praise or blame, and he remained aloof from 'mixing with the troops', as he liked to call it. (Although not a military man himself, his favourite reading revolved around the Africa Korps in Egypt in World War II.) Leadership was by example. Even when he was due holidays he tended to come in to see how the land was lying.

The work group as a whole resented him. Some were outspoken about his lack of real knowledge about what they were doing. Others disliked his diktats. All complained to one another about his endless memos and his calls for them to 'come up to my office for a chat' – no matter what they were doing. There was some grudging acceptance about his task leadership, but all believed that he was going about things the wrong way.

He had favourites – often female supervisors. This upset most of the staff. Above all, though, he did not involve the group in decisions, and his action towards the group seemed to minimize its role and to maximize his authority. He made some token remarks to some individuals (his favourites) while neglecting the others. He gave his friends more responsibility and called them his team. His team got more recognition, more authority, more responsibility and more opportunity to shine. Discontent was now open and resentment about Collins was never far from the surface. The senior management began to hear of his activities, as they had deliberately left him to get on with it while they had been looking to international markets. They would have to see him about his leadership.

Task

1 Analyse the leadership ability of Des from several perspectives. You may wish to include: characteristics or traits, functions, style and situation.
2 What can be done to amend his approach?

Defining conflict

The traditional perspective on conflict is negative. According to this, the presence of conflict indicates that something is wrong, and therefore it should be eliminated.

The contemporary perspective describes conflict as neither inherently good nor bad but as inevitable. Too much can have negative consequences; too little can also be negative in that such a state can lead to apathy and lethargy and provide little or no impetus for change and innovation.

Evidence suggests that conflict can improve the quality of decision making in organizations.[44] Thus the crucial issue is not conflict itself but how it is managed. We can therefore define conflict as 'functional' or 'dysfunctional' in terms of the effect it has on the organization. *Dysfunctional* conflict can have serious consequences for the organization's ability to achieve its goals; however, *functional* conflict can be thought of in terms of organizational innovation, creativity and adaptation.[45] In fact, the failure of some organizations can be traced back to too much harmony: it may be caused by complacency.[46]

We could therefore argue that dysfunctional conflict should be discouraged and functional conflict encouraged. In reality, however, most organizations attempt to eliminate all types of conflict.

Behavioural scientists have spent more than three decades researching and analysing how dysfunctional intergroup conflict affects those who experience it.[47] They have found that groups placed in a conflict situation tend to react in fairly predictable ways:

- within groups: increased group cohesiveness, emphasis on loyalty, rise in autocratic leadership, focus on activity;
- between groups: distorted perceptions, negative stereotyping, decreased communication.

Effective conflict management involves more than specific techniques. The ability to understand and diagnose conflict correctly is the first step in managing it.

In this section we examine conflict from a variety of perspectives. First we consider three views of conflict and the levels and sources of conflict that can occur in organizations. Then we outline styles in conflict management and the conditions under which each style may be appropriate.

Views of conflict

There are three views of conflict: positive, negative and 'balanced'.

Positive view
Conflict in organizations can be positive. The creation and/or resolution of conflict often leads to constructive outcomes; the need to resolve conflict can cause people to search for ways of changing how they do things; the conflict-resolution process is often a stimulus for positive change within an organization; and the search for ways to resolve conflict may not only lead to innovation and change, but make change more acceptable.[48]

The intentional introduction of conflict into the decision-making process can be beneficial. It is natural for us to hold different opinions, attitudes and values from others on a given situation. A positive view of conflict encourages us to work out our differences.

Positive outcomes of conflict can take the form of increased motivation and commitment, high-quality work and personal satisfaction.

Negative view
Conflict can have serious negative effects and divert our efforts from goal attainment. Furthermore, it can have a negative effect on our psychological wellbeing. Conflicting ideas, thoughts and beliefs can result in resentment, tension, stress and anxiety. Over a period of time, conflict may be detrimental to individual and group development.[49]

Negative outcomes of conflict may manifest themselves in labour turnover, sabotage, low-quality work, absenteeism and stress.

'Balanced' view

A 'balanced' view of conflict is preferable from a managerial perspective. Conflict may sometimes be highly desirable and at other times destructive; so managing conflict becomes an essential ingredient in the art of management.

Levels of conflict

There seem to be four major levels of conflict within organizations:

1 intrapersonal (within an individual)

2 interpersonal (between individuals)

3 intragroup (within a group)

4 intergroup (between groups)

Conflict can also occur at an intraorganizational level (within an organization) or an interorganizational level (between organizations). These levels are often interrelated.

Intrapersonal conflict

Conflict can exist within an individual when a choice has to be made between two diametrically opposed goals. We may be faced with the choice of acting in our own interests or in the organization's.

There are three basic types of intrapersonal conflict:

1 *approach–approach* conflict, in which an individual must choose between two or more alternatives that have positive outcomes (for example, choosing between two jobs that appear to be equally attractive);

2 *avoidance–avoidance* conflict, in which an individual must choose between two or more alternatives that have negative outcomes (for example, threatened demotion or increased travelling);

3 *approach–avoidance* conflict, in which an individual must decide whether to do something that has both positive and negative outcomes (for example, accepting a promotion but having to move).

The intensity of intrapersonal conflict generally increases under one or more of the following conditions:

■ There are several alternative courses of action for coping with conflict.

■ The positive and negative consequences of these alternatives are perceived as roughly equal.

■ The source of conflict is perceived as important to the decision maker.

Interpersonal conflict

Interpersonal conflict results when two individuals disagree about issues, actions or goals – the concept of confrontation comes into play. Many interpersonal and intrapersonal conflicts are based on some type of role conflict or role ambiguity.

A role is the bundle of tasks and duties that others expect a person to perform in doing a job. Role conflict, therefore, occurs when what we consider to be our role is incompatible with that of our manager. Role ambiguity, on the other hand, refers to the situation where we have no clear idea as to what is required of us.

Intragroup conflict

This may take many forms; for example, substantive and affective conflicts. *Substantive* conflict refers to intragroup conflict that is based on intellectual disagreement among group members, as when the tasks of one group member interfere with those of another. *Affective* conflict is intragroup conflict that is based on emotional responses to a situation. This refers to clashes among some or all of the group's members, which often affect the group's processes and effectiveness.[50]

Intergroup conflict

This refers to opposition and clashes between two or more groups. Intergroup conflict often occurs in union–management relations. Under extreme conditions, the groups develop and, perhaps, consolidate attitudes towards and relationships with each other that are characterized by distrust, rigidity, a focus only on self-interest, a failure to listen, etc.

Intraorganizational conflict

Three forms of conflict can be identified within organizations. *Vertical* conflict exists between managers and subordinates. *Horizontal* conflict exists between employees or departments at the same level. *Line–staff* conflict occurs over resources or the involvement of staff people in line decisions.

Interorganizational conflict

This is conflict between organizations where some form of inter-dependency exists; for example, they have the same suppliers, customers, competitors, government agencies, etc. Organizations in conflict frequently demonstrate either co-operative or competitive behaviours. The extent to which conflict arises may depend on the extent to which one organization creates uncertain conditions for the others, attempts to access or control the same resources, encourages communication with others, attempts to balance power in the marketplace and develops procedures for resolving existing conflict.[51]

Now tackle Activity OB3.5.

Stages of conflict

One way to understand conflict is to view it as a dynamic rather than a static concept. It can be seen as a sequence of conflict stages – latent, perceived, felt, manifest and aftermath.[52]

- *Latent:* Conflict begins when the conditions for it exist. Individuals or groups may have power differences, compete for scarce resources, strive for autonomy, have different goals, or experience diverse role pressures. These are the foundations for disagreement, competition and conflict.
- *Perceived:* Individuals or group members know that conflict exists.
- *Felt:* When one or more parties feel tense or anxious, conflict has moved beyond the perceived stage. Conflict becomes personalized to the individuals or groups involved.

ACTIVITY OB3.5

CONFLICT: CREATING A BALANCE SHEET

Activity code
- ✓ Self-development
- ✓ Teamwork
- ✓ Communications
- ☐ Numeracy/IT
- ✓ Decisions

Task

Draw up a balance sheet for the impact of conflict on an organization. Examine the negative and positive aspects of conflict and weight the factors in your individual or group conclusion. An example is provided on the grid.

NB: You and/or your group should adopt the neutral position of an OB analyst.

Negatives

Conflict disrupts the production flow.

Positives

Conflict makes the ground rules more clear and explicit.

■ *Manifest:* Overt behaviour whose intention is to place obstacles in the path of those pursuing a particular goal occurs. Open aggression and withdrawal of support illustrate manifest conflict. At this stage conflict must be resolved or used constructively in order for effective organizational performance to continue.

■ *Aftermath:* The final stage of conflict is the situation after it has been resolved or suppressed. The conflict aftermath describes the outcome of the conflict – it may result in supportive, paternalistic or adversarial relationships. It could revert back to a latent stage or continue unabated at the manifest stage – perhaps taking a new twist or direction.

Conflict is inevitable in organizational life, but it need not be destructive. Depending on how it is managed, the negative effects may be minimized and positive ones may result. Effective conflict management is based, in part, on a solid understanding of the different ways that conflict emerges and can be resolved.

Conflict management

There are a large number of techniques that can be used to deal with conflict between two or more individuals. They range from the use of force by a manager or a trade union to a problem-solving approach. Possible ways of handling interpersonal conflict are as follows:

■ *Force* – a manager may demand the acceptance of a certain situation.

■ *Withdrawal* – withdraw from or avoid the person with whom the conflict exists. Conflict is reduced but the original cause remains.

■ *Smoothing* – a manager or subordinate attempts to provide an image of co-operation.

■ *Compromise* – neither party gets all it wants, but an agreement is reached.

■ *Conciliation, mediation and arbitration* – outside, neutral parties enter the situation to assist in resolving the conflict.

■ *Problem solving* – this is characterized by an open and trusting exchange of views. The approach here is a joint decision-making focus which can take the sting out of relationship conflicts, if not out of major institutional conflicts. Some time ago, Oldfield[53] advocated this approach.

The physical layout of work, new procedures, new institutions and structures as well as different attitudes can help in the management of conflict. This is developed at length in another volume of this series, *Effective Labour Relations*.

In part, the institutionalization of conflict occurs through the integrating mechanisms of learning, communications and power sources/structures within the organization. We now turn to these mechanisms, not only from the context of managing conflict but from a wider perspective of managing the effective organization.

Notes

1 Crozier, *The Bureaucratic Phenomenon*.
2 Handy, *Understanding Organizations*.
3 Warr and Wall, *Work and Well Being*.
4 Shaw, *Group Dynamics*.
5 Schein, *Organizational Psychology*.
6 Bales, *Interaction Process Analysis*.
7 McDavid and Harari, *Social Psychology*.
8 Bass, *Leadership Psychology*.
9 Homans, *Human Group*.
10 Alcorn, 'Understanding groups at work'.
11 For a fuller discussion see Mayo, *Human Problems of an Industrial Civilization*.
12 Shaw, *Group Dynamics*.
13 Tuckman, 'Developmental sequence in small groups'.
14 Kormanski, 'Situational leadership approach'.
15 Napier and Gershenfeld, *Groups*.
16 T.R. Davis, 'Influence of the physical environment in offices'.
17 Mackie and Goethals, 'Individual and group goals'.
18 Sneizek et al., 'Social uncertainty and interdependence'.
19 Berelson and Steiner, *Human Behavior*.
20 George and Bettenhausen, 'Understanding prosocial behavior'.
21 Bettenhausen and Murnigham, 'Development and stability of norms'.
22 Porter et al., *Behavior in Organizations*.
23 Staw, *Psychological Dimensions*.
24 Hemphill and Coons, 'Development of the leader behavior description questionnaire'.
25 Tannenbaum et al., *Leadership and Organization*.
26 Yukl, *Leadership in Organizations*.
27 Conger, 'Inspiring others'.
28 Stogdill, 'Personal factors'.
29 Ghiselli, *Explorations in Managerial Talent*.
30 Stogdill, 'Personal factors'.
31 Summarized in Katz and Kahn, *Social Psychology of Organizations*.
32 Lewin et al., 'Patterns of aggressive behaviour'.
33 For example, Korman, 'Consideration, initiating structure, and organizational criteria'; Sales, 'Supervisory style and productivity'.
34 Fleischman and Hunt, *Current Developments in the Study of Leadership*.
35 Katz and Kahn, *Social Psychology of Organizations*.
36 Blake and Mouton, *New Managerial Grid*.
37 Vroom and Yetton, *Leadership and Decision Making*.
38 House, 'Path–goal theory of leader effectiveness'.
39 Yukl, *Leadership in Organizations*.
40 Fiedler, *Theory of Leadership*.
41 Rice, 'Construct validity of the Least Preferred Co-worker score'.
42 Kabanoff, 'Equity, power and conflict'.
43 Filley, 'Some normative issues in conflict management'.
44 Cosier and Schwenk, 'Agreement and thinking alike'.
45 Thomas, 'Conflict and conflict management'.

46 Robbins, *Essentials of Organizational Behavior.*
47 Sherif and Sherif, *Groups in Harmony and Tension.*
48 Cosier and Dalton, 'Positive effects of conflict'.
49 Baron and Richardson, *Human Aggression.*
50 Kabanoff, 'Equity, power and conflict'.
51 Pfeffer, *Power in Organizations.*
52 Pondy, 'Organizational conflict'.
53 Oldfield, *New Look Industrial Relations.*

Unit Four

Focus on Integrating Mechanisms

Learning Objectives

After completing this unit, you should be able to:

- understand the concept of integrative mechanisms;
- explain the role of learning and describe learning approaches;
- understand the communication process and gained insight into non-verbal communication factors;
- explain the concept of organizational power and identify the sources of power;
- apply the generic skills.

Contents

Overview

Learning

► Defining learning

► Historical perspectives on learning

Behaviourist approach

Cognitive approach

Social learning approach

► Developing and changing work behaviour through training

Communication

► Defining communication

► The communication process

What should be communicated?

How can we communicate more effectively?

► Non-verbal communication

Non-verbal behaviour

Power

► Defining power

► Sources of power

► Effective use of power

Unit Four

> " The effective organisation has integrating devices consistent with the diversity of its environment. The more diverse the environment and the more differentiated the organization, the more elaborate the integrating devices. "
>
> *Lawrence and Lorsch*[1]

Overview

The mechanisms an organization adopts to achieve its goals and objectives are many and varied. Furthermore, the integrating mechanisms within an organization largely determine how effective an organization is in reality. The primary purpose of these integrating mechanisms is to place individual employee behaviours into an organizational context and to focus them on the achievement of organizational goals and objectives. The secondary purpose is to maximize the individual's own contribution to his or her development.

Desirable work behaviours contribute, in no small way, to achieving organizational goals, just as, conversely, undesirable work behaviours may hinder their attainment. It is therefore important that desirable work behaviours are nurtured and encouraged through appropriate integrating mechanisms. Again, a motivated employee with his or her own development plans further integrates these mechanisms.

The focus of this unit is on examining how managers can encourage desirable work behaviours through three commonly used integrating mechanisms, by exploring the development, maintenance and change of work behaviours in the broader context of learning, communication and power.

Learning

A good manager does not try to change an employee's basic personality or fundamental beliefs. Rather, he or she should be more concerned with all employees learning productive behaviours. To a great extent, learning new work behaviours depends on environmental factors. Therefore the manager's goal is to provide learning experiences in an environment that will promote employee behaviours desired by the organization. Again, this should meet employee objectives as well as ensuring less transient behavioural patterns.

Learning, therefore, can be seen as a useful management tool for developing and changing employee behaviours as well as a key developmental tool for employee satisfaction.

Defining learning

Learning is a word that we all use in our everyday conversations, and when we do, everyone seems to know what it means. Still, 'learning' is one of those common terms that most of us would have difficulty defining precisely. This difficulty is partly due to the fact that we use the term to describe at least two different kinds of activity.

First, we use 'learning' to describe the mental activities that are involved when we acquire new meanings for stimuli; for example, 'learning the names of our peers and subordinates'. Here we are talking about acquiring new information. When we learn a person's name, we are actually giving the name greater significance by associating it with a person's face. Thus, we commonly use the term 'learning' whenever we refer to the activity of attaching new meaning or significance to a stimulus.

We also use the term 'learning' to refer to situations in which we develop some new response. We talk, for example, about 'learning to type' or about 'learning to use a computer'. Here we use the term to describe the acquisition or modification of some behaviour. The notion here is that by practising or experiencing a response over and over, one becomes capable of refining or changing the response being made. We assume that learning is the process responsible for this change.

Since both definitions are so common, which one is technically more correct? The answer is that both are correct, as both these uses seem to capture what psychologists mean when they use the term.

So, simply, 'learning is a relatively permanent change in the frequency of occurrence of a specific individual behaviour.'[2] Therefore, learning refers to the acquisition of skills, knowledge, abilities and attitudes through patterned actions and practice, which changes our behaviour.

Individuals can learn in a variety of ways. However, to understand contemporary thinking on learning we need to be aware of its historical roots.

Historical perspectives on learning

Historically, there have been many different attempts to explain this complex process. Essentially, these fall into three discrete approaches:

1 *Behaviourist approach* – these attempts emphasize the reinforcement between behaviours through trial-and-error experiences.
2 *Cognitive approach* – these are primarily concerned with the significance of cognitive environment cues and expectations.

3 *Social learning approach* – these attempt to integrate both behaviourist and cognitive approaches.

We develop other approaches, related and not so related, later in Box OB4.1.

Behaviourist approach

Behaviourist theorists emphasize the link between a given stimulus and response. One of the most influential behaviourist approaches to learning is *classical conditioning*. This involves reflexive responses or behaviours.

In classical conditioning an unconditioned stimulus (environmental event) elicits a reflexive response. Sometimes a neutral environmental event (conditioned stimulus) can be paired with the unconditioned stimulus that elicits the reflex. Eventually the conditioned stimulus alone elicits the reflexive behaviour.

In classical conditioning, environmental events that precede a reflexive response control it. The classic experiment by Pavlov[3] illustrates this. He noted that upon presentation of a piece of meat (unconditioned stimulus) to a dog, the dog salivated (unconditioned response). The ringing of a bell (neutral stimulus) initially yielded no salivation response. After pairing the ringing bell with the piece of meat, the dog salivated (conditioned response). In classical conditioning, after repeated pairing of neutral and unconditioned stimuli, solitary presentation of the neutral stimulus leads to a conditioned response.

The question which arises is: can this be related to human behaviours? Simple kinds of human conditioning similar to this process occasionally occur. For example, we learn that fire alarms are indicators of danger. Smoke, flames or other evidence of fire serve as the unconditioned stimulus; running away is the unconditioned response. As we grow up we associate fire alarms with fires. Thus, the alarm becomes the conditioned stimulus and movement the conditioned response. Similarly, companies frequently attempt to get customers to associate certain images with their products and services; for example, we have been conditioned to associate brown bread with healthy living.

Although classical conditioning provides some insights into the learning process, from a managerial perspective, classical conditioning is usually not considered applicable to the work setting. Managers do not have to deal with reflexive responses. Instead, managers are interested in the voluntary behaviour of employees and how it can be changed through the use of other techniques.

Operant or instrumental conditioning extends classical conditioning to focus on the consequences of behaviour.[4] A stimulus still causes a response, but what happens after the response – a desired or undesired consequence – determines whether the response will recur. In other words, operant conditioning involves the modification of voluntary responses through rewards, punishments and consequences of other kinds. Therefore, in operant conditioning situations, we learn to alter our behaviours depending on what their consequences are. For example, an individual who receives a bonus (positive consequence) after reaching his or her work targets (stimulus) is more likely to repeat the behaviour than if his or her performance is ignored (negative consequence).

Operant conditioning attempts to provoke change in voluntary or operant work behaviours of the employee. The consequence that follows the behaviours partly controls them. Virtually all employee behaviours in organizations are operant behaviours.

Operant work behaviours are of interest to managers because they can be controlled or managed by their environmental consequences. The frequency of an employee behaviour can be increased or decreased by changing its environmental consequences. The consequences of behaviour, therefore, act as *reinforcers*.

A *contingency of reinforcement* is the relationship between a behaviour and the preceding and following environmental events that influence that behaviour. It consists of an antecedent, a behaviour and a consequence,[5] where the antecedent precedes and is a stimulus to a behaviour (sets the scene for behaviour to occur) and the consequence is the result of behaviour. A consequence of a behaviour can either be positive or negative in terms of goal or task accomplishment. Managers may be able to use various kinds of reinforcement to affect employee behaviour.

Reinforcement is a behaviour contingency that increases the frequency of a particular behaviour that it follows. Positive reinforcement presents a pleasant consequence for occurrence of a desired behaviour; that is, a manager provides a positive reward contingent on the employee's behaviour that the manager views as desirable or leading toward achievement of the organization's goals.[6]

Several factors can influence the intensity of positive reinforcement.[7] For example, the reinforcer should only be given if the desired behaviour occurs. The larger the amount of reinforcer delivered, the more effective the reinforcer. Depriving the employee of the reinforcer will ensure that when desired behaviours occur and reinforcers are given, their effect will be that much greater. Common organizational reinforcers and rewards are shown in table 4.1.

Negative reinforcement is where an unpleasant event is presented before the employee behaviour and is then removed when the behaviour occurs. Negative reinforcement is not synonymous with punishment. Punishment refers to a 'penalty' being incurred *after* the event by employees if they do not behave in the desired way.

Operant conditioning theory is the most widely used theory of learning. It has organizational implications for designing effective reward and punishment systems whose express purpose is to encourage desired work behaviours and discourage undesirable work behaviours.

Table 4.1 Reinforcers and rewards used by organizations

Type	Examples
Material rewards	Pay, bonuses, profit sharing, incentives
Fringe benefits	Pensions, company car, insurance, discounts, expense accounts
Status symbols	Nice office, carpet, curtains
Social rewards	Praise, pats on the back
Task rewards	Achievement, responsibility
Self-rewards	Self-praise

Cognitive approach

In contrast to the stimulus–response links that are key in behaviourist theories, cognitive theorists look at the significance of cognitive environmental cues and expectations.[8] In other words, there is a change in what learners know rather than what they do. The processing of knowledge is therefore important. Cognitive learning consists of two components: insight learning and latent learning.

Insight learning involves understanding what is being learnt and thinking about it. In a normal experiment in insight learning, a problem is presented, followed by a period of time when no apparent progress is made and finally a solution suddenly emerges. A feature of insight learning is that it can be generalized to other situations.

Latent learning is not manifest at the time learning takes place. Learning goes on in the absence of reward, but when a suitable reward is available, the information previously learnt can be used. We tend to store knowledge about positive and negative reinforcements acquired through past experiences; for example, some previous behaviours have been a source of satisfaction whereas others have not. Cognitions from several different learning experiences may be integrated so that we can adapt to new situations to achieve personal goals.

An early contribution to the concept of latent leaning was made by Tolman.[9] In Tolman's early experiments, rats learned to run through a maze to a goal of food. Repeated trials allowed the rat to develop cognitive connections that identified the correct path to the goal. Each time the rat reached its goal, the connections between the cognitive cues and the expectancies of reaching the goal were strengthened. According to Tolman, the rat developed a cognitive map of the path to the goal, so that one cue or stimulus led to the next cue or stimulus, rather than to a response.

The final approach to learning which is considered is the social learning approach. This extends beyond both behaviourist and cognitive learning theories.

Social learning approach

Social learning theory suggests that learning results from modelling behaviours. Using observations to gather information, learners imitate the behaviour of others.[10] According to Bandura,[11] a learner first watches others and develops a mental picture of the behaviour and its consequences. The observer then tries out the behaviour. If positive consequences result, the behaviour is repeated, but if negative consequences occur, no repetition takes place. The learner's assessment of response consequences parallels behaviourist theories. The learner's development of a cognitive image of the situation incorporates ideas of cognitive learning.

A central part of social learning is the concept of self-efficacy. This refers to the belief that one can perform adequately in a situation.[12] Employees with high self-efficacy believe that they have the ability needed, they are capable of the effort required to achieve the goal, and no outside events will prevent them from obtaining a desired level of performance. If workers have low self-efficacy, they believe that no matter how hard they try something will happen to prevent them from reaching their desired level of performance. Self-efficacy influences our choice of tasks and how long we will try to reach our goals.

A manager's expectations about a subordinate's behaviour can affect a person's self-efficacy. If a manager holds high expectations of the person and gives him or her the proper training to succeed, the person's self-efficacy is likely to increase. If a manager holds low expectations of the subordinate, the subordinate performs poorly, and the manager gives little constructive advice, then the poor behaviour might persist because the employee is likely to form an impression that he or she cannot achieve the task. When people believe that they are not capable of doing the required work, their motivation to perform the task will be low, potentially resulting in lower performance.

Applications of social learning theory for improving behaviour in organizations are beginning to emerge.[13] Researchers have suggested that managers should consider the following:

- identify the behaviours that will lead to improved performance;
- select the appropriate model for employees to observe;
- make sure that employees are capable of meeting the technical skill requirements of the required new behaviours;
- structure a positive learning situation to increase the likelihood that employees will learn the new behaviours and act in the proper manner;

■ provide positive consequences (praises or bonuses) for employees who engage in proper modelling behaviours;

■ develop management practices that maintain these newly learned behaviours.

Although none of the above approaches comprehensively explains the learning process, they are useful in that each provides managers with clues about different aspects of learning. Activity OB4.1 will help you identify how you learn.

ACTIVITY OB4.1

LEARNING

Activity code
✓ Self-development
☐ Teamwork
✓ Communications
☐ Numeracy/IT
✓ Decisions

How do you learn? Which style of learning do you prefer? Do you have a range of styles?

This is not a test on learning, merely an exercise on how best you learn. In each group of statements A–D, give each statement, (a), (b), (c) and (d), a grade 1–4: 4 means that this summarizes your learning style, while 1 means that this is least characteristic of your approach to learning (for example, in training or at college). See the *Handbook* for an interpretation of your 'score'.

Group			Grade (1–4)
A	(a)	I like new experiences.	
	(b)	I like to think things over.	
	(c)	I like to be intellectually pushed.	
	(d)	I like to see a link between what we are learning and my job.	
B	(a)	Learning methods must have a practical advantage	
	(b)	Learning methods must allow you to question basic assumptions.	
	(c)	Learning methods should allow you to take in information before commenting.	
	(d)	Learning methods must be action-oriented.	

Group			Grade (1–4)
C	(a)	I like to review events.	
	(b)	I like to be in the limelight.	
	(c)	I like to practise with an expert.	
	(d)	I like to be involved with structured events.	
D	(a)	Relationships and associations should be explored in a methodical manner.	
	(b)	Practical issues must be used.	
	(c)	Decisions on issues should not be made in haste.	
	(d)	A difficult issue should be used to tax people.	

Source: Concept (not questions) adapted from a combination of Kolb, 'Towards an applied theory of experiential learning', and Honey and Mumford, *Manual of Learning Styles*

A different perspective on learning characteristics and learning theories and their relationship with training can be found in Box OB4.1. Activity OB4.2 will enable you to fuse learning schools of thought and learning characteristics.

BOX OB4.1

Learning characteristics and learning theories

Learning, or behavioural change, lies at the heart of education, development and training. Learning theories are therefore used by both sides in the education debate between the traditionalists and the radicals, between a more didactic input approach on the one hand and student-centred activities and participative methods on the other. In training and development, particularly of the higher-order skills of comprehension and judgement, the student-centred approach with its experience-based learning seems to have routed the opposition. The didactic approach, if applied, seems restricted to lower-order skills, such as motor response, and to non-managerial training. It is felt that there is no clear-cut answer, in either education or training, as to whether one theory or another can justify a participative view or a more structured input. Indeed, the use of one theory will tend to emphasize some learning characteristics rather than others, including participation or structure, so the argument is cyclical: the theory justifies the argument, but the theories themselves give different weightings to the characteristics of learning.

It will be suggested that some characteristics of learning, while not separated from the values or premises of the school of thought, may be more common across the schools that we would imagine from a top-down approach.

The approach

M. Jones, writing in 1979,[1] related the practice of training to the mainstream theories of learning and showed very well how these main theories influenced training methods. The three main learning theories were identified as:

1 behaviourist or social learning
2 phenomenological or humanist
3 cognitive or Gestalt

Jones used the method of expanding on these three main theories and then examining their implications for training methods. The slant here is to examine the main characteristics of learning adapted from the core theories of learning and then relate these characteristics to Jones' three main schools of thought, with their respective implications. So a bottom-up approach is being used here.

Common learning characteristics

The main aspects which were extrapolated from many learning theories were as follows.[2]

- *Motivation:* This concerns commitment to the task and can be inferred from behaviour. It can be classified as intrinsic – that is, within the individual – or extrinsic – that is, with some form of goal orientation outside the task in hand.
- *Results:* Feedback or knowledge of results is linked to positive motivation. We all like to know how we are doing.
- *Rewards:* Again, these are linked to goal-directed behaviour, or motivation, and tied in with knowledge of results.
- *Trial and error:* An unsystematic and costly approach, but it has a positive side if learners are given parameters within which to 'discover' principles etc. for themselves.
- *Insight:* This is linked to trial and error. We can lie awake for hours trying to solve a problem, and it may come in a flash the next morning. A creative framework helps such learning.
- *Practice:* We do and we learn. This can be either by trial and error or by a more systematic form of 'structured experience'.
- *Scale:* Some learning, such as learning to recite a verse of poetry, must be learned as a whole, while other types, such as biology at A-level, must be broken down into part learning owing to its complexity.
- *Individual differences:* We are all different social animals, so age, intelligence, level of previous knowledge, etc., must all be taken into account.
- *Periods of learning:* Learning is tiring and it is not a steady upward curve, so we need to plan accordingly.
- *Repetition:* Recall may be stimulated by constantly repeating formulae, etc., but it can often be short-term and not remembered by the individual in the long term.
- *Interference:* In many ways learning is a form of communication between A and B, so blockages can occur.
- *Transfer:* Learning a principle or whatever has no merit unless it can be applied to different scenarios. Perhaps this is where a real division could occur between trainers and educationalists, as the application may be the realm of the trainer while 'art for art's sake' may exist more in educational circles.

Sources:
1   M. Jones, 'Training practices and learning theories'
2   A.H. Anderson, *Successful Training Practice*

ACTIVITY OB4.2

FUSION: SCHOOLS AND CHARACTERISTICS

Activity code
- ☑ Self-development
- ☑ Teamwork
- ☑ Communications
- ☐ Numeracy/IT
- ☑ Decisions

Task

1 Read Box OB4.1.

2 Using the chart here, relate these main learning characteristics to the three main schools of learning, noting the respective importance of each characteristic.

3 Provide a rationale for your matrix.

Learning characteristics	Schools of thought		
	Behaviourist or social learning	Phenomenological or humanist	Cognitivist or Gestalt
Motivation Extrinsic Intrinsic			
Knowledge of results			
Reward and punishment			
Trial and error			
Discovery and insight			
Learning by doing or active practice			
Scale: part or whole			
Individual differences			
Period of learning			
Structured repetition			
Interference			
Transfer			

Developing and changing work behaviour through training

Training involves a systematic set of procedures and experiences that are planned and implemented. The express purpose of training is to bring about some change in the skills, knowledge and attitudes of employees that will result in improved job performance. If an organization finds itself with a need for increased performance, efficiency, better methods of work, lower labour turnover, wastage of materials and ultimately greater profitability – training *might* be the answer.

It is important to determine whether training is actually necessary, since there may be other factors which are contributory to such problems rather than a lack of training. For example, there may be a negative attitude among the workforce due to a lack of feedback on job performance, insufficient information about the duties of their job, a non-supportive work environment, poor job design or personal problems inside or outside work.[14]

Generally, training can improve an individual's performance only when:

■ the employee does not have the skill or knowledge to do the job;

■ low performance is not due to lack of practice;

■ low performance is not due to other causes.

For training to be worthwhile, it is imperative that learning takes place. Training, if it is to be successful, therefore depends on an understanding of the learning process.[15]

As stated earlier, learning is a relatively permanent change in behaviour that occurs as a result of practice or experience. Therefore, we can say that training is equal to a learning experience. The trainee will bring to any learning situation a range of knowledge, skills and attitudes previously acquired. The trainer must build on these previously acquired attributes, which will vary from person to person, so that each trainee can gain new knowledge, skills and attitudes. However, no two trainees will necessarily learn in quite the same way. In practice, the trainer will try to provide a learning situation that appears to meet the needs of the greatest number of trainees.

Trainees may also vary in the degree of motivation they possess and in their level of self-esteem. Those with low motivation or low self-esteem will normally take longer to complete a training programme than the well-motivated trainee.

Finally, although training may improve performance, it costs money. The organization, therefore, must ask whether the costs of *not* training sufficiently outweigh the costs of learning and the costs of training before implementing the training solution.

BOX OB4.2

Generalizations from learning theory

1 Trainees learn best by making active responses. People learn best by doing and getting involved, not just listening.
2 The responses that the trainees make are limited by their abilities and by the sum total of their past responses.
3 Learning proceeds most effectively when the trainees' correct responses are promptly reinforced.
4 The frequency with which a response is reinforced will determine how well it will be learned.
5 Practice in a variety of settings will increase the range of situations in which learning can be applied.
6 Motivated trainees are more likely to learn and to use what they have learned than an unmotivated trainee.
7 Trainees should be encouraged to find summarizing or governing principles to help to organize what they are learning.
8 Trainees should be assisted to learn to discriminate the important stimuli in every situation so that they can respond appropriately.
9 Trainees will learn most effectively when they can learn at their own pace.
10 There are different kinds of learning and they may require different learning conditions.

Source: Adapted from Silverman, 'Learning theory applied to training'

Box OB4.2 gives a different insight on the main learning characteristics we have covered to date.

Understanding the learning process and its influence on training can help the manager make informed decisions about learning experiences as well as providing an effective tool for maintaining and developing desirable work behaviours.

In the next section, we continue to explore integrating mechanisms for changing and developing desirable work behaviours by focusing on the important process of communication.

Communication

In an organization, communication provides the means by which employees may be stimulated to accomplish organizational goals. Therefore, effective communication should be considered not an end in itself, but a means of achieving organizational objectives.

Many organizational problems can be explained in terms of communication problems. The ability to communicate well is critical to effective management. In fact, it has been estimated that managers spend over 75 per cent of their time involved in communication activities in one form or other.[16] Given that communication is such an important activity, it is good to know that communication skills can be learnt.

Defining communication

Communication is probably one of the few areas in organizational behaviour where there is a commonly held view of what it is about. Communication is the transmission and reception of ideas, information, opinions, attitudes and feelings, through more than one medium, that produce a response.[17] This definition suggests that communication is a multi-stage process between at least two people – the sender and the receiver.

The communication process

There are four basic steps that we should be aware of if we wish to communicate effectively. We need to:

1 attract people's attention to our communication;

2 ensure that they understand and comprehend our message;

3 influence others to accept as true the information we have given them;

4 ensure that they remember the information we have given them and hope that they modify their behaviour on the basis of that communication.

See Activity OB4.3.

ACTIVITY OB4.3

COMMANDMENTS OF GOOD COMMUNICATION

Activity code

☑ Self-development
☑ Teamwork
☑ Communications
☐ Numeracy/IT
☑ Decisions

We are all familiar with communications. As an individual or in a group, your task is to list what you or your group feel are the ten key aspects of organizational communications.

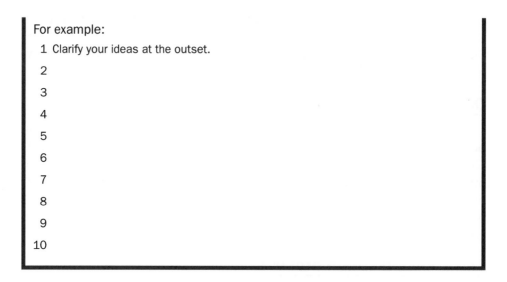

For example:

1 Clarify your ideas at the outset.

2

3

4

5

6

7

8

9

10

On the basis of the meaning transmitted, the receiver will act in response to the communication. This action can be to ignore the message, perform some task, store the information for some future use, or something else.

What should be communicated?

Some managers limit their communication with subordinates to giving instructions, but communication should have a much larger scope, as it is an essential requirement of good management. Behavioural scientists have shown that employee motivation is impossible without effective communication.

Research has also shown the need for subordinates to be heard, consulted and understood by their managers. The need for an effective communication system that advances the goals of the organization is quite obvious, particularly in times of economic recession and increased competition. The responsibility to maintain a good communication climate clearly falls on management.

Deciding precisely what should be communicated is often difficult. The manager who believes that everything is open to communication will invariably find that the channels of communication become jammed with a whole host of irrelevancies that ultimately may prove detrimental to the organization's effectiveness. Employee needs must also be considered, and how those needs are to be addressed must be communicated effectively, if managers wish to ensure employee co-operation. Employees want to know certain things; for example:

■ their standing in relation to the official, formal authority structure;

■ their standing in relation to the informal organization, with respect to individual status, power, acceptance and so forth;

- events that have a bearing on their own and the company's future economic security;
- operational information that will enable them to develop pride in their job.

How can we communicate more effectively?

Effective communication means that the receiver correctly interprets the message of the sender. This often fails to occur due to breakdowns in communication. Let us concentrate on some of the common barriers to the multi-stage process of communication.

When communication is attempted, messages are transmitted through such means as speaking, writing, acting and drawing. A number of channels may be used to transmit any message. Words can be communicated orally, through such methods as face-to-face conversations, telephone conversations, radio and television. Reports, letters, memos, books and articles can serve as written channels. The senses of touch, smell and taste are non-verbal channels. A great deal of meaningful communication takes place without a word being spoken. However, many of these are ignored; so what attracts our careful attention?

Research into perception has shown that the situation or context in which we receive information and the nature of the information itself influence whether or not we 'notice' the attempt at communication. The situation or context is important in terms of the *amount of information* we receive. Too much information could lead to information overload, as a person can absorb only so many facts and figures at any one time. When excessive information is provided, a major breakdown in communication can be caused by the person's filtering or selecting only certain types of information.

The *direction of the communication* will also affect it. It has been found that upward communication normally filters out negative data and downward communication filters out task-irrelevant data.[18]

The *pattern or network of information* affects whether or not the information attracts our attention. There are essentially two patterns of communication: formal (this resembles organization structure) and informal (commonly referred to as the grapevine). All of us have a role in formal and informal networks, and these two roles strongly influence how much and what type of information we will receive.[19]

A variety of organizational factors, such as centralization v. decentralization, the sender's status within the organization, physical location, etc. will also affect the amount of information we receive.

The nature or characteristics of the message affect whether or not we notice the information. This is based on our perceptions of the message (see Unit Two). The *novelty or newness of information* draws our attention, as do its degree of *importance to us personally*, and its *intensity*.

Unless the sender attracts the receiver's attention to the message, it does not matter how good the message is – it will not be received.

The second stage of the communication process is to ensure that the receiver comprehends and understands our message. There are two factors which determine how completely we comprehend the message: the semantics of the message and the perceptual set of the receiver.

The receiver must 'decode' the message by converting the symbols into meaning. Like senders, receivers have diverse backgrounds, experiences and aspirations. Communication is effective only to the extent that the receiver's decoding matches the sender's encoding.

Language problems can result from the vocabulary used and from different meanings applied to the same word (semantics). A manager must appreciate and understand the type of audience being addressed. Breakdowns in communication often occur when the sender does not tailor the message to match the knowledge base of the receiver. This problem is most severe when someone deliberately uses fancy words just to seem more knowledgeable. When a sender uses words to which a receiver attaches different meanings from those intended by the sender, a semantic – or meaning-of-words – communication breakdown is likely to occur.

The problem of misinterpretation is further exacerbated by the perceptions and past experiences of the receiver. These tend to be the major cause of miscommunication. They include various forms of distortion of the message by drawing unwarranted conclusions through perceptual bias, filtering data into preconceived beliefs, stereotyping, projection and simplification (see Unit Two for fuller explanation).

Once the receiver has noticed and understood our communication, it is important that he or she accept this information as true. Much of our communication is aimed at converting others to our point of view. There are two sets of variables which most strongly influence whether the communication to others is accepted as true: first, certain characteristics of the communicator that may increase its credibility (such as expertise, trustworthiness, attractiveness); second, the extent to which the receiver is defensive towards the communication – that is, to which the communication is personally threatening and is dissonant information that poses some threat to the individual receiving it.

The ultimate objective of any communication is that the information is remembered and that the receiver modifies his or her behaviour on the basis of that communication.

How the message is presented and the nature of organization's reward systems both influence the long-term effectiveness of our communications and whether or not the desired work behaviours occur.

Box OB4.3 offers some presentational issues which we all should consider before attempting to communicate.

BOX OB4.3

Presentational issues

- *Logical v. emotional* – decide on whether you are appealing to people's minds or hearts.
- *Explicit v. implicit conclusions* – it tends to be more effective to draw conclusions explicitly to avoid misinterpretation.
- *One-side v. two-sided arguments* – by and large it is more effective to present both sides of the argument.
- *Primacy v. recency effects* – speaking first or last.
- *Extreme v. moderate positions* – depend on you: if you have high credibility adopt an extreme position; if you have less credibility adopt a more moderate one.
- *Oral v. written* – oral tends to be more effective: employees seem to prefer it, as they are able to get feedback.
- *Single presentation or repetition* – repetition is attention-getting and increases sensitivity and alertness to information.
- *Timing of the communication* – it is important for a manager to determine the most appropriate time to transmit a message.

To summarize. Box OB4.4 suggests some concrete ways of improving communication in organizations.

BOX OB4.4

Improving communication in organizations

Mechanisms

1 Control the flow of information through such means as the 'exception' principle (upward), the 'need to know' principle (downward), queuing, critical timing, off-site meetings, and preventing the isolation of subordinates.
2 Increase repetition. Use multi-channels for the whole message.
3 Reduce ambiguity. Use simple and direct language.
4 Use as much face-to-face oral communication as possible. Obtain feedback and listen effectively, limiting your talking, putting the other talker at ease, removing distractions and being empathetic.
5 Avoid putting listeners on the defensive. Do not overdo argument and criticism, use descriptive, non-evaluative language, and do not try to overwhelm subordinates with your status.
6 Address objections and arguments to the communication head on. Argue both sides of the question, repeat main points, draw explicit conclusions, take an extreme position if you are highly credible, and make explicit recommendations or action.
7 Reinforce words with actions.

In our discussion so far we have been implicitly referring to oral or written communication. However, it has been said that 'we speak with our vocal organs but we converse with our whole body'.[20] In fact research has shown that our meaning is derived one-third from words and two-thirds from non-verbal communication. In other words, the old adage that actions speak louder than words seems to be true.

The next section looks at how non-verbal communication can help us to communicate more effectively.

Non-verbal communication

This includes non-language human responses, such as body motions and personal physical attributes, and environmental characteristics, such as a large or small office. Non-verbal cues may contain many hidden messages and can influence the process and outcome of face-to-face communication. Even a person who is silent or inactive may be sending a message which may or may not be the intended one, such as boredom, fear, anger or depression. Most of this is unconscious, but by trying to understand it, we can attempt to avoid sending the wrong or unintended messages as well as gaining some insight into what others are thinking.

Non-verbal communication performs many roles:

- It can replace speech; for example, sign languages are used by people who are deaf and dumb, and by bookmakers at a race track.

- It complements speech; for example, we interpret a smile as meaning that the person is pleased, a gasp as an indication of surprise.

- It clarifies speech; for example, when trying to explain directions on how to get from A to B, pointing helps the receiver see clearly whether we mean left or right.

- It emphasizes meaning; for example, stressing words and pausing highlights those words.

- It regulates conversations; for example, we can identify when it is our turn to speak through the rise and fall in a speaker's voice pitch and volume.

- It provides feedback; for example, we can tell if someone is uncomfortable. It provides clues as to whether to drop a subject or pursue it.

- It indicates the nature of relationships between people; for example, someone speaking loudly, having a focal position in the room, sitting behind a desk or at the head of the table, and using long glances suggests the dominant figure.

Non-verbal behaviour

Table 4.2 outlines the basic types of non-verbal cue and illustrates the numerous ways in which we can and do communicate without saying or writing a word.

In conclusion, we can say that communication is the lifeblood of organizations. When individuals engage in effective communication, they

Table 4.2   Non-verbal cues

Type	Examples
Body motion	Gestures, facial expressions, eye behaviour, touching and other movement of limbs and body
Personal physical characteristics	Body shape, physique, posture, body or breath odours, height, weight, hair colour, skin colour
Paralanguage	Voice qualities, volume, speech rate, pitch, non-fluencies (such as 'um' or 'uh'), laughing, yawning, etc.
Use of space	Ways people use and perceive space, including seating arrangements, conversational distance and the 'territorial' tendency to stake out a personal space
Physical environment	Building and room design, furniture and other objects, decoration, cleanliness, lighting, noise
Time	Being late or early, keeping others waiting, cultural differences in time perception, relationship between time and status

increase their own sense of wellbeing and become more effective. When managers engage in effective communication, they are providing the means by which the goals and objectives of the organization may be accomplished. Activity OB4.4 provides you with the opportunity to put this into practice.

ACTIVITY OB4.4

COMMUNICATIONS: ASSERTIVENESS

Activity code
- ✓ Self-development
- ✓ Teamwork
- ✓ Communications
- ☐ Numeracy/IT
- ✓ Decisions

We are manipulated daily. Management is there to 'utilize resources', which can be translated into using people. Our organizational peers and subordinates can also take advantage of us, let alone our family and friends. We are all at risk from such manipulation, but especially so are those from a non-dominant ethnic culture, and, perhaps most of all, women.

We need to become less passive and more assertive while not being seen as too aggressive. The passive–aggressive continuum may be part of the behavioural pattern: frustration, poor self-image, inability to control self, disliking self, disliking others. The assertiveness aspect means standing up for yourself in a controlled fashion and treating others as you wish to be treated.

Some working concepts

Our behavioural pattern may indicate one thing but our body language gives away our innermost thoughts. So the body language and the overt behaviour need to be as one. Examples of assertiveness in body language include:

- controlled body movements and the cultivation of a relaxed 'style';
- steady (not fixed) eye contact;
- feet on the ground and shoulders back.

Examples of behavioural assertiveness include:

- the 'Thatcher technique' or 'broken record' approach – stating your position and sticking to it;
- the 'cloudy technique' of agreeing with the proposal content but not accepting any personal critique – for example, 'Yes I lost that report';
- the 'disarming the enemy technique' of tackling the opponent by recognizing the issue and seeking some joint solution – for example, 'I appreciate that I caused problems losing that memo, but we can sort it out. I'll talk to John, the originator of the note';
- the 'kicking for touch technique' – a favourite of parents when they say 'I'll see', which is a kind way of saying 'No.'

Application of concepts

This exercise is designed to give you a personal insight into your behavioural pattern. It involves first developing an awareness of body language by classifying it into distinct categories, and second a more personal reflection on your behaviours at work or college or in leisure. The behaviours may differ according to place, so start off thinking about work and/or college.

Body language: when you demonstrate the following non-verbal signals, what are you telling the world? Tick one behavioural type for each signal.

	Behavioural Type		
	Aggressive	Passive	Assertive
1 Round shoulders, knees together (locked)			
2 Finger jabbing or pointing			
3 Intense eye contact			
4 Mumbling and sighing			

	Behavioural Type		
	Aggressive	Passive	Assertive
5 Jerky body movements such as shuffling			
6 Eye contact avoidance, such as floor watching			
7 Shoulders back, chest out			
8 Staring at the ceiling			
9 Loud, fast speech			
10 Swift, quick, darting body movements			
11 Controlled body movements			
12 Feet on the floor			
13 Shoulders back slightly but relaxed			
14 Quiet, hesitant speech			
15 Steady eye contact			

Behavioural patterns: how often do you do the following?
Rank each from 1 to 4 (1 = Never; 2 = Sometimes; 3 = Usually; 4 = Always).

	1	2	3	4
1 Ask questions at a meeting				
2 State your views to others in a clear fashion				
3 Elaborate on your ideas to others				
4 Speak to a group of people with ease				
5 Ask for clarification in areas of ambiguity				
6 Criticize someone openly to his or her face				
7 Discuss someone else's criticism of you or your views				
8 Say no to a demand that is difficult to meet				
9 Prepare to argue your case				
10 Prepare to say 'You are attempting to manipulate me'				
11 'Kick for touch' and not give an on-the-spot response				
12 Confront a problem by recognizing your own personal contribution to its making				

In the final part of this unit, we focus on the role of power in improving individual and organizational performance.

Power

The idea of 'power' is central to the understanding of organizations. Power is a multi-faceted concept which has been analysed from numerous perspectives: as a characteristic of the individual, as an interpersonal influence process, as a commodity to be traded, as a type of causation and as an issue in the study of values and ethics.[21] Our concern here is to discuss power as an influence process within the confines of developing desirable work behaviours.

Defining power

Power is the potential or actual ability to influence others in a desired direction. It is the ability to get things done the way one wants them.[22] 'Power' is an emotionally laden term, particularly in cultures that emphasize individuality and equality.

Power can be a highly effective instrument. Organizational researchers increasingly cite the value of identifying and using it to improve individual and organizational performance.[23] They have transformed the view of power as a wicked instrument of force[24] into that of it as an instrument of positive action. However, the fact still remains that aggressive power behaviour can create conflict, which is frequently dysfunctional for the organization.

Both individuals and groups within and outside the organization can exert power. Individual employees can influence the actions an organization takes to reach its goals, and formal as well as informal groups can exercise power. People and institutions outside the organization may also influence its behaviour, for example, owners, suppliers, clients, competitors, employee associations (unions, professional bodies), etc. all exert power.[25] It is an inescapable part of an effective organization, and therefore must be carefully managed to benefit all concerned.

Sources of power

Given that power is such an important aspect of organizational life and such a vital asset for managers, how is it acquired? French and Raven[26] put forward six bases of power:

1 *Rewards:* This base is derived from the person's control over resources; for example, control over personnel and the ability to give pay increases, promotions, etc. An individual who has control over organizational rewards,

including pay raises, status and desirable jobs, as well as praise recognition or group sanctions, may use rewards to encourage others' compliance with desired behaviours and goals. Managers effectively use this power if their subordinates believe that complying with their requests will result in extrinsic or intrinsic rewards. Caution must be used when rewarding employees: providing virtually the same reward to all employees regardless of their performance frequently causes high-level performers to become disenchanted with the reward system, and subsequently they produce less. At the same time, collective equity needs to be reconciled with rewarding the best performers.

2 *Coercive:* This refers to the power to punish, reward or threaten and to use one's position to force others to take action. A manager with coercive power can force individuals to behave in certain ways, by demoting or dismissing them or by increasing the direction provided to them. Coercive power must be used with extreme caution: misplaced coercion can negatively affect the manager's effectiveness, and coercion may well beget coercion from subordinates and trade unions.

3 *Legitimate:* This power is derived from the position or job the individual holds in the organization. Possessing legitimate power means that managers can exert influence over others simply because of the authority associated with their jobs. Among the most powerful individuals in business are those who possess both legitimate power and expertise.

4 *Referent:* This is dependent on the charisma or personal attraction of the individual. Interpersonal skill and emotional support from others are the source of power for this person. Individuals with charisma often exert referent power because they attract others to follow.

5 *Expert:* This source of power derives from knowledge and is based on the acknowledgement of another's expertise. An individual who has unique or special knowledge and experience may use this expertise as a source of influence and as a way of building personal power. Expertise in an area, especially in a firm where few others possess similar knowledge, can result in significant power for the experienced person.

6 *Information:* (set in context about people, events or other facts): Access to information or resources provides a source of influence by helping individuals or subunits cope with uncertainty. An employee who has obtained information that others do not possess, but desire, has a certain degree of power. Power may also come from the control of scarce resources of information. Hence, 'editing' of information or interfacing with information sources can lead to greater power.

Power only exists within the interaction between those exercising and those responding to it. The effective use of power is, therefore, about the capacity to mobilize these sources for effective use.

At this stage, you should carry out Activity OB4.5.

ACTIVITY OB4.5

THE ALBION HOLIDAY CENTRE, OR THE CAMBRIDGE BLUE

Activity code
✓ Self-development
✓ Teamwork
✓ Communications
☐ Numeracy/IT
✓ Decisions

Tomson and Smythe had started working in the hotel sector some twenty years ago. Tomson's family wealth and Smythe's industry had allowed the two friends to buy a medium-sized three-star hotel near Duxford in Cambridgeshire. Their initial motive had been to provide a stopover facility on the A505 for passing trade and to act as an overspill hotel for the tourist-infested city of Cambridge, a pleasant fifteen to twenty minutes' drive from the hotel. The Albion, as it was called (George Tomson and Phil Smythe being quite patriotic), had prospered over the last few years. It had a further shot in the arm with the opening of the north-bound London motorway, the M11. More passing trade came off at the Duxford exit for a comfortable night's rest, a reasonably priced meal and a soothing drink. Duxford is fairly close to the expanding third 'London' airport at Stanstead.

Both men were ambitious – not only for themselves but for the hotel. There was a division of opinion over where the hotel business was going and both partners had fairly fixed ideas on the matter.

George: Look Phil, for goodness' sake, here we are doing quite nicely. But if we stand still we're dead – competition will come in and take every-thing. All we need is some big company to come around here, build a motel and there goes our pension.

Phil: I understand that – I don't want to sit about all day, either. You appointed the manager, Des Reeves ... you pushed for him ... I would have been happy keeping my hand in on the operations.

George: We're partners, we are the entrepreneurs here, not managers. Let someone else get on and manage the detail. We need to look at the big picture. You must agree.

Phil: Yes, yes, I can see that, but we must agree on the picture.

George: Absolutely. So what do you think of the plan, eh? We're three-star at the moment. It's okay for the middle-of-the-road traveller.

Phil: The A505 is bad enough for safety without travelling in the middle of the road!

George: Quite. Anyway, I've made an inventory (with the manager's help of course) of where we're at now. Once we know that, it's easier to plan.

Phil: I should have been involved in this stock taking ...

George: Yes, you are – of course you are. Stop being so sensitive about everything. There is no fait accompli. I'm just taking a snapshot of the present to help us deal with the future. Come on Phil, give it a shot ... we'll need to look at what we've got even if you have something else up your sleeve.

Phil: Well, as a matter of fact, I've been doing a lot of thinking as well. [George interjects: 'Oh yeah!' Phil ignores him and keeps going as George does this to him all the time.] Well, it's like this. We've got acres and acres of space out at the back there. We could expand and I know old Farmer Wells has some land up for sale as well – he's never away from the pub anyway – and I'm sure that we can get a deal.

George: We don't need more land, surely. We must upgrade what we've got – go for a better marketplace.

Phil: We would need more land. Look, for years and years Mary and I used to get in the car, hitch up the caravan and go. It was great away from the city doing your own thing – and plenty of different scenery – every day if you wanted, you could be somewhere else.

George: Memories, memories.

Phil: No – you miss the point. Caravan holidays are expanding. I'm still a member of the club. Once a quarter I get the booklet. I know what caravan people want. I know the prices they'll pay and the amenities they look for. Look, what we do is to screen the Albion off with pine trees two or three thick – the trees will grow in no time, so the holiday park will be separated from the hotel. A path will lead down to the lounge and restaurant, of course. We'll have a captive audience in the summer. We could have some 60 pitches (that's 60 separate pieces of land for each caravan or trailer tent).

George: Tents! For goodness' sake, what is this all about? This is crazy. We need to go upmarket – not become some refugee camp for the displaced.

Phil: They are not displaced. Most of these people are wealthy 'townies' who want to escape in their Volvos and their BMWs. These cars and caravans together can cost up to £30,000, if not more. The potential is immense. Cambridge is not far. Thetford and Thetford Park are within travelling distance, there is only one site and a couple of CLs around there.

George: CLs – what's that, then?

Phil: A CL is a small stopover place for a couple of vans (as we call them), usually without electricity and often linked to a farm or a pub.

George: We're in a different market.

Phil: All the more reason for diversifying, then.

> *George:* Yes and no. Let me have my say now. [He passes Phil the inventory.] We're half way there already. At the moment we're really a three-and-a-half star, although we have a three-star category. We must go for a four-star and later a five-star rating to attract a wealthy clientele. A health farm, a country retreat, a bit of old England – the foreigners will love it – so will the executives from London and those passing through the airport.
>
> *Phil:* Let's focus on this inventory thing, but it has an equal application for my idea as well.
>
> *George:* Sure, sure. The reception has to be manned at all times by uniformed staff. No change. We've got old Harry, the night porter, and we can give him a uniform. The lift system is fine.
>
> **Task**
> 1 To what extent do the communication flows between these two men illustrate logical coherent debate or power ploys?
> 2 Who seems to have the real power and why?
> 3 Can you speculate as to the likely outcome of this discussion?

Effective use of power

When we are faced with a situation where we wish to influence the behaviour of others, we have a number of strategies which may be effective. There is considerable research interest in identifying effective influence strategies and understanding the situations where each might be used.[27] An example is the work of Kipnis et al.,[28] who surveyed managers in England, the USA and Australia in an attempt to measure the ways in which they try to influence their superiors and their subordinates.

The study concentrated on seven influence strategies:

1 assertiveness – the use of the direct and forceful approach;
2 bargaining – the use of negotiation through the exchange of benefits;
3 coalition – the mobilization of other people within the organization;
4 friendliness – the use of flattery and the creation of goodwill;
5 higher authority – gaining the support of higher levels in the organization to back up requests;
6 reason – the use of facts and data to support the development of a logical argument;
7 sanctions – the use of rewards and punishments.

Interestingly, the frequency with which managers used each of the influence strategies was almost identical in each of the countries studied. When attempting to influence their superiors, managers tended to adopt the 'reason' strategy most often, followed by 'coalition', and then by 'friendliness'. The strategies used for influencing subordinates were different: managers still used 'reason' most frequently, but resorted to 'assertiveness' next. This is not a surprising finding, as managers can use their positions more legitimately and be more aggressive when seeking compliance from subordinates than when they are trying to influence their superiors.

The effective use of power is a difficult challenge for managers, employees and organizations. (See Box OB4.5.) The goal is to influence the behaviour of others in ways that are consistent with the needs of the organization and the needs of its members.

BOX OB4.5

Power ploys

If an organization is a political system,[1] it follows that we must at least live with organizational politics, while others may wish to exploit them for their own benefit. Korda[2] gives us some illustrative examples of how to develop this power vision for our own benefit:

- Stir the pot through ownership of the ladle.
- Grandiose titles emanate importance.
- The more time you have and the less work you do, the more powerful you become.
- Bad news should be accepted with a cool, detached air (you did not care anyway).
- Do not quite turn on the tears, but turn on the hysteria (people do not like scenes).
- Every time you say 'no', your power increases.
- Look powerful – plant your feet firmly on the ground to give an air of solidity.

Sources:
1   See Robbins, *Organizational Theory*, and Box OB1.6
2   Adapted from Korda, *Power! How to Get It*

Now carry out Activity OB4.6, which illustrates the dynamics of power.

We have looked at three common integrating mechanisms: learning, communication and power. Each of these, if used effectively, can help managers maintain, develop and change employee behaviours with a view to achieving organizational objectives and to reconciling individual needs with organizational aims.

ACTIVITY OB4.6

THE COLLEGE OF EDUCATION: THE POWER AND NO GLORY

Activity code
☑ Self-development
☑ Teamwork
☑ Communications
☐ Numeracy/IT
☑ Decisions

This state-funded College of Education is based at four sites within a 15-mile radius in the south of England. It has approximately the following number of students: 1,900 full-time students, predominantly school leavers undertaking technician-type courses; 600 day-release students from local industry and commerce, undertaking professional and technician-type courses; 2,800 students who attend one afternoon and two evenings per week from their place of work; and 6,000 students who attend in the evenings only. It has some 220 full-time academic staff, 195 part-time-cum-associate help, and 150 administrative staff, technicians, porters and so on.

In many ways it is a community college rather than an academic centre of excellence. It is involved in adult education in the broadest sense, although it is becoming increasingly vocation-oriented, with a strong presence in business studies, finance and languages for business. The specialisms are reflected in the organizational structure, although older specialisms are still predominant, perhaps at the expense of the newer growth areas of business and languages. There are five faculties:

1 TAD – technology, art and design
2 communications and media
3 social studies (English literature, sociology and psychology)
4 business and finance
5 languages

The support areas include learning resources, which is supposed to keep academics abreast of 'best practice'; student counselling and welfare; and a new innovation for the College, the marketing liaison group. This marketing group reflects the educational changes at national level, whereby funding from government is being slowly and deliberately reduced per student, while the number (and, arguably, the quality) of students is increased. The marketing team's role is to find additional funding from short courses and language seminars, and from encouraging the enrolment of overseas students, with or without English as their first language, as they pay the full tuition fees without government funding or support. The marketing team would like all students to pay the full tuition fees and envisage this happening as the government increasingly withdraws financial support from the education sector. An administrative section co-ordinates all non-academic staff.

There is a senior management team of administrators with personnel and labour relations support from the human resources team. The senior management (six in all) are joined by the five faculty heads to form the directorate. Each head of faculty is supported by the set leader, who hires deputies and assists with resources, timetabling, staff management and academic development. In addition, there is a range of standing committees and subcommittees of the directorate covering areas from academic standards to sexual and racial equality. The organizational structure is shown in figure 4.1.

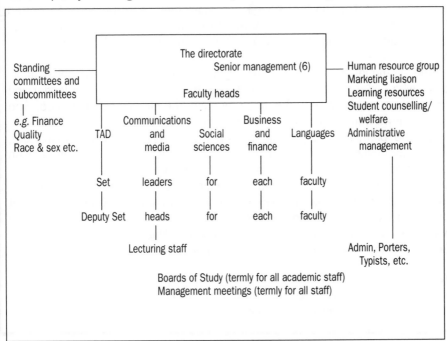

Figure 4.1 College of Education organizational structure.

Thomson had not been lecturing long. His first role was part-time, then he moved up to a full-time position. He was not particularly able and he knew it; but he had other skills – he was a charmer and an opportunist.

The decision-making system at the college worked through a network of endless committees. Unlike his colleagues, he put himself forward to serve on these committees, on anything from academic standards to student-based learning. He latched on to the innovative work of another lecturer in the social science area who used simulated exercises across the main business functions. Papers appeared with her ideas but with his name. He attended obscure conferences and made sure that he circulated his notes to the directorate of the college.

The new faculty head of Social Sciences came into the post. Here was another opportunity. Thomson was always in college from 9 to 5, and he began popping in to see the head for a cosy chat. They got on well and the head, also not a particularly able man, did not feel threatened by Thomson, for after all he had no real academic background. Thomson started to do little tasks for the busy head, who was not greatly interested in routine administration.

By this time, Thomson had ingratiated himself with every senior person in the institution, much to the disgust of his colleagues. He now floated the idea of a student counselling role with the head – for himself, of course. In spite of his lack of knowledge in this area, a job was created for him. It brought no extra money but it did mean a bigger job title, with greater access to resources (very finite in the college), so more memos and reports emanated from his desk. Staff grumbled that this fellow had been given the job without a formal advertisement and selection procedure. None the less, welfare was added to his remit.

The promotion round started up again. In spite of better qualified applicants who had researched, published, taught and administered for longer and far better than Thomson, the head pushed for him to be promoted. The head's views were decisive, and Thomson was duly promoted.

On the premise that you must keep moving before you are found out, Thomson sought another role in co-ordination of distance learning and liaison with the social services – a new job and no interview. He got it and moved on. Oram, an able administrator and academic, sought Thomson's old job. He was told there would be an open selection – an interview. Oram did not get the job; a friend of the head was redeployed into it from another faculty. Oram was disillusioned. The head went off on a fact-finding trip to the French Social Services in the south, taking Thomson with him.

Task

1 Analyse the power dynamics between Thomson and the head.
2 What can Oram do about this situation?

Notes

1 Lawrence and Lorsch, *Organization and Environment*.
2 Akin, 'Varieties of managerial learning'.
3 Pavlov, *Conditioned Reflexes*.
4 Skinner, *Analysis of Behavior*.
5 Luthans and Kreitner, *Organizational Behavior Modification*.
6 Miller, *Principles of Everyday Behavior Analysis*.
7 Thorndike, *Educational Psychology*.
8 Tolman, 'Cognitive maps'.
9 Ibid.
10 Davis and Luthans, 'Social learning approach'.
11 Bandura, *Principles of Behavior Modification*.
12 Gist, 'Self efficacy'.

13 Zalesny and Ford, 'Extending the social information processing perspective'.

14 Laird, *Approaches to Training and Development.*

15 Bass and Vaughan, *Training in Industry*, and more recently, A.H. Anderson, *Successful Training Practice.*

16 Mintzberg, *Nature of Managerial Work.*

17 Krone et al., 'Communication theory and organizational communication'. See also A.H. Anderson and Kleiner, *Effective Marketing Communications.*

18 O'Reilly, 'Individual and information overload in organizations'.

19 Wexley and Yukl, *Organizational Behaviour and Personnel Psychology;* Reitz, *Behavior in Organizations.*

20 Abercrombie, 'Paralanguage'.

21 Cavanagh, *Ethical Dilemmas.*

22 Salancik and Pfeffer, 'Examination of need satisfaction models'.

23 Kanter, 'Power failure in management circuits'.

24 Kaplan, 'Power in perspective'.

25 Mintzberg, *Nature of Managerial Work.*

26 French and Raven, 'Bases of social power'.

27 Schreisheim and Hinkin, 'Influence tactics used by subordinates'; Yukl and Falbe, 'Influence tactics and objectives'.

28 Kipnis et al., 'Patterns of managerial influence'.

Unit Five

Focus on The Organization

Learning Objectives

After completing this unit, you should be able to:

- understand the concepts of organizational design and structure;

- describe the various approaches to organizational structure and its key determinants;

- understand the concept of organizational culture;

- explain the relationship between organizational culture and performance;

- understand the nature of decision making and identify the stages to effective decision making;

- apply the generic skills.

Contents

Overview

Organizational Structure

▶ Defining organizational structure

▶ Organizational design

▶ Approaches to organizational structure

The classical school

The human relations school

Situational approaches

Organizational Culture

▶ Defining organizational culture

▶ Factors that impact on organizational culture

▶ Evidence of organizational culture

▶ Performance and organizational culture

Decision Making

▶ Types of decisions

▶ Decision-making models

Rational model

Bounded rationality model

Political model

▶ Stages of managerial decision making

▶ Behavioural influences on individual decision making

▶ Barriers to effective decision making

Unit Five

❝ An organization does not make decisions; its function is to provide a framework, based on established criteria, within which decisions can be fashioned in an orderly manner.❞

Sloan[1]

Overview

Up to now we have concentrated on organizational effectiveness in terms of individuals, groups and integrating mechanisms. It is important, however, not to lose sight of the fact that the organization itself plays an important role in determining the effectiveness of each of these processes. To work effectively, all members of the organization must have a clear understanding of the organization's structure, its goals and its culture.

The way that we learn about what the organization expects of us is through the organization's culture: the set of shared values about how things are actually achieved in the organization (that is, the policies, practices and norms that are really important). Organizational design or structure is the ultimate outcome of organizational strategy – it is what gives the organization its coherence, from which culture develops.

This unit will consider organizational structure, culture and decision making in order to determine the broader concept of organizational effectiveness.

Organizational Structure

Organizations influence the behaviours of their members. Therefore, if we can design organizations in such a way as to promote greater efficiency and higher levels of motivation, this will go a long way to achieving their ultimate goals. An organization's structure provides the context for work. Though most of us have little influence on how an organization is structured, it is important for us to understand the constraints and opportunities provided in different organizations in order to use them to full effect.

Defining organizational structure

As discussed in Unit One, different organizations can have very different structures. Structure relates to the pattern of relationships between positions in the organization and the people assigned to those positions. The primary function of structure is the division of work among members of the organization, and the co-ordination of their activities so that they are directed towards achieving the goals and objectives of the organization.

The structure, therefore, defines tasks and responsibilities, work roles, relationships, and channels of communication. Structure creates a framework of order and authority through which the activities of the organization can be planned, organized and controlled. In other words, the structure of an organization largely determines how the organization is managed.

Despite the variety of structures available to organizations, a framework was proposed by Mintzberg[2] suggesting that every organization has five parts:

1 top management
2 middle management
3 technical support staff
4 administrative support staff
5 technical core

Top management is located at the top of the organization, middle management is at the intermediate levels, and the technical core includes those who do the basic work of the organization. Technical support staff are those who are responsible for the formal planning and control of the technical core, and administrative support staff include indirect services and clerical and maintenance employees.

The five parts may vary in size and importance depending on the overall environment, strategy and technology. Mintzberg suggests that these organizational parts can fit together in five basic configurations, where environment, goals, power, structure, formulation, technology and size hang together in identifiable clusters. This framework defines key organizational variables and tells managers the appropriate configuration for specific environments and strategies.

The structure of an organization affects not only productivity and economic efficiency but also the morale and job satisfaction of the workforce. An organization's structure should, therefore, be designed so as to encourage the willing participation of the organization's members to achieve effective performance. See Box OB5.1 for an alternative approach to structuring an organization.

Organizational design

One key task of an organization is to decide on its goals and strategy and then to design the organizational form appropriate for the strategy. The idea is that by fitting the pieces together in the 'right' configuration, an

---

BOX OB5.1

Organizational structure

Is there a 'best way' of structuring the organization? Galbraith tackles the question in an interesting paper.[1]

For Galbraith, the organization structure exists to:

- increase the pre-planning ability of the overall organization;
- increase the adaptability if the pre-planning phase has not occurred;
- maintain continued viability.

He begs the question of whether strategy follows the organization structure or vice versa. Various approaches are used in this 'information-processing' role of the organization structure, including the following:

- *Rules:* Task-related behaviours are predicted and scheduled in advance (depending on their complexity), and rules or programmes allow these to be carried out. This is very much a functionalist approach, like rule making in a labour relations system.[2]
- *Hierarchy:* The hierarchy is used in cases of exception, where the established rules do not meet the unprogrammed situations, encountered by the organization.
- *Targets and goals:* As a direct correlation to this growing uncertainty (unprogrammed situations), the hierarchy gets overloaded, so goal accomplishment is met through specific targets being set. Planning and budgetary control become important.

To Galbraith, this uncertainty of situations creates stresses and strains within the organization, and information processing becomes difficult. The hierarchy has difficulty absorbing the uncertainty, and the critical rules are inadequate. Either the capacity for information dissemination is upgraded and/or the need for certain types of information is questioned. We end up with the 'programmable events' being absorbed lower down the hierarchy, and the non-routine issues being dealt with via a form of 'management by exception'.

If Galbraith is correct, the potential for overload, particularly with a turbulent external environment clouding decisions, is very important for more senior managers, while much of the organizational structure exists to absorb the more programmable events. Lesser animals in the bureaucracy seem destined to deal with these programmable decisions.

Sources:
1 J.R. Galbraith, 'Organization design'
2 See the work of Dunlop, *Industrial Relations Systems*, as an example of such 'rule' making

---

organization can develop and maintain a high level of effectiveness. So the starting point for defining organizational design is strategy; that is, the current set of plans, decisions and objectives that have been adopted to achieve the organization's goals.

Strategy formulation includes the activities that lead to the establishment of a firm's overall goals and mission and the development of a specific strategic plan. Strategy formulation typically begins with an assessment of the opportunities and threats in the external environment and an assessment of strengths and weaknesses within the organization; and this leads to the definition of an organization's distinctiveness compared with other organizations.

Strategy implementation is the use of managerial and organizational tools to direct and allocate resources to accomplish strategic objectives. In other words, it is the administration and execution of the strategic plan.

The direction and allocation of resources are accomplished with the tools of:

- organizational structure
- control systems
- culture
- technology
- human resources

The *entrepreneurial* structure is typically found in new, small, entrepreneurial organizations. It consists of a top manager and workers in the technical core with only a few support staff. There is little specialization or formalization, and co-ordination and control is from the top. The founder has the power and creates the culture. Employees have little discretion, but work procedures are typically informal. The organization is suited to a dynamic environment, as it is adaptable in its response to change.

Machine bureaucracy refers to large, routine, technologies organizations, often oriented to mass production. There is extensive specialization and formalization. Key decisions are made at the top and there is a large core of technical and administration support staff. Technical support staff are used to routinize and formalize work, and tend to be the dominant group. This configuration is often criticized for lack of control by lower employees, lack of innovation, weak culture and an alienated workforce; however, it is suited to a large organization in a stable environment.

Professional bureaucracy is where the production core is composed of professionals (for example, hospitals, universities and consulting firms). Although it is a bureaucracy, people within the production core have some autonomy. Long training and experience encourage 'clan control' and strong culture, thereby reducing the need for bureaucratic control structures. Organizations of this type often provide services rather than tangible products. They exist in complex environments and most of the power rests with the professionals. Technical support groups are small or non-existent, but a large administration support staff is needed to handle routine administration affairs. Now tackle Activity OB5.1.

ACTIVITY OB5.1

BUREAUCRATIC ROLES

Activity code
✓ Self-development
✓ Teamwork
☐ Communications
☐ Numeracy/IT
✓ Decisions

From the knowledge gained to date complete the following (group or individual) task.

The essence of bureaucracy lies in the concept of the 'office-holder'. The roles are formalized and codified in a fairly meticulous manner. These bureaucratic roles, visible in most large organizations, private or public, include the following (1–13):

1

2

3

4

5

6

7

8

9

10

11

12

13

The *diversified* form occurs in extremely large organizations subdivided into product and market groups. There are few liaison devices for co-ordination between divisions. They are quite formalized within the division, because technologies are often routine. The environment tends to be simple and stable for any division, although the total organization serves a diverse market (for example, Ford, General Motors, Procter & Gamble, etc.). Each division is more or less autonomous, with its own subculture.

The *ad-hocracy* organization develops to survive in a complex, dynamic environment. Technology is sophisticated, as in the aerospace and electronic industry. This configuration occurs in quite large organizations with the need to be adaptable. It has a team-based structure which typically emerges with horizontal linkages and empowered employees. Both technical support staff and the production core have authority over key production elements. Elaborate division of labour occurs, but it is not formalized, and professionalism is high. Cultural values are strong and clan control is stressed. With decentralization, people at any level may be involved in decision making. Ad-hocracy is almost the opposite of machine bureaucracy in terms of structure, power relationships and environment.

All organizations have to make provision for continuing activities towards the achievement of given aims; hence processes of task allocation, supervision and co-ordination are developed. These constitute the organization's structure, and the fact that these activities can be arranged in various ways means that organizations can have differing structures.

Now tackle Activity OB5.2.

ACTIVITY OB5.2

ORGANIZING THE ORGANIZATION

Activity code
☑ Self-development
☑ Teamwork
☐ Communications
☐ Numeracy/IT
☑ Decisions

The work to be carried out by an organization must be broken down into specific responsibilities. This occurs at job level. In addition, it occurs at divisional, sectional and unit levels.

Task

Below we note five possible ways (there are others) of grouping activities. Your role, as an individual or in a group, is to examine the intrinsic merits and drawbacks of each method.

1 *Function:* The enterprise is organized through disciplines, such as marketing, finance, personnel management and operations.

2 *Product:* Each division has a focus on a product, such as pens, paper and printing material.

3 *Geography:* The organization could be administered on the basis of geographical areas.

4 *Customer:* The class of customer makes for the division; for example, 'industrial' and 'consumer' users.

5 *Number:* This is done by a head count; divisions are based on having equal groups of people in each division or unit.

The variety may be related to variations in such factors as:

- the objectives of the organization
- size
- ownership
- geographical location
- technology
- environment

These factors produce the characteristic differences in structure of a bank, a hospital, a mass production factory or a local government department.

Approaches to organizational structure

There have been a number of approaches to organizational structure, but these can be classified into two broad approaches: universalist and situational. The *universalist* approaches suggest 'one best way' explanations to organization structures. The two main schools of thought are the *classical* and the *human relations* schools, each offering a different perspective but within the confines of a universalistic solution. The *situational* approaches offer no universal solution and answer the question 'What determines an organization's structure?' with 'It depends.' There are those who say that technology is the key determinant, while others say it is the environment in which the organization operates.

The classical school

Major contributors to this school of thought were Taylor,[3] Gulick,[4] Urwick[5] and Fayol.[6] From such contributors, a representative set of statements is given below:

- Employees should be formally grouped and organized in specialist functional departments.

- These departments should have a hierarchical structure with authority focused and disseminated from the board of directors.
- An organization chart should be indicative of structure, depicting the chain of command and channels of communication.
- Each employee should report to only one 'superior'.
- The span of control of subordinates by 'superiors' should be limited to permit effective supervision; that is, no more than eight.
- Jobs should be described and the nature of duties prescribed.
- The number of levels of authority in the organization should be kept to a minimum to ensure effective control and communication.
- Authority should be commensurate with responsibility.
- Departments should be categorized as either 'line' (marketplace, such as production and sales) or 'staff' (specialist advice and services, such as personnel).

The basic assumptions about behaviour are that individuals are isolated and chiefly motivated by money, and that the authority of management to give orders is taken for granted.

At the time, these 'principles' helped a large number of managers and contributed to efficiency. However, by the 1920s, evidence was mounting that the behavioural assumptions on which they were based were wrong. In spite of criticisms, large, formal organizations still use some of these guidelines.

The human relations school
Major early contributors to this school of thought were Mayo,[7] and Roethlisberger and Dickson.[8] The general conclusion drawn from the Hawthorne Experiment (see Unit One) was that the key to increased productivity lay not in individual incentive schemes and traditional authoritarian management, as advocated by the classical school of thought, but in fostering better relations with employees.

This emphasis on individuals and work groups continued during the 1950s and 1960s, with the contributions of Maslow,[9] Herzberg,[10] McGregor,[11] Likert[12] and Argyris.[13] The emphasis was placed on factors such as job satisfaction, group dynamics, participative leadership styles and motivation (discussed in greater detail in other units).

Situational approaches
Major contributors of the 'It depends' school of thought were Burns and Stalker,[14] Woodward,[15] and Lawrence and Lorsch.[16] Each tried to identify the key determining factor of organizational structure, looking especially at size, technology and the environment.

There is a dearth of empirical and theoretical literature relating to *size* and its effect on organizational structure. Blau and Scott[17] found that:

- increasing organizational size was positively related to increasing differentiation (measured by number of levels, departments, job titles, etc.);
- *but* the rate of differentiation decreases with increasing size;
- *but* the relative size of the administrative component is lower in larger organizations;
- the span of control of supervisors is positively related to size.

So, size leads to differentiation, which in turn leads to an increased need for control and co-ordination, leading to an increased requirement for administrative overhead. But (empirically) the administrative component is conversely related to size, which, coupled with increased supervisory spans of control, suggests economies of scale.

Therefore, there is an anomaly in which greater size appears to lead to *both* a larger and a smaller administrative component. This is partly resolved by the work of Haas et al.,[18] which suggests that the size–administrative-component relationship is curvilinear; that is, the relative size of administration is greater in organizations that are small (under 700 employees) or large (over 1,400 employees). Pugh et al.[19] concluded that increased size is related to increased structuring of organizational activities and decreased concentration of authority, while Mahoney et al.[20] found that as size increased, managerial practices changed. There was greater flexibility in personnel assignments, greater delegation of authority, and greater emphasis on results rather than procedures.

However, the findings of Hall and Tittle[21] are rather less straightforward. They found only a small relationship between size and the *perceived* degree of bureaucracy. In a more extensive study, Hall et al.[22] found:

- a slight tendency for larger organizations to be more complex and more formalized (but the relationship was strong on only a few variables);
- complexity variables with a strong relationship to size were: spatial dispersion, number of hierarchical levels and functional specificity of department (but not number of departments).

  So the relationship between size and complexity indicators was limited to a few factors. Even here, enough deviant cases existed to cast doubt on the assumption that large organizations are reasonably more complex than small ones.

- formalization variables which had a strong relationship to size were formalization of the authority structure, of penalties for rule violation and of training procedures.

Hall et al. conclude (in opposition to Blau) that structural differentiation is not necessarily a consequence of expanding size, their study finding the relationship to be partial and weak. They suggest that the direction of causality may be the reverse of that suggested by Blau (in other words, that complexity causes size).

Argyris[23] has also criticized Blau's findings. He questions Blau's reliance on official (senior management and organization charts) descriptions of organization structures, pointing out that these are often inaccurate, and argues that *context* may be more influential than size (for example, Civil Service units are complex because of Civil Service regulations, not size).

Aldrich[24] argues that size is, in fact, a dependent variable: 'the more highly structured firms, with their greater degree of specialisation, formalisation and monitoring of role performance, simply need to employ a larger work force than less structured firms.' In his analysis, *technology* emerges as a major determinant of structure.

There has been a great deal of discussion on what we actually mean by the term 'technology'. However, it is generally accepted that it is 'the means by which an organization transforms inputs into outputs'. This includes the techniques and processes used to transform labour, knowledge, capital and raw materials into finished goods and services. All organizations, irrespective of what they produce, have technologies.

The relationship between technology and an organization's structure has been the subject of continual debate for over forty years. A major influence in this area has been the work carried out by Woodward.[25]

Woodward studied the relationship between production systems, technology and structure in manufacturing concerns. She investigated specific features of organizations; for example:

- The number of levels of authority between top and bottom.
- The span of control or the average number of subordinates of supervisors.
- The clarity of duties.
- The amount of written communication.
- The extent of division of functions among specialists.

Woodward found that organizations had considerable differences in these features. The question was: why? She compared organizations of different sizes and historical background and found that these were not significant factors. But when differences in technology were studied, there seemed to be a relationship between the technology used by an organization and its structure.

In unit and small-batch organizations, there was a shorter hierarchy; in large-batch and mass-production organizations, there were shorter lines of command, fewer managers and clerks, and a large number of production operatives; and in process-production organizations, there were taller hierarchies, longer lines of command (managed through committees rather than instructions down the line), more trained graduates, and largely administrative and managerial personnel.

In conclusion, Woodward found that the type of structure an organization develops (and should develop) is influenced by its technology, whether the technology is unit, mass production, or a continuous process. She suggested that a mechanistic type of organization fits best with mass-production technology. A more organic form of organization responds best to a unit (craft) or continuous process (for example, gas refinery) technology. Therefore, while there was no universal 'best way' to design an organization, there did appear to be a particular structure appropriate to each technical situation.

Further work in this area has been undertaken by Thompson[26] and Perrow.[27] Whereas Woodward was concerned with technological determinism, Thompson and Perrow attempted to explain why the relationship between technology and structure existed.

While technology appears to be a major factor in determining an organization's structure, it is not the only one. Early contingency research looked at the fit between an organization's structure and its *environment*. Burns and Stalker[28] were concerned with the impact of changing technology and the attempts of old-established organizations to adjust to new environments. Their study attempted to determine how changes in the technology and environment affected management processes. By examining the environmental settings of each of the organizations in their study, Burns and Stalker were able to distinguish five different kinds of environment, ranging from 'stable' to 'least predictable'. They were also able to identify the management processes and structures used by each.

The most important contribution of the Burns and Stalker study is the mechanistic organization–organic organization dimension it provides for analysing organizations. Placed on a continuum, it looks like this:

Mechanistic  Organic

In classifying organizational structures, each can be placed somewhere along this continuum. Mechanistic organizations would be highly structured, bureaucratic forms of organization, conforming very closely to scientific and classical management traditions, while the organic organization would be highly unstructured and flexible. Those organizations moving into dynamic or turbulent environments would have to make a transition from a mechanistic to an organic structure, and vice versa.

Another important research study related to the environment was conducted by Lawrence and Lorsch.[29] This has provided important insights into the way in which departments in a structure relate to their environments.

Spurred on the work of Burns and Stalker, Lawrence and Lorsch attempted to go one step further by seeking to answer the question: 'What kind of organization does it take to deal with various economic and market conditions?'. They did this by looking not only at the overall structure but also at the way in which specific departments within the organizations were organized. They introduced two central concepts: differentiation and integration.

By *differentiation*, Lawrence and Lorsch referred to the fact that, within all organizations, there are suborganizations, each of which develops a particular unique structure to cope with its environment. Divisions and departments will behave differently because of the demands of their own particular environment.

There is the risk, in a highly differentiated organization, that each unit might develop a strong substructure which results in each going its own way. Lawrence and Lorsch suggest that organizations have developed sophisticated methods for overcoming such potential conflicts. They referred to these methods as *integration*. It is not unusual for these methods, as in the case of mechanistic structures, to take the form of rules, policies and procedures, which aim to 'control' the behaviours of all. In organic structures, integration is normally achieved through co-operation and teamwork.

As discussed above, the earlier approaches to organization and management believed in one best form of structure and tended to concentrate on limited aspects of the organization. The classical and human relations approaches also tended to study the organization in isolation from its environment. The situational or contingency approach takes the view that there is no one best structure and there are a large number of variables which influence organizational design and performance. Therefore, all we can say is that the most appropriate structure is dependent on the contingencies of the situation for each organization.

Now tackle Activity OB5.3, which is concerned with restructuring.

Organizational Culture

Every organization has its own unique way of reflecting its shared values and goals. All have their own ambience, feeling and style, which influence the responses of both customers and employees. This phenomenon is often referred to as the organization's culture.

As with so many other concepts in organizational behaviour, there is no universally accepted definition of culture. However, there are broad assumptions we can make.

ACTIVITY OB5.3

MALMÖ COMMUNICATIONS: A RESTRUCTURING EXERCISE

Activity code
- ☑ Self-development
- ☐ Teamwork
- ☑ Communications
- ☐ Numeracy/IT
- ☑ Decisions

Tom Smith, an affable fellow, bilingual in English and Swedish, was the relatively new MD of the UK subsidiary of Malmö Communications, a Swedish-based telecommunications company. Recently Malmö had taken over the systems firm of Peripheral (UK) in Cambridgeshire. The UK firm employed some 220 people, of whom 123 were involved with services, software support and in-house repair work, under the banner of 'customer care'.

The products ranged from powerful minicomputers, with economical standard configurations and built-in expansion capability suitable for introductory levels, to the powerful System 95, ideally suited for signal conditioning, process control and mass data applications.

The labour force was highly qualified and accustomed to a fair degree of autonomy. The firm had been informal and even the dress code of the administration people had shocked Smith when he first arrived. The sales people were quite high-powered but disorganized. The R&D people were mostly long-haired boffins, while the manual workers were said to be 'troublesome and unaccustomed to being managed'.

Great labour difficulties had been experienced. Many of the top managers had left, and an attempt to introduce human resource practices had fallen away. Cost-cutting exercises had trimmed excess. The time was not ripe for reorganization.

Smith believed in structure. The aim of any organizational structure was goal attainment, and this was very close to Smith's vision of work. Structure was not everything, of course, but work allocation, the grouping of functions, decision making, co-ordination and control would all be facilitated by structural solutions. Smith had been brought up in the old school, and although he was quite open-minded, all this 'contingency management' left him cold.

The whole structure needed to reflect both authority and responsibility. A plan was needed whereby the job responsibilities of people dovetailed into departmental objectives and in turn related closely to the mission and goals of the firm. His preference was for tighter control and the avoidance of sloppy procedures, job overlap and ambiguous lines of responsibility. At the same time he recognized the need, particularly in this industry, to keep up to date with the marketplace so that they could react accordingly. This might mean a more fluid approach to structures at both organizational and job level. Could he find a balance?

He jotted down his own preference. People needed to know what they were about, so there should be a formal structure with job descriptions. Some chain of command would be necessary from his desk to the shop floor, for it was lost at the moment in the matrix structure. Customers demanded competence and so did he; so each job would have its set sphere of competence. Recruitment should be stricter and based on this competence.

The reward system should give some security as well as incentive. It was good to promote people from within. The existing channels of communication were too fluid and often people bypassed their immediate boss. More discipline was needed: procedures were adhered to in the technical area with specifications, etc., but administrative procedures were openly flouted. These procedures should be more codified. All this would mean better efficiency and the possibility of a lifetime career for all competent officials at Malmö Communications. A tight ship would mean that the goals of the organization would be met and all would benefit.

Task

Critically examine Smith's views on structure and comment on the application of his structural solutions to this case.

Defining organizational culture

Organizational culture is the system of shared values, beliefs and habits within an organization that interacts with formal structure to produce behavioural norms.[30]

'Culture gives people a sense of how to behave and what they ought to be doing.'[31] The definitions vary:

■ symbols, language, ideologies, rituals and myths;[32]

■ is a product;

■ is historical;

■ is based upon symbols;

■ is an abstraction from behaviour and the products of behaviour;[33]

■ is a pattern of basic assumptions created by an organization as it struggles with adapting to the external environment and internal integration.

The culture of an organization represents a complex pattern of beliefs and expectations shared by its members. More specifically, organizational culture is defined as shared philosophies, ideologies, values, beliefs, assumptions, expectations and norms.[34] It includes the following:

■ overt similarities in employee behaviour; for example, rituals, ceremonies and the language commonly used;

■ shared common norms throughout the organization; for example, a fair day's work for a fair day's pay;

■ strong values held by an organization; for example, product quality;

■ the underlying philosophy of the organization;

■ the rules of the game for 'getting along' in the organization;

■ the manifestations of organizational climate, such as physical layout and the interactions with customer.[35]

All these definitions suggest that organizational culture consists of a number of elements, such as assumptions, beliefs, values, rituals, myths and languages.

Schein[36] points out that culture involves assumptions, adaptations, perceptions and learning. He goes on to suggest than an organization's culture has three layers:

1 artifacts and creations which are visible but often not interpretable (for example, decor, furnishings, etc.);

2 values or things that are important to people;

3 the basic assumptions people make that guide their behaviour.

As organizational culture is essentially concerned with organizational values and attitudes, it influences the behaviour of individuals, groups and organizational processes in general. For example, if quality is important in the culture, then employees are expected to demonstrate behaviour which goes some way to achieving this objective.

It has been suggested that organizational culture provides employees with a sense of stability through identification with the organization's culture.[37]

Given the importance of organizational culture for individual and group behaviour as well as for organizational processes, it is useful to differentiate between 'strong' and 'weak' cultures.[38] A strong culture exists where the main values of the organization are shared by employees. The stronger the culture the more influential it is on behaviour. For example, Japanese companies such as Toyota and Nissan illustrate 'strong', influential cultures.

Many have written about the powerful influence culture has on individuals, groups and processes; for example, Ouchi,[39] Peters and Waterman,[40] and Deal and Kennedy.[41] However, little empirical and theoretical research exists to support this stance, and there is no evidence to suggest that one form of culture is more effective than another.

Cultures seem to evolve over a period of time. As Schein described it: 'the culture that eventually evolves in a particular organization is ... a complex outcome of external pressures, internal potentials, responses to critical events, and, probably to some unknown degree, chance factors that could not be predicted from a knowledge of either the environment or the members'.[42] Therefore imposing a culture would probably be met with resistance, as it is difficult to impose core values.[43]

Factors that impact on organizational culture

Among the factors that impact on organizational culture are work groups, organizational characteristics, supervision and administration.[44]

Our interactions and experiences shared with other members of our *work group* will affect our perceptions of the organization's culture. Likewise, factors such as group values, attitudes, norms, commitment, morale, etc., colour our outlook on life and determine to what extent we share the core values of the organization, which in turn affects the culture of the organization itself.

The leadership style of managers influences the culture of the group and vice versa. If a manager adopts a distant attitude, this could well have a negative affect on the group and, consequently, the organization. If the manager is task-oriented,[45] this alters the environment. In an ideal situation, the manager should adopt a people-oriented leadership style to have a positive impact on group effectiveness.

Organizational characteristics such as size, technology, etc., can significantly affect the culture of an organization. For example, large bureaucratic organizations require greater specialization than their smaller counterparts, which means that they tend to be more impersonal than small enterprises. Technologically advanced organizations employ a larger number of technical specialists than less technologically advanced organizations, which determines to a large extent the way in which problems are solved.

An organization's culture can be affected by the *supervisory* and *administrative* processes in place. For example, organizations that have clear rewards systems related to performance have a greater tendency to develop achievement cultures than those that do not have such systems. Open communication systems promote greater participation, thereby impacting on organizational culture.

Evidence of organizational culture

We have focused on a number of factors which potentially have an impact on organizational culture. It should be noted, however, that within most large organizations both a dominant culture and many subcultures may exist (similar to the state of affairs discussed under the heading 'organizational structure'). *Dominant culture* refers to the majority view of the organization, whereas *subcultures* refer to various subunits within an organization. For example, it is not unusual for the production department to have a very different culture to the marketing department. Although members of both departments may share the dominant culture, they develop shared values unique to their particular unit.

Most management gurus would advocate an open and participative culture as being most effective. These cultures are characterized by such factors as trust, openness in communications, considerate and supportive leadership, group problem solving, work autonomy, and information sharing. The antithesis of the open and participative culture is the closed and autocratic one. These cultures are characterized by greater rigidity, a formal chain of command, shorter spans of control, and stricter individual accountability.

Determining exactly what type of culture exists in an organization can be difficult. The evidence of an organization's culture can be found in its status symbols, traditions, history, rituals, jargon and physical environment. None of these components alone represents the culture of an organization; taken together, however, they reflect and give meaning to the concept of organizational culture.

Performance and organizational culture

One of the primary reasons that culture has received such attention is the underlying assumption that there is a relationship between the culture of an organization and its effectiveness.

Many popular books have been written recently which suggest that 'strong', well-developed cultures are a key factor in effective, high-performing organizations. It is suggested that this is the case for two fundamental reasons:[46] first, a strong culture often suggests a tighter relationship between an organization's strategy and its culture; second, a strong culture equally implies a greater commitment on the part of the organization's employees. Given these two factors, culture is seen as an essential characteristic for organizational success.

Despite this commonly held view, however, the research evidence supporting the strong-culture–performance relationship is mixed. Denison[47] found that organizations with a 'participative' culture performed better than those without it, whereas Cameron and Freeman[48] suggested that there was no difference in organizational effectiveness between those with strong and weak cultures.

In summary, the effects of organizational culture on an organization's performance are as follows: understanding the culture of an organization provides vital clues to expected behaviours for employees and thereby to fostering desired employee behaviours. Organizational culture establishes commitment to the organization's shared value system of working towards common goals. Finally, organizational culture can have an effect on the organization's performance.

Now complete Activity OB5.4.

ACTIVITY OB5.4

CULTURE AT THE *FREE PRESS* LTD

Activity code
- ✓ Self-development
- ✓ Teamwork
- ✓ Communications
- ☐ Numeracy/IT
- ✓ Decisions

The *Free Press* newspaper does not have a single 'culture'. Instead there seem to be different if not divergent 'personalities'.

The editorial stress on independence and the search for truth is shared by the journalists, the librarians and most of the production team, who have an immense pride in their newspaper. To a great extent this pride in what they are doing permeates the whole place.

The circulation people have this pride as well, but it is tempered by the more commercial pressures of increasing sales and the logistical problems of distribution.

The commercial vision dominates advertising, both classified and display, for the people working there know that without advertising there would be no newspaper. It is also hard work, particularly on the display side, for as a cynic once remarked, they are only selling blank spaces. Of course, this is not a fair assessment, for they are the commercial arm of the newspaper. Their view is shared by the promotions people, but this team has longer to reflect between sales pitches and there is less panic to fill up the spaces than among their advertising colleagues. Publicity, competitions and photo sales all have this commercial approach.

The maintenance, administration, computing, and personnel and training sections tend to share some of the values of the newspaper, with its intellectual rigour, and there is a general awareness at induction, for example, of the commercial realities of life.

The senior management team balance the intellectual product with the marketing vision. At the end of the day, though, these managers believe that the marketplace dictates life – although they would be careful to couch their marketeering in terms compatible with editorial independence and so forth.

The culture is also highly unionized, with people very conscious of their rights and obligations. This unionism spreads through every department.

Newspapers like the *Free Press* exist in very competitive climates. Radio, television, computerized updates on television, other newspapers, weekend papers and magazines all compete for news, and any medium is an alternative for advertising. The influx of 'free' papers crammed full of advertising has knocked the revenue of the *Free Press*.

Task

It has been decided to go for a marketing culture across the whole of *Free Press* Ltd to stimulate greater commercial awareness among the staff. How would you do it?

Decision Making

Decision making is the process of identifying and solving problems. Problem solving is the process of decision making. QED!

Decision making is the process of generating and evaluating alternatives and making choices between them. It is not just about problem solving: it is also about exploiting opportunities. It is part of everyday life; we make decisions on the spur of the moment, after much thought, and in between these two extremes. The quality of the decisions that managers make is the yardstick of their effectiveness.[49]

Types of decisions

Simon[50] made the distinction between two types of decision: programmed decisions and non-programmed decisions. The former refers to repetitive and routine decisions where a set procedure has been established for handling a particular situation, and the latter refers to non-routine situations where the decision is, therefore, new and unstructured.

Traditionally, programmed decisions have been handled through rules and standard operating procedures that the organization develops for dealing with them. Their advantages are that they simplify and speed up the decision-making process. They reduce uncertainty, are consistent, and enhance co-ordination and control. Non-programmed decisions are usually handled by general problem-solving processes, judgement, intuition and creativity, as they tend to be a response to complex and changing situations.

The main concern of top management should be non-programmed decisions, while first-level management should be concerned with programmed decisions. In other words, the nature, frequency and degree of certainty surrounding a problem should dictate the level of management at which the decision should be made.

A further distinction can be made between personal and organizational decisions. Personal decisions are personal to the individual. Some have little relevance to the job (for example, what film to see) while others have more (for example, career decisions, participating at work, whether to go to work or stay at home). Therefore, it can be said that personal decisions can have an impact on one's personal life as well as the organization. Organizational decisions, on the other hand, are decisions made about the issues, problems, policies and practices of the organization itself. These vary from trivial to extremely important decisions, and these latter have a profound impact on the organization.

Another distinction, made by Ansoff,[51] is that between strategic, operating and administrative decisions. Strategic decisions are long-term ones which determine the main goals and objectives of the organization in the light of its relationship with its environment. These tend to be non-routine, non-repetitive and complex – in Simon's terminology, non-programmed decisions.

Operating decisions, on the other hand, are short-term and concerned with such matters as output levels, pricing and inventory levels. There are fewer variables involved, so these tend to be routine and repetitive (programmed decisions).

Administrative decisions arise from the interaction between strategic and operating decisions. They are principally concerned with harmonizing the organization's structure; for example, by establishing lines of authority, communication lines, etc.

Decision-making models

Outlines below are three influential decision-making models, which reflect the variations in how decision making has been perceived and interpreted. All three models are useful in helping us to understand the complexity and variety of decision-making situations found in organizations.[52]

Rational model
The rational or classical model assumes that decision making is a rational process whereby decision makers seek out and choose the best available alternative course of action, with the express aim of maximizing the achievement of goals and objectives. The model requires the goals or problem to be clearly defined, and to be followed by an exhaustive search for alternative solutions and thorough data collection and analysis. The basic assumptions of this model are that all the information regarding the alternatives is available; that objectively ranking these alternatives is possible; and that the alternative which is finally chosen will provide the maximum gain possible for the organization.

There are particular problems with the rational model. It operates on the false assumption that goals can be clearly identified. Even in situations where they are apparent, they often conflict with other goals. In addition, decision makers are unable, for a variety of reasons, to consider all alternatives and outcomes, and the necessary information is not always available. Therefore, we can say that, under most circumstances, managers do not make decisions in this way.

Bounded rationality model

As a result of the criticisms associated with the rational model, many felt the need for a decision-making model that provided a more accurate representation, as well as offering some guidance on how we should approach decisions.

The bounded rationality model takes into account the limitations of the rationality model and offers a clearer explanation of the decision-making process. It goes some way to explaining why different people make very different decisions based on the same information. It incorporates our tendency not always to opt for the 'best' alternative solution – that is, to 'satisfice' – a tendency which is often based on a limited search for alternative solutions. The model also recognizes the reality that reliable information is not always available, regardless of time or resources.

Satisficing is the means of selecting an acceptable alternative solution. 'Acceptable' often comes down to 'easier to identify and achieve, and less controversial, than the best available alternative'. This works on the premise that decision making continues to generate and evaluate alternatives until one alternative is 'good enough' to be acceptable, rather than, as in the rational approach, until the 'best' alternative is identified.

The following quotation suggests that decisions will always be based on incomplete and inadequate comprehension of the real situation: 'The capacity of the human mind for formulating and solving complex problems is very small compared with the size of the problems whose solution is required for objectively rational behaviour in the real world – or even for a reasonable approximation to such objective rationality.'[53]

Political model

The political model works on the assumption that organizational decisions reflect the decisions of individuals to satisfy their own interests. The preferential interests are determined at an early stage and do not tend to change when new information becomes available. The process of defining the goals, searching for alternatives, collecting and analysing data is adhered to only to influence the decision in individuals' favour. Decisions are seen as the result of the distribution of power in the organization and the effectiveness of the tactics used by the various participants in the process.[54]

Stages of managerial decision making

Managerial decision making begins with the recognition of a problem or opportunity and concludes with an assessment of the results of actions taken to solve those problems or exploit the opportunities. McCall and

Kaplan[55] provide a model of the different stages of managerial decision making (see figure 5.1). Although there appears to be a logical sequence, managerial decision making is often a messy process.

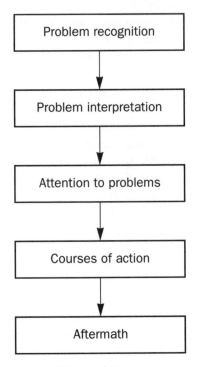

Figure 5.1 Stages of managerial decision making.

Source: Adapted from McCall and Kaplan, *Whatever it Takes.*

Behavioural influences on individual decision making

There are a number of behavioural factors which influence the decision-making process, such as our values, personality, attitudes, etc.

Our values have a great effect on how we make decisions. We make judgements all the time based on our values; for example, in establishing objectives, in developing alternatives, in choosing an alternative, in implementing a decision, and in evaluating that decision.

The decisions we make strongly reflect our personality. Some studies have focused on personality variables and their effect on decision making.[56] Many of us find taking risks easier than others. Therefore, those of us who have an aversion to risk taking will establish different objectives, evaluate alternatives differently, etc., from those of us who do not.

Many behavioural scientists have focused attention on what has been referred to as 'post-decision anxiety'. Such anxiety is also known as *cognitive dissonance*.[57] When there is a conflict between the decision made and our own cognitions (attitudes, beliefs, etc.), we suffer from this affliction, because we have doubts about the choice made.

Barriers to effective decision making

There are several barriers to making informed and effective decisions. An awareness of these can help to improve the decision-making process.

'Tunnel vision' refers to a narrow focus on alternative solutions. We can say that those of us who suffer from tunnel vision have 'mental blinkers' which restrict our choices to a relatively small range of alternatives. Tunnel vision can, therefore, have a detrimental effect on the decision-making process.[58] Previous commitments to a particular decision make it increasingly difficult to evaluate other alternatives objectively and to change any actions already taken.

Research by Soelberg[59] indicates that many people choose a 'favourite' alternative early on in the decision-making process, but continue to play the game by evaluating additional solutions. The consequences are clear: other alternatives are distorted and evaluations that take place emphasize the preferred solution as being the 'best'.

An organization's structure, culture and decision-making style affect individuals, groups and organizational processes every day. Therefore, understanding each of these is imperative for the effective organization. Further, when we attempt to implement change (see Unit Six), we need a sound understanding of structure, culture and decision-making processes.

Activity OB5.5 draws together these three important elements.

ACTIVITY OB5.5

DECISIONS ON ORGANIZATIONAL CULTURE AND AUTHORITY

Activity code
☑ Self-development
☐ Teamwork
☐ Communications
☐ Numeracy/IT
☑ Decisions

The OB advisor was charged with introducing cultural change within the organization. He decided to focus, initially, on its authority structure. The organization was divided into:

■ *Line authority* – this was the usual 'top-to-bottom' legitimate authority running from the boss to the subordinate, following the principle of the 'unity of command'.

- *Staff authority* – this was the advisory role of specialists, who could give assistance and conduct investigations. The advice was given to the line managers, but the latter could accept or reject it.
- *Functional authority* – this involved the right to seek information from other sections or departments not under the direct control of the authority holder. For example, the data processing manager had to have monthly returns from each department.

The decisions revolved around the staff–line interface. The organization was moving away from a mechanistic mode to a more organic format. The layers of officials on the line hierarchy had always been serviced by an army of specialists, from management accountants to labour relations officers. Now the push in the new culture was for decentralized power structures and making all managers responsible for their decisions, which would encompass the traditional staff advisory roles. Indeed, the new line managers would be their own staff specialists, particularly when dealing with people. Research and development, legal services, finance and management accounting would remain as staff specialists, although slimmed down quite considerably. The personnel and training department would now be 'devolved'.

This was the aim, but the OB advisor was troubled. He was a personnel specialist, but he was not thinking about his role, which would continue anyway at the director's level of giving policy advice. He was concerned about the swamping of the people specialism by line management, as expertise would be diluted. He would oppose it or at least modify it – now he needed more supportive arguments to back up his decisions.

Task

1 Provide the OB advisor with arguments for retaining the specialist people advisory/staff role.
2 Note possible counter-arguments as well, so that the OB advisor is well armed.

Notes

1 Sloan, *My Years with General Motors.*
2 Mintzberg, *Nature of Managerial Work.*
3 Taylor, *Principles of Scientific Management.*
4 Gulick, 'Notes on the theory of organization'.
5 Urwick, 'Executive decentralization'.
6 Fayol, *General and Industrial Management.*
7 Mayo, *Human Problems of an Industrial Civilization.*
8 Roethlisberger and Dickson, *Management and the Worker.*
9 Maslow, *Motivation and Personality.*
10 Herzberg, *Work and the Nature of Man.*
11 McGregor, *Human Side of Enterprise.*
12 Likert, *New Patterns of Management.*
13 Argyris, *Personality and Organization.*
14 Burns and Stalker, *Management of Innovation.*
15 Woodward, *Industrial Organizations.*
16 Lawrence and Lorsch, *Organization and Environment.*

17 Blau and Scott, *Formal Organizations*.
18 Haas et al., 'The size of the supportive component in organizations'.
19 Pugh et al., 'Dimensions of organization structure'.
20 Mahoney and Frost, 'Role of technology'.
21 Hall and Tittle, 'A note on bureaucracy and its correlates'.
22 Hall et al., 'Examination of the Blau–Scott and Etzioni Typologies'.
23 Argyris, *Personality and Organization*.
24 Aldrich, *Organizations and Environments*.
25 Woodward, *Industrial Organizations*.
26 Thompson, *Organizations in Action*.
27 Perrow, 'Framework for the comparative analysis of organizations'.
28 Burns and Stalker, *Management of Innovation*.
29 Lawrence and Lorsch, *Organization and Environment*.
30 Sharplin, *Strategic Management*.
31 Schwartz, 'Matching corporate culture'.
32 Pettigrew, 'On studying cultures'.
33 Jongeward, *Everybody Wins*.
34 Gordon, 'Industry determinants of organization culture'.
35 Schein, *Organization Culture and Leadership*.
36 Schein, 'How culture forms'.
37 Smircich, 'Concepts of culture'.
38 Saffold, 'Culture traits, strength and organizational performance'.
39 Ouchi, *Theory Z*.
40 Peters and Waterman, *In Search of Excellence*.
41 Deal and Kennedy, *Corporate Cultures*.
42 Schein, 'How culture forms'.
43 Reynolds, 'Imposing a corporate culture'.
44 Halpin, *Organizational Climate of Schools*.
45 See Unit Three for a fuller explanation of leadership styles.
46 O'Reilly, 'Corporations, culture and commitment'.
47 Denison, 'Bring corporate culture to the bottom line'.
48 Cameron and Freeman, 'Cultural congruence'.
49 Bass, *Organizational Decision Making*.
50 Simon, *New Science of Management Decisions*.
51 Ansoff, *Strategic Management*.
52 Dean, *Decision Processes*.
53 Simon, *New Science of Management Decisions*.
54 Pfeffer, *Power in Organizations*.
55 McCall and Kaplan, *Whatever it Takes*.
56 Renwick and Tosi, 'Effects of sex'.
57 Festinger, *Theory of Cognitive Dissonance*.
58 White and Bednar, *Organizational Behavior*.
59 Soelberg, 'Unprogrammed decision making'.

Unit Six

Focus on Change Processes

Learning Objectives

After completing this unit, you should be able to:

■ understand some of the concepts of change from a number of perspectives;

■ explain individual and organizational resistances to change;

■ appreciate some of the models and processes for organizational change;

■ apply the generic skills.

Contents

Unit Six

"An organization has two choices – adapt or die.**"**

Anon

Overview

Change is an inherent part of life, and a major challenge facing organizations is to manage it effectively.[1] The management of change involves adapting an organization to the demands of a changing environment and modifying the actual behaviours of its employees. If its members do not change their behaviours, the organization cannot change. A manager needs to consider many things when undertaking organizational change, including the types of pressure being exerted on the organization to change and the kinds of resistances to change that are likely to be encountered.

All organizations exist in a changing environment and they themselves are constantly changing. In this unit we examine the goals of planned organizational change, pressure for and resistance to change, and some models and processes for implementing organizational change.

The Importance of Change

When organizations fail to change, the costs of that failure may be quite high. Organizational change can be difficult, but adaptive, flexible organizations have a competitive advantage over rigid, static ones.

It is important to distinguish between change that inevitably happens to all organizations and change that is planned by the organization.[2] The latter refers to a series of planned activities designed to change individuals, groups, and organization structure and processes.[3]

We have all been members of changing organizations at some time or other, whether at school, at college or at work. Activity OB6.1 provides you with the opportunity to identify some of the triggers of change. It acts as a brainstorming session for you as an individual or a member of a group. You may wish to think of an organization with which you are familiar to give you some context to these triggers.

Planned organizational change is a conscious attempt to improve the way in which groups, departments or the whole organization function.

197

ACTIVITY OB6.1

CHANGE TRIGGERS

Activity code
- ✓ Self-development
- ✓ Teamwork
- ✓ Communications
- ☐ Numeracy/IT
- ✓ Decisions

The need for change is often triggered by factors internal to the organization and by characteristics external to the organization. Your task is to identify some of these factors which trigger change.

Internal:

External:

There are essentially two underlying objectives to such change:

1 to improve the ability of the organization to adapt to changes in its environment;
2 to change patterns of employee behaviours.

Change is inevitable and is a continuing process. Even minor changes may have major repercussions, and what appears to be a minor change to a manager may seem major to those affected by it.

It is necessary before any change programme is put into action that a thorough investigation is undertaken to determine the individual's and organization's capacity for change. Two key indicators of individual willingness to change are how satisfied they are with their current situation and the extent to which they perceive the proposed changes as being risky for them personally. When employees are unhappy with the status quo and feel little personal risk from a change, it is likely that they would welcome it, whereas if employees are happy with the current situation and feel threatened by the proposed changes, they are less likely to welcome them.[4]

Resistance to Change

Pressures on organizations to change are never-ending. These pressures can be both internal and external in direction. It is inevitable that change will be resisted, at least to some extent, by both individuals and organizations. Resistance to change can take many forms. Examples of *overt* resistance are strikes, reduction in productivity, poor-quality work, sabotage, etc. *Covert* resistance examples are absenteeism, resignations, loss of motivation, lower morale, and higher accident and error rates. Resistance to change can be traced to many sources: individuals, groups, departments, the organization itself. Therefore, it is important for us to understand the reasons for and sources of resistance to change.[5]

Individual resistance to change

Resistance from individuals is very often nothing to do with the change itself but relates more specifically to the implications of such change. It means people adjusting themselves to a changed situation, which brings with it a certain amount of uncertainty and therefore fear about, for example, job loss, deskilling, loss of earnings, loss of status, loss of companions due to reorganization, or even loss of familiar surroundings. We can classify these into a variety of sources of individual resistance to change, namely: selective perception, habit, dependence, fear of the unknown, and economic reasons.

- *Selective perception:* As discussed in Unit Two, we tend to perceive selectively those things that conform most closely to our current understanding of our world. Once we 'paint our picture' of reality, we tend to resist changing it.
- *Habit:* We are all creatures of habit to some extent, so we tend to respond to situations in our own customary way. Whether a habit becomes a major source of resistance to change depends largely on whether we see some mileage in changing our habitual behaviour.
- *Dependence:* Dependence on others can lead to resistance to change. If we rely heavily on others, we may resist change until those we depend upon embrace it.
- *Fear of the unknown:* The unknown often makes people anxious, and change in the work situation, as in any other aspect of life, carries with it an element of uncertainty.
- *Economic reasons:* If the changes are seen as a threat to our economic security, we are more likely to resist them.

Another source of resistance is from the organization itself.

Organizational resistance to change

To a certain extent, an organization by its very nature resists change. Organizations standardize and systematize tasks in order to ensure efficiency and effectiveness, so they create defences against change. Significant sources of organizational resistance to change are: threats to power and influence, organization structure, and resource limitations.

■ *Threats to power and influence:* Those who possess power or influence in organizations may consider change to be a potential threat to these. Once a power position has been established, individuals or groups often resist changes that are perceived as reducing it.

■ *Organization structure:* Organizations need stability and continuity in order to function effectively. This need results in individuals being allotted roles, establishing procedures of work, etc. However, this essential need can be a strong source of resistance. Therefore we can say that the greater the rigidity in structure, the more likely it is that change proposals would be resisted. On the other hand, flexible, adaptive organizations are designed to reduce the resistance to change.

■ *Resource limitations:* Change inevitably requires resources, be they financial, time, or the acquisition of essential skills. It is not uncommon for desirable changes to be forsaken because of the lack of resources.

Activity OB6.2 highlights some of the likely blockages to change.

ACTIVITY OB6.2

RESISTANCE TO CHANGE

Activity code
✓ Self-development
✓ Teamwork
☐ Communications
☐ Numeracy/IT
✓ Decisions

Almost inevitably, changes in organizations are going to be resisted. Below is a list of likely blockages.[1] Your task, as an individual or a group, is to develop a policy on how to overcome these points of resistance to change.

Resistance point	How to overcome
1 Security in status quo	
2 No need to change	
3 Interests threatened	
4 Timing	
5 Disagreement on interpretation	
6 Unknown quantity	
7 Resources inadequate	

Source:
1 Adapted from Schermenhorn et al., *Managing Organizational Behaviour*

Overcoming resistance to change

Managers and employees need to identify and overcome resistance to change and to become more effective change agents. Understanding and overcoming resistance is complex, owing to the many variables which need to be taken into account. Lewin[6] developed a model which sees change as a dynamic balance of forces working in opposite directions. He referred to this as a 'force field analysis', and suggested that any situation can be considered to be in a state of equilibrium resulting from a balance of forces constantly pushing against each other. Certain forces in the situation – various resistances to change – tend to maintain the status quo. At the same time, various pressures for change are acting against these forces and are pushing for change.

In order to initiate change, a manager must act to modify the current equilibrium forces. The manager might attempt to change the situation by:

- increasing the strength of pressure for change;
- reducing the strength of the resisting forces or removing them completely from the situation;
- changing the direction of a force – that is, changing a resistance into a pressure for change.

There are distinct advantages in adopting this model in order to understand change processes. The depth of analysis required to appreciate the current situation fully enables managers to identify the aspects relevant to change. Perhaps more importantly, the variables that can be changed and those that cannot are clearly determined. It is not uncommon for managers to squander a great deal of time, money and energy on actions which they have little or no control over. It is only by focusing on the 'forces' that they do have control over that managers will be more able to effect change.

Often, the most effective way to make changes is to identify existing resistance to change and to focus efforts on removing or reducing as much resistance as possible. An important part of Lewin's approach to changing behaviours comprises a three-phase process:

1 *Unfreezing:* This phase requires the forces that maintain the organization at its current level to be reduced. This can be achieved by providing information that reveals the mismatch between current employee behaviours and those that are desirable.

2 *Moving:* This phase moves the organization's behaviour to a new plane by developing new behaviours, values and attitudes through changes in the organization's structures and processes.

3 *Refreezing:* The final phase establishes the organization's new equilibrium. This is commonly achieved through such means as organizational culture, norms, policies and structures.[7]

Let us now look at some models and processes for organizational change.

Models and Processes for Organizational Change

Many models and processes can be used to effect organizational change. A convenient way of classifying these is to focus on individuals, jobs and the organization.

Focus on people

To change an organization means changing the pattern of recurring behaviour.[8] Focusing on people as an approach to change relies heavily on changing employees' recurring behaviour. The most effective way of tackling this is by involving members of the organization in the process by creating a climate of participation. This approach can improve both individual and group processes in such areas as decision making, identifying and solving problems, communication, etc. Four popular approaches to organizational change which focus on people are: surveys, team building, process consultation, and quality of working life.

Surveys can prove to be an effective way of fostering closer relations between individuals, groups and departments through the identification of common fears and problems. They are particularly important at the organizational analysis stage, as they are a mechanism by which problems and issues are highlighted: this may provide vital information on the changes needed. The information is legitimized by the fact that it is concerned with the goals and problems of each employee, thereby going some way to eliminating potential individual resistances to change. Surveys in themselves, however, do not introduce change.

Team building, on the other hand, enables individuals, as part of a work group, to plan the changes needed to improve their effectiveness. This process increases the involvement and participation of individuals, which is essential if significant changes need to be introduced and maintained in the organization. Team building can provide a useful way to involve employees in an organizational change programme and to increase collaborative behaviour.

Process consultation is guidance provided by a consultant to help members of an organization perceive, understand and act on process events that occur in their work environment.[9] It is often effective in changing attitudes and group norms, improving interpersonal and decision-making skills, and increasing group cohesiveness and teamwork.

Quality of working life (QWL) programmes are concerned with the improvement of working conditions which affect the employee's experience with the organization. QWL programmes often focus on such issues as security, health and safety, participation, equal opportunities, and the work itself.

Each of these approaches would normally be used within the context of a broader organizational change programme.

Focus on task

The task-focused approach to change emphasizes changes in employees' work. This is commonly referred to as job design or redesign. Simply job design 'is the organization of a job to satisfy the technical–organizational requirements of the work to be accomplished and the human requirements of the person performing the work'.[10]

Ultimately, job design is concerned with restructuring the way work is performed, with the specific purpose of improving job performance by increasing employee motivation and involvement. This has been the focus of a great deal of research over the last twenty years. Why is this?

It is argued that much of the twentieth century has been dominated by the general principles of scientific management,[11] which has resulted in extensive division of labour, work simplification and tight managerial control systems – essentially, concentrating on only one half of the equation: 'to satisfy the technical–organizational requirements of the work'. However, this traditional approach to job design has been called into question, and there is now a necessity for alternative systems to be found. Two fundamental reasons for this need for change are as follows:

1 The socio-technical systems concept argues for a balance between social and technical requirements. An overemphasis on technical requirements, it is claimed, has led to increasing opposition from employees.

2 The motivational assumptions of the traditional approach to the design of jobs is, simply, that workers are basically lazy, irresponsible and instrumentally

oriented; hence the need for machine pacing, managerial controls and incentive payment schemes. The alternative view, put forward by many,[12] is that average employees like their work, will behave in a responsible manner if given the opportunity, and are likely to be motivated by the job itself. These two extremes are presented in McGregor's Theory X and Theory Y.[13]

It is, therefore, worth reiterating that job design is the integration of two primary aims: first, to satisfy the organization's requirements for productivity, efficiency and service; and second, to satisfy the needs of the individual for interest, challenge and accomplishment.

Hackman and Lawler[14] were primarily concerned with the relationship between job content variables on the one hand and individual work attitudes and behaviour on the other. They examined and described this relationship in terms of four key variables: variety, autonomy, task identity and feedback. Their research indicated that the greater the variety involved in a job, the greater was the overall satisfaction reported by employees. There were consistent positive relationships between each of the four job content variables and the measure of employee attitudes. That is to say that individuals in jobs offering greater variety, autonomy, task identity and feedback tended to exhibit more positive work attitudes. The fact that attitude towards pay is unrelated to three of the job characteristics weighs against the interpretation that as pay varies systematically with the nature of work, it is the cause of the observed relationships.

Evidence of this nature has led many[15] to the conclusion that job simplification leads almost inevitably to monotony, boredom and job dissatisfaction. There seems to be a need to avoid the consequences of 'simplified' jobs while at the same time allowing the economic goals of the organization to be attained.

Alterations that can be made in the social and technological work environment range from minor modifications to major changes. A wide variety of terms is used to describe changes in job design, and to add to the confusion they are often used interchangeably. However, the conceptual distinctions are important. Common approaches are:

- job rotation, which increases the variety of activities undertaken while not affecting the content of any single job;
- job enlargement, which increases the variety of the job but without moving the individual;
- job enrichment, which increases the opportunity for achievement and recognition;
- job extension, which allows additional jobs of a similar nature;
- autonomous working groups which involve a group of workers being given control over a significant unit of work.

Job rotation, enlargement and extension involve a change in job design by operating on the range of tasks involved, whereas, job enrichment and autonomous work groups focus on the discretionary element of work. The two last are the most significant job design approaches.

Job enrichment

This approach was developed by Herzberg[16] and has found most success in non-union organizations in the USA. However, it has also been successfully tried out in the UK.[17]

As an approach it is concerned with the job of the individual employee and seeks to build into it more responsibility, achievement, opportunity for growth and advancement, interest and recognition (it is very much based on Herzberg's motivating and satisfaction factors, outlined in Unit Two). The work group and the payment system are not involved, since Herzberg's two-factor theory argues that they are irrelevant to motivation and positive satisfaction. The change process and the boundaries of the redesign into management territory are controlled by management. The introduction of change is explicitly not seen as a subject for participation. Within the UK, this approach has met with success with shopfloor workers only when pay is involved in some sort of productivity bargain.

Autonomous work groups

Davis and Taylor[18] define autonomous work groups as being 'effectively leaderless teams of employees working together in the completion of the group's primary task'. Davis[19] describes the key elements of autonomous behaviour as: self-adjustment to changes required by technological variability, self-evaluation of performance, self-regulation of work content and structure within the job, and participation in setting up goals or objectives for job outputs. The overall aim is to provide a job which is complete, in the sense that the group sees it through from beginning to end and also has the responsibility for planning, co-ordinating and evaluating its own work activities, within broad constraints reached through the participation of the group members in joint decision making with their superiors.

This perspective focuses on the need to optimize the socio-technical and economic systems. Coal-mining studies[20] and the Norwegian industrial democracy programme[21] provide good illustrations. The approach contains a number of implications:

- The changes are open-ended – one change may lead to another.
- No issues are necessarily precluded from the change.
- Those involved in the newly designed work system should also be involved in its design.
- There is an assumption that workers want to have more control over their day-to-day work.

A number of issues arise from the introduction of autonomous work groups. The industrial relations climate within an organization crucially determines the outcome of attempts to redesign jobs. Union attitudes are often ambivalent or clearly hostile. They see a number of reasons to oppose or resist these types of changes. For example, such changes distract attention from pressing issues, and call for more effort without commensurate additional rewards; they can upset traditional distinctions, particularly between craft and operative workers; fewer workers may eventually be required; the whole approach is seen as a form of sophisticated management manipulation; there is a danger that group loyalties could override union loyalties; and workers do not want to take on added responsibility – management should solve its own problems.

This last issue of 'management solving its own problems' leads us to the question: if a group of workers have demonstrated their ability to exercise responsibility and to control their own work, where does the process stop? A form of participation and reorganization from the bottom up is created, which spreads into the supervisory role and could extend to middle management.

The traditional activities of the personnel function require reappraisal in the context of autonomous work groups. Individual job descriptions, job evaluation and incentive payment schemes are less appropriate, and monitoring of individual performance is less feasible. Questions are also raised about who should select, train and discipline group members. So autonomous work groups are not necessarily the right kind of task change for all organizations.

For an overview of some of the job design experiments undertaken, see Box OB6.1.

BOX OB6.1

Experiments in job design

1 *Biggane and Stewart* did an early study on job enlargement.[1] This involved several changes, including an increased variety of operations and responsibility, and increased control over work pace. They concluded that 'a large majority of operators came to prefer job enlargement in a relatively short time.' The outcomes were that there were lower labour costs and the quality of work improved.

2 *Paul, Robertson and Herzberg*[2] describe the effects of job enrichment. Their studies are methodologically superior to Biggane and Stewart's as they used an experimental design on sales reps, design engineers, factory supervisors and lab technicians. This involved increased autonomy and responsibility. The results were that the control group did not change, while the experimental group reported more favourable attitudes.

3 *Davis and Valfer*[3] introduced autonomous work groups. Personnel costs in terms of absenteeism, grievances, transfers and injuries were unaffected. There was some

improvement in the quality of work and the costs were reduced. Employee and supervisory attitudes improved and were favourable towards changes.

4 *Buitendam*[4] compared self-regulating autonomous work groups with individual attitudes, and found that autonomous work groups were more satisfied with their jobs, had a more positive attitude towards their peers, and the communications with other departments and quality of product were improved. However, although there were fewer complaints generally, there were more complaints with regard to work flow.

The introduction of a greater variety and autonomy is not always accompanied by a change in employee attitudes.

5 *Lawler, Hackman and Kaufman*[5] undertook job enrichment research in a telephone company. This failed to reveal any of the anticipated increases in satisfaction. The workers did not feel more involved in their work and there was greater dissatisfaction with interpersonal relationships.

Sources:
1   Biggane and Stewart, 'Job enlargement'
2   Paul et al., 'Job enrichment pays off'
3   Davis and Valfer, 'Intervening responses'
4   Buitendam, *Deverticalization in Production Organizations*
5   Lawler et al., 'Effects of job redesign'

Both approaches – job enrichment and autonomous work groups – are limited by a given technology and based on doubtful assumptions about worker motivation. A review of the evidence suggests that the process of change, and in particular worker involvement and attention to the payment system, are crucial to the success of job design.

Another task approach is *quality circles*. These are work groups, generally containing fewer than a dozen volunteers from the same area, who meet regularly to monitor and solve job-related quality and/or production problems. Quality circles may also be utilized to improve working conditions, increase the level of employee involvement and commitment, and encourage employee self-development.

There is considerable overlap between the various approaches with respect to the changes in the work situation required for their implementation. In introducing one form of job design, changes are often made which correspond to those emphasized by another. The implementation of any one form of job design typically involves modifications to other aspects of the work environment; for example, it may change the relationship between subordinate and superior.

Each of these job design techniques has been found to be an effective approach to organizational change under certain conditions. All can positively affect task performance, absenteeism, turnover and job satisfaction. It is important to note, however, that job redesign is not a universal cure. It involves a continuing process of learning and opinion change and its success is very much dependent on the organizational culture and structure.

Focus on the organization

A common approach to focusing on the organization is through organizational development. This is a planned, systematic process of organizational change based on behavioural science technology, research and theory.[22] It relies heavily on motivation theory and personality theory (see Unit Two) and learning theory (see Unit Four), as well as on research on group dynamics, leadership and power (see Unit Three) and organization design (see Unit Five).

Organizational development is not a single technique but a collection of techniques that have a certain philosophy and body of knowledge in common. It comprises a set of actions undertaken to improve both organizational effectiveness and employees wellbeing.[23] 'Organizational development' refers to the process of preparing for and managing change. It has certain distinguishing characteristics:[24]

- It is planned. It involves goal setting, action planning, implementation, monitoring, and taking corrective action where necessary.
- It is problem-oriented. It attempts to apply theory and research from a number of disciplines to the solution of organizational problems.
- It reflects a systems approach. It is a way of linking the human resources and potential of an organization to its technology, structure and management processes.
- It is an integral part of the management process. It is a way of managing organizational change processes.
- It is a continuous process, not a series of ad hoc activities designed to implement a specific change.
- It focuses on improvement. It is something that can benefit almost any organization, not just ineffective ones.
- It is action-oriented, focusing on accomplishments and results.
- It is based on sound theory and practice.

Is there one best way for an organization to develop? Many different approaches have been used successfully in organizational development efforts, but an approach that works in one organization may not necessarily do so in another. Therefore, there is no one best approach to change.

Successful organizational development programmes use a variety of approaches. The determining factor in deciding which approaches to use is the nature of the problem the organization is trying to solve. Therefore, an accurate diagnosis of organizational problems is absolutely essential as a starting point for an effective organizational change programme.[25]

An organizational diagnosis involves four basic steps:

1 recognizing and interpreting the problem and assessing the need for change;

2 determining the organization's readiness and capability for change;

3 identifying managerial and workforce resources and motivations for change;

4 determining a change of strategy and goals.[26]

Box OB6.2 looks at organizational change from the organization's perspective.

BOX OB6.2

Organizational change

A lot of the work on changing the organization seems to be a retreat from bureaucracy into more fluid and organic or flatter structures. The dynamic is change in the external environment, and the slower mechanistic bureaucracy is seen as less adaptable than its organic alternative.

The *mechanistic* version is more appropriate to stable conditions, and is seen as having:

■ specialized tasks broken down into functions;

■ technical functions and tasks that may be pursued at the expense of the wider organizational objectives;

■ a tightly defined hierarchy of roles;

■ rights and obligations that transfer to functional positions;

■ a dominating hierarchy;

■ prevailing instructions and orders;

■ an expectation of loyalty and obedience;

■ great regard for internal knowledge and expertise.

The *organic* version is seen as having:

■ specialist knowledge and experience that is tapped for the benefit of the organization;

■ a wider job framework, not bound by strict functional demarcation lines;

■ more fluid tasks that can be constantly redefined;

■ wider commitment;

■ a network of decisions that replace a hierarchical order;

■ lateral communications joining with the vertical communications of the mechanistic format;

■ a flow of information and advice, not diktats from above;

■ a commitment to the tasks of the organization;

■ a value for external know-how and experience.

These lists do sound a little like the 'before' and 'after' parts of some advertisements, but they are extrapolations from the steady state to the more dynamic state which underpins much of organization development and its structural variants.

Source: Adapted from Burns and Stalker, *Management of Innovation*

We have looked at organizational change from three perspectives: focusing on people, on the task, and on the organization. What are the key factors required to introduce and manage change?

Managing Change

Box OB6.3 highlights the main criteria for introducing change. In terms of the successful management of change, be it at a people, task or organizational level, it is important that the full co-operation of all concerned is obtained, an effective method of communication which is two-way at all levels and stages is in place, and there is effective feedback to the decision-making process.

BOX OB6.3

Introducing change

Communication and consultation are particularly important in times of change. The achievement of change is a joint concern of management and employees and should be carried out in a way which pays regard both to the efficiency of the undertaking and to the interests of employees. Major changes in working agreements should not be made by management without prior discussion with employees or their representatives.[1]

The philosophy of a consultative style of management runs through the Industrial Relations Code of Practice and the participative approach to human relations.[2]

In the UK for example, The Industrial Society embraces this view of change management. The plan of change once established stands or falls by its methods of delivery from explanations of the need for change, consultation and negotiation with those affected, communicating the process of change, putting it into effect and consulting after the event to ensure readjustment and transition.

Sources:
1   Department of Employment, *Industrial Relations Code of Practice*
2   A.H. Anderson, *Effective Labour Relations*

Change has very often to be effected while maintaining present procedures, and if this is to be achieved it requires the full co-operation of the participants. Gaining willing consent throughout the course of effecting change is positive motivation.

Activity OB6.3 requires you to examine some aspects of organizational change.

ACTIVITY OB6.3

ORGANIZATIONAL CHANGE

Activity code

☑ Self-development
☑ Teamwork
☑ Communications
☐ Numeracy/IT
☑ Decisions

As the organization almost takes on a life of its own, a parallel with the animal kingdom is often drawn, claiming that its very survival and growth are at stake if it fails to adapt. Indeed, a 'survival of the fittest' biological race can be seen in some organizations.[1]

Pressures for change can occur from the turbulence of the external environment or from within the organization. One such pressure for change is about learning, which we started to develop in Unit Four. The concept of the 'learning organization' is increasingly with us, and even though there is some significant debate about the concept's validity, the organization does need to adjust its learning or training needs.

Task

We have adapted some research into triggers on learning and training in organizations.[2] Your role is to examine these triggers and determine whether they are external to the organization, internal, or both. Thereafter you must rank in importance what you would expect these pressures to be upon the three types of organizations – large, medium and small.

The top ten external and internal factors that were seen to trigger training were:

- Local labour market (existing)
- The views of the line manager
- Loss of a key employee (unforeseen)
- The anticipated demand for product/services
- The views of the training department
- Expected labour market (local)
- Forecast profitability (allowing for environment)
- Recent company profitability
- National labour market (existing)
- Plans to change method/technology

As an aside, trade union policies, shopfloor views, local educational facilities and government grants trailed in at the bottom of the league table.

Sources:
1   See Williams, 'Organizational development'
2   Argyris and Schon, *Organizational Learning*; Research Bureau Ltd, *Research on External and Internal Influences*

The 'depth' of intervention in this structured attempt to manage change may be seen beyond the levels of the people, task or organization. Harrison[27] divides the change interventions into two: a 'deep change strategy', which attempts to change people's values, and a 'shallow change strategy', which is more open and based on structures, ideas, technologies, etc.

Examples of the 'deep-end' approach include biodata (biographical data) feedback, the Grid (placing oneself on a grid for self- and group reflection), and some form of T or training group in a laboratory or fish-bowl environment. More rational problem-solving approaches, like key result areas or joint problem-solving seminars, are examples of the 'shallow end'. Harrison argues for the depth to be as shallow as possible. Perhaps value changes, by definition, are going to be more difficult and it is easier to change attitudes – 'behaviour modification programmes' abound in training and development to sustain this process of attitudinal change.

Williams[28] takes another perspective. Change and its subsequent method of operation or intervention can be divided into 'structure' and 'process'. 'Structure' involves a technical intervention at the level of the organization – changing from mechanistic to organic, for example – while 'process' is a 'softer' technique aimed at groups and individuals.

The methods used must reflect the type of intervention sought. The structural dimension (or 'techno-structural' as he refers to it), may involve job redesign, greater autonomy for work groups, and applying models to restructure the organization. The process dimension involves norm changes, teamwork, goal setting, and feedback sessions on values and attitudes.

Whatever classification scheme of interventions and the respective methods we apply, change management is probably one of the most demanding aspects of organizational behaviour. We have touched upon some of the mechanisms and methods of change, so we will not elaborate on these any further. Instead, we will look at some common approaches used by management in an attempt to implement change.

The work of Kotter and Schlesinger[29] can be useful in the actual *approach* of change management, rather than the specific model, method or technique. See Activity OB6.4.

In *Effective Personnel Management* and *Effective Labour Relations* in this series,[30] we also note some of the shortcomings of managing change. Stephenson,[31] for example, is cited when he argues that much of organizational development can be oversimplistic and based on human relations philosophies rather than a total systems approach. The value system is also questioned.

This latter point is developed in the labour relations aspects of change. So many of these initiatives assume a unitarist perspective:[32] taking a managerialist stance at the expense of the employees, forcing a core value

ACTIVITY OB6.4

STRATEGIES FOR CHANGE MANAGEMENT

Activity code
☑ Self-development
☑ Teamwork
☑ Communications
☐ Numeracy/IT
☑ Decisions

Kotter and Schlesinger have suggested six key approaches to implementing change strategies. Your task, as an individual or in a group, is to define what you think that this strategy means in practice and to make a meaningful comment on its value in introducing change.

The strategies are:

■ Education and communication
■ Facilitation and support
■ Participation
■ Negotiation
■ Manipulation
■ Coercion

Source: Adapted from Kotter and Schlesinger, 'Choosing strategies for change'

system down the throats of workers with little or no negotiation or concession to the legitimate interest of workers. Hence, change management must take more of a pluralistic vision to be truly effective, taking account of the diversity of interests at the workplace. Therefore, we advocate an emphasis, wherever possible, on the people and process side of things, using co-operative methods of change and employing such techniques as training and development, full consultation and negotiation, and job redesign. The structural side should not be forgotten, of course, but we need to stop treating people like machines or robots, for change will be inhibited, 'breakdowns' in the existing status quo will continue to occur unabated, and the organization will continue to be ineffective.

To conclude this unit: change is constant. The pace of change in the last twenty to thirty years has never been surpassed even during the early stages of the Industrial Revolution. Environmental turbulence[33] and internal revolutions and evolution[34] within the organization all mean that change management on this unprecedented scale may continue for some time. Change is difficult to manage, but we have tried here to evoke the climate of an effective organization which will facilitate it. The philosophies, the techniques and the approaches to change must all be in tandem and built on the solid bedrock of a sound understanding and analysis of organizational behaviour.

Now tackle Activity OB6.5, which ties the issues of change together.

ACTIVITY OB6.5

LESSONS OF CHANGE

Activity code
- ✓ Self-development
- ✓ Teamwork
- ✓ Communications
- ☐ Numeracy/IT
- ✓ Decisions

The British Institute of Management (BIM) noted that there are 'widespread changes in working patterns' taking place. These changes include:

- alterations in hours
- more part-time work
- increased job splitting and job sharing
- changes in the design of jobs
- contracting out and outworking away from the core labour force

Task

Comment on these trends and the types of problem that you or the group feel that management will encounter.

Derive sound 'principles of change' for managers to handle these changes. Write a report on these guidelines.

Source: Adapted from: British Institute of Management, Managing New Patterns of Work

Notes

1 Carnell, *Managing Change in Organizations*.
2 Cummings and Huse, *Organizational Development and Change*.
3 Goodman and Kurke, 'Studies of change in organizations'.
4 Zeira and Avedisian, 'Organizational planned change'.
5 Argyris, *Management and Organizational Development*.
6 Lewin, 'Frontiers in group dynamics'.
7 Cummings and Huse, *Organizational Development and Change*.

8 Kahn, 'Organizational development'.

9 Schein, *Process Consultation*.

10 L.E. Davis et al., 'Current job design criteria'.

11 Taylor, *Principles of Scientific Management*.

12 McGregor, *Human Side of Enterprise*; Herzberg, *Work and the Nature of Man*; Argyris, *Personality and Organization*.

13 McGregor, *Human Side of Enterprise*.

14 Hackman and Lawler, 'Employee reactions to job characteristics'.

15 Argyris, *Personality and Organization*; Blauner, *Alienation and Freedom*; K. Davis, *Human Society*; Kornhauser, *Mental Health of the Industrial Worker*; Likert, *Human Organization*; McGregor, *Human Side of Enterprise*; Whyte, *Money and Motivation*.

16 Herzberg, *Work and the Nature of Man*.

17 Paul et al., 'Job enrichment pays off'.

18 L.E. Davis and Taylor, *Design of Work*.

19 L.E. Davis, 'Design of jobs'.

20 Trist and Bamforth, 'Some social and psychological consequences'.

21 Emery and Thosrud, *Form and Content in Industrial Democracy*.

22 Burke, *Organizational Development*.

23 Beer and Walton, 'Organization change and development'.

24 Marguiles and Raia, *Conceptual Foundations of Organizational Development*.

25 Burke, *Organizational Development*.

26 Beckhard, *Organizational Development*.

27 Harrison, 'Choosing the depth of organizational intervention'.

28 Williams, 'Organizational development'.

29 Kotter and Schlesinger, 'Choosing strategies for change'.

30 A.H. Anderson, *Effective Personnel Management*; A.H. Anderson, *Effective Labour Relations*.

31 Stephenson, 'Organizational development'.

32 See, for example, Fox, *Man Mismanagement*, for a debate on unitarism and pluralism.

33 A.H. Anderson and Barker, *Effective Business Policy*, take this perspective further.

34 Greiner, 'Patterns of organizational change'.

Conclusion

As we have seen, an organization is a group of people coming together to achieve a common purpose. An effective organization should not be seen as only task- or goal-oriented. It must also take full account of the needs and wants of its constituent members – its people. This is not to advocate a modern-day Theory Y[1] approach; nor is it advocating the Theory Z of Ouchi,[2] a combination of Type A (American) and Type J (Japanese) firms with formal control mechanisms, management by objectives, formal planning and sophisticated financial and information systems. This is not enough, as the Z firms would be too task-oriented. Organizations need task and goal planning and control, as well as a more liberal and liberated people philosophy. Perhaps the combined Y of McGregor and Z of Ouchi will make for the type of organization that we are advocating.

For the sake of analysis, we have organized this book into containable units. These units in turn reflect organizational reality with their emphases on the individual, on interpersonal and group processes, on integrating mechanisms, and on the organization. Of course, by breaking down the subject in such a way, we simplify the complexity of the whole, so a synthesis is needed of all these variables.

We have also looked at the concepts, the approaches and the methods of organizational behaviour. These philosophies and methodologies of how we go about studying people in organizations are a critical component of the subject. We have sought an objective stance for the book and advocated it as a method of work for the practitioner in an organization. Organizational need and greed as well as the politics and individual careers of people will dilute objectivity, but we should still strive for some vision that allows us to stand back and see a more objective reality.

Finally, we have looked at change. We have deliberately made this unit shorter than the rest, for the subject is covered elsewhere in the series.[3] Change and its pace compound the difficulties of managing effectively. Economic competition with globalized economies and challenges from the Pacific Rim can be allied to rapid technological innovation to give ever-increasing turbulence. Longer-term social change from a desire for sexual and racial equality as well as in other areas, with a growth of 'knowledge workers', can be linked to the fortunes of changing state policies.

Within the organization too, there are the demands of and for change. The social responsibility of business figures large, with flexible working and homeworking continuing at a great pace, while people at work, who are citizens in their non-working life, demand a greater say in involvement, participation and co-determination of their conditions of work, if not of work itself.[4]

The main purpose of this book has been to provide you with the basic knowledge, skills, techniques and insights of organizational behaviour. It was and is a wide brief – if we have contributed in some way to making you a more effective manager of organizations, we will have succeeded.

Notes

1 McGregor, *Human Side of Enterprise*.
2 Ouchi, *Theory Z*.
3 See A.H. Anderson and Barker, *Effective Business Policy*, for an environmental analysis of change from a strategic perspective; A.H. Anderson, *Effective General Management*, for an overview of 'change management'. The human aspect of change is covered in A.H. Anderson, *Effective Personnel Management*, while the negotiation of change is covered in A.H. Anderson, *Effective Labour Relations*.
4 See, for example, Steade, *Business and Society in Transition*.

Bibliography and Further Reading

Abercrombie, K., 'Paralanguage', *British Journal of Diseases of Communication*, 3 (1968).

Adams, J.S., 'Toward an understanding of inequity', *Journal of Abnormal Social Psychology*, 67 (1963).

Adams, J.S., 'Inequity in social exchange', in *Advances in Experimental Social Psychology. Vol. 2*, ed. L.Berkowitz (Academic Press, New York, 1965).

Ajzen, I. and Fishbein, M., *Understanding Attitudes and Predicting Social Behaviour* (Prentice Hall, Englewood Cliffs, NJ, 1980).

Akin, G., 'Varieties of managerial learning', *Organizational Dynamics*, Autumn (1987).

Albrow, M., 'The study of organizations: objectivity or bias', in *Social Science Survey*, ed. J. Gould (Penguin, Harmondsworth, 1968).

Alcorn, S., 'Understanding groups at work', *Personnel*, August (1989).

Alderfer, C.P., *Existence, Relatedness and Growth: human needs in organizational settings* (Free Press, New York, 1972).

Aldrich, H.E., *Organizations and Environments* (Prentice Hall, Englewood Cliffs, NJ, 1979).

Allport, F.H., *Theories of Perception and the Concept of Structure* (Wiley, New York, 1955).

Allport, G.W., 'The historical background of modern social psychology', in *Handbook of Social Psychology: theory and method. Vol. 1*, ed. G. Lindzey (Addison-Wesley, Reading, MA, 1954).

Anderson, A.H., 'The learner without clothes: the need for a training system', *Training Officer*, June (1993).

Anderson, A.H., *Successful Training Practice: a managers' guide to personnel development* (Blackwell, Oxford, 1993).

Anderson, A.H., *Effective General Management* (Blackwell, Oxford, 1994).

Anderson, A.H., *Effective Labour Relations* (Blackwell, Oxford, 1994).

Anderson, A.H., *Effective Personnel Management* (Blackwell, Oxford, 1994).

Anderson, A.H. and Barker, D., *Effective Business Policy* (Blackwell, Oxford, 1994).

Anderson, A.H. and Kleiner, D., *Effective Marketing Communications* (Blackwell, Oxford, 1994).

Anderson, B.F., *Cognitive Psychology: the study of knowing, learning and thinking* (Academic Press, New York, 1975).

Ansoff, H., *Corporate Strategy* (Penguin, Harmondsworth, 1987).

Ansoff, H.I. (ed.), *Strategic Management* (London, Macmillan, 1981).

Argyris, C., *Personality and Organization* (Harper, New York, 1957).

Argyris, C., *Integrating the Individual and the Organization* (Wiley, New York, 1964).

Argyris, C., *Management and Organizational Development: the path from XA to YB* (McGraw-Hill, New York, 1971).

Argyris, C. and Schon, A., *Organizational Learning: a theory of action perspectives* (Addison-Wesley, Reading, MA, 1978).

Bales, R.F., *Interaction Process Analysis: a method for the study of small groups* (Addison-Wesley, Reading, MA, 1950).

Bandura, A., *Principles of Behavior Modification* (Holt, Rinehart and Winston, New York, 1969).

Barker, D., 'Action learning in management development', *Assessment and Evaluation in Higher Education*, 18 (1993).

Barnard, C.I., *The Functions of the Executive* (Harvard University Press, Cambridge, MA, 1938).

Baron, R.A. and Richardson, S.R., *Human Aggression*, 2nd edition (Plenum Press, New York, 1991).

Bass, B.M., *Leadership Psychology and Organizational Psychology* (Harper and Row, New York, 1960).

Bass, B.M., *Organizational Decision Making* (Richard D. Irwin, Holmewood, IL, 1983).

Bass, B.M. and Vaughan, J.A., *Training in Industry: the management of learning* (Wadsworth, Belmont CA, 1966).

Beckhard, R., *Organizational Development: strategies and models* (Addison-Wesley, Reading, MA, 1969).

Beer, M. and Walton, A.E., 'Organization change and development', *Annual Review of Psychology*, 38 (1987).

Belbin, R.M., *Management Teams: why they succeed or fail* (Heinemann, London, 1981).

Bennis, W.G. and Shepard, H.S., 'A theory of group development', *Human Relations*, 9 (1965).

Berelson, B. and Steiner, G.A., *Human Behavior: an inventory of scientific findings* (Harcourt, Brace and World, New York, 1964).

Bettenhausen, K.L. and Murnigham, J.K., 'The development and stability of norms in groups facing interpersonal and structural challenge', *Administrative Science Quarterly* (1991).

Biggane, J.F. and Stewart, P.A., 'Job enlargement: a case study', Research Series of Labor and Management, State University of Iowa, 25 (1963).

Blake, R.R. and Mouton, J.S., *The New Managerial Grid* (Gulf Publishing, Houston, 1964).

Blau, P.M. and Scott, W.R., *Formal Organizations* (Chandler, San Francisco, 1962).

Blauner, R., *Alienation and Freedom* (University of Chicago Press, Chicago, 1964).

Braverman, H., *Labor and Monopoly Capitalism* (Monthly Review Press, New York, 1974).

Brayfield, A.H. and Crockett, W.H., 'Employee attitudes and performance', *Psychological Bulletin*, 52 (1955).

Buitendam, A., *Deverticalization in Production Organizations* (Philips Industries, Eindhoven, n.d.).

Burgess, R., 'Research methods in the social sciences: book survey', *British Book News*, April (1987).

Burke, W.W., *Organizational Development: principles and practices* (Little Brown, Boston, 1982).

Burnham, J., *The Managerial Revolution* (Penguin, Harmondsworth, 1962).

Burns, T. and Stalker, G.M., *The Management of Innovation* (Tavistock, London, 1961).

Burns, T., 'Industry in a new age', *New Society*, 18 (31 January 1963).

Business Technician and Education Council (BTEC), 'Common skills and experience of BTEC programmes' (BTEC, London, n.d.).

Cameron, K.S. and Freeman, S.J., 'Cultural congruence, strength and type: relationships to effectiveness', in *Research in Organizational Change and Development. Vol. 5*, eds R.W. Woodman and W.A. Passmore (JAI Press, Greenwich, CT, 1991).

Capel, I. and Gurnsey, J., *Managing Stress* (Constable, London, 1987).

Carnell, C.A., *Managing Change in Organizations* (Prentice Hall, Englewood Cliffs, NJ, 1990).

Carr, E.H., *What is History?* (Macmillan, London, 1968).

Cattell, R.B., *The Scientific Analysis of Personality* (Penguin, Baltimore, 1965).

Cavanagh, G.F., *Ethical Dilemmas in Modern Corporations* (Prentice Hall, Englewood Cliffs, NJ, 1988).

Cherrington, D.J., *Organizational Behavior: management of individual and organizational performance* (Allyn and Bacon, Boston, 1989).

Conger, J.A., 'Inspiring others: The language of leadership', *Academy of Management Executive*, 5 (1991).

Cooper, C.L. and Marshall, J., 'Occupational sources of stress: a review of the literature relating to coronary heart disease and mental ill health', *Journal of Occupational Psychology*, March (1976).

Cooper, C.L. and Marshall, J., *Understanding Executive Stress* (PBI, New York, 1977).

Cooper, C.L. and Marshall, J., *White Collar and Professional Stress* (Wiley, New York, 1980).

Cosier, R.A. and Dalton, D.R., 'Positive effects of conflict: a field experiment', *International Journal of Management*, 1 (1990).

Cosier, R.A. and Schwenk, C.R., 'Agreement and thinking alike: ingredients for poor decisions', *Academy of Management Executive*, February (1990).

Cronbach, L.J., 'The two disciplines of scientific psychology', *American Psychologist*, 12 (1957).

Crozier, M., *The Bureaucratic Phenomenon* (Tavistock Publications and University of Chicago Press, Chicago, 1964).

Cummings, T.G. and Huse, F.F., *Organizational Development and Change*, 4th edition (West, St Paul, Minn., 1989).

Davis, K., *Human Society* (Macmillan, New York, 1950).

Davis, L.E., 'The design of jobs', *Industrial Relations*, 6 (1966).

Davis, L.E. and Taylor, R.N., *The Design of Work* (Penguin, Harmondsworth, 1972).

Davis, L.E. and Valfer, E.S., 'Intervening responses to changes in supervisor job designs', *Occupational Psychology*, 39 (1965).

Davis, L.E., Canter, R.R. and Hoffman, J., 'Current job design criteria', *Journal of Industrial Engineering*, 6 (1955).

Davis, T.R., 'The influence of the physical environment in offices', *Academy of Management Review*, 9 (1984).

Davis, T.R.V. and Luthans, F., 'A social learning approach to organizational behavior', *Academy of Management Review*, 5 (1980).

Deal, T.E. and Kennedy, A.A., *Corporate Cultures: the rites and rituals of corporate life* (Addison-Wesley, Reading, MA, 1982).

Dean, J.W., *Decision Processes in the Adoption of Advanced Technology* (Pennsylvania State University, University Park, PA, 1986).

Dearborn, D. and Simon, H.A., 'Selective perception: a note on the departmental identifications of executives', *Sociometry*, 21 (1958).

Denison, D.R., 'Bring corporate culture to the bottom line', *Organizational Dynamics*, Autumn (1984).

Department of Employment, *Industrial Relations Code of Practice* (HMSO, London, 1972).

Digman, J.M., 'Personality structure: emergence of the five factor model', *Annual Review of Psychology*, 41 (1990).

Drucker, P.F., *The Practice of Management* (Harper and Row, New York, 1954).

Dubin, R., 'Work in modern society', in *Handbook of Work, Organization and Society*, ed. R. Dubin (Rand McNally, Chicago, 1976).

Dunlop, J.T., *Industrial Relations Systems* (Holt, Rinehart, New York, 1958).

Dunnette, M.D., Campbell, J.P. and Hakel, M.D., 'Factors contributing to job dissatisfaction in six occupational groups', *Organizational Behavior and Human Performance*, 2 (1967).

Emery, F. and Thosrud, E., *Form and Content in Industrial Democracy* (Tavistock, London, 1951).

Evans, M.G., 'Conceptual and operational problems in the measurement of various aspects of job satisfaction', *Journal of Applied Psychology*, 53 (1971).

Eysenck, H.J., *Dimensions of Personality* (Routledge and Kegan Paul, London, 1947).

Eysenck, H.J., *Structure of Human Personality* (Methuen, London, 1960).

Eysenck, H.J., 'Development of a theory', in *Personality, Genetics and Behavior: selected papers* (Praeger, New York, 1982).

Fayol, H., *General and Industrial Management*, trans. C. Stors (Pitman, London, 1949).

Feldman, D.C. and Arnold, H.J., *Managing Individual and Group Behavior in Organizations* (McGraw-Hill, New York, 1983).

Feldman, D.C. and Arnold, H.J., *Organizational Behavior* (McGraw-Hill, New York, 1986).

Festinger, L., *A Theory of Cognitive Dissonance* (Peterson, Evanston, IL, 1957).

Fiedler, F.E., *A Theory of Leadership* (McGraw-Hill, New York, 1967).

Fiedler, F.E., Chelmers, M.M. and Mahar, L., *Improving Leadership Effectiveness* (Wiley, New York, 1976).

Filley, A.C., 'Some normative issues in conflict management', *California Management Review*, 21 (1978).

Fleischman, E.A. and Hunt, J.G. (eds), *Current Developments in the Study of Leadership* (Southern Illinois University Press, Carbondale, 1973).

Fox, A., *A Sociology of Work in Industry* (Collier Macmillan, London, 1971).

Fox, A., *Man Mismanagement* (Hutchison, London, 1974).

French, J.R.P. and Caplan, R.D., 'Psychosocial factors in coronary heart disease', *Industrial Medicine*, 39 (1970).

French, J.R.P. and Raven, B., 'The bases of social power', in *Studies in Social Power*, ed. D. Cartwright (University of Michigan Institute of Social Research, Ann Arbor, 1959).

Freud, S., *The Ego and the Id* (Norton, New York, 1960).

Galbraith, J.K., *The Affluent Society* (Penguin, Harmondsworth, 1967).

Galbraith, J.R., 'Organization design: an information processing view', *Interfaces*, May (1974).

Gellerman, S.W., *Behavioural Science in Management* (Penguin, Harmondsworth, 1974).

George, J.M. and Bettenhausen, K.L., 'Understanding prosocial behavior, sales performance and turnover: a group level analysis in a service context', *Journal of Applied Psychology*, October (1990).

Ghiselli, E.E., *Explorations in Managerial Talent* (Goodyear, Pacific Palisades, CA, 1971).

Gist, M.E., 'Self efficacy: implications in organizational behavior and human resource management', *Academy of Management Review*, 13 (1989).

Goldthorpe, J.H., Lockewood, D., Bechhofer, F. and Platt, J., *The Affluent Worker: industrial attitudes and behaviour* (Cambridge University Press, Cambridge, 1968).

Goodman, P.A. and Friedman, A., 'An examination of Adams' theory of equity', *Administrative Science Quarterly*, 16 (1971).

Goodman, P.S. and Kurke, L.B., 'Studies of change in organizations: a status report', in *Change in Organizations*, ed. Goodman PS and Associates (Jossey-Bass, San Francisco, 1982).

Gordon, G.G., 'Industry determinants of organization culture', *Academy of Management Review*, 16 (1991).

Gouldner, A.W., *Patterns of Industrial Democracy* (Free Press, New York, 1954).

Gouldner, A.W., 'Cosmopolitan and locals: toward an analysis of latent social roles', *Administrative Science Quarterly*, December (1957).

Greenberg, J., 'Cognitive reevaluation of outcomes in response to underpayment inequity', *Academy of Management Journal*, 32 (1989).

Greiner, L.E., 'Patterns of organizational change', *Harvard Business Review*, May–June (1967).

Greiner, L.E., 'Evolution and revolution as organizations grow', *Harvard Business Review*, July–August (1972).

Gross, B.M., *Organizations and their Managing* (Free Press, New York, 1968).

Gulick, L., 'Notes on the theory of organization', in *Papers on the Science of Administration*, eds L. Gulick and L. Urwick (The Institute of Public Administration, 1937).

Gyllenhammar, P., *People at Work* (Addison-Wesley, Reading, MA, 1977).

Haas, J.E., Hall, R.H. and Johnson, N., 'The size of the supportive component in organizations: a multi-organizational analysis', *Social Forces*, 42 (1963).

Hackman, J.R. and Lawler, E.E., 'Employee reactions to job characteristics', *Journal of Applied Psychology*, 55 (1977).

Hall, R.H., *Organizations: Structures, Processes and Outcomes*, 5th edition (Prentice Hall, Englewood Cliffs, NJ, 1991).

Hall, R.H. and Tittle, C.R., 'A note on bureaucracy and its correlates', *American Journal of Sociology*, 72 (1966).

Hall, R.H., Haas, J.E. and Johnson, N.J., 'An examination of the Blau–Scott and Etzioni typologies', *Administrative Science Quarterly*, 12 (1967).

Halpin, A.W., *The Organizational Climate of Schools* (US Office of Education, Department of Health, Education and Welfare, Washington, DC, 1962).

Handy, C., *Understanding Organizations* (Penguin, Harmondsworth, 1983).

Handyside, J., 'The 16PF', *Personnel Management*, March (1984).

Harrison, R., 'Choosing the depth of organizational intervention', *Journal of Applied Behavioural Science*, 6 (1970).

Hellriegel, D., Slocum, J.W., Jr, and Woodman, R.W., *Organizational Behavior* (West, St Paul, Minn., 1992).

Hemphill, J.K. and Coons, A.E., 'Development of the leader behavior description questionnaire', in *Leader Behavior: its description and measurement*, eds R.M. Stodgill and E.A. Coons (Bureau of Business Research, Ohio State University, Columbus, 1957).

Herzberg, F., *Work and the Nature of Man* (World, Cleveland, 1966).

Herzberg, F., Mausner, B. and Snyderman, B., *The Motivation to Work* (Wiley, New York, 1959).

Hill, J.M.M. and Trist, E.L., 'Industrial accidents, sickness and other absences', Tavistock Pamphlet No. 4 (Tavistock, London, 1962).

Hinkle, L.E., Whitney, L.H., Lehman, E.W., Dunn, J., Benjamin, B., King, R., Plakun, A. and Fleshinger, B., 'Occupation, education and coronary heart disease', *Science*, 161 (1968).

Hollenbeck, J.R. and Brief, A.P., 'The effects of individual differences and goal origins on goal setting and performance', *Organizational Behavior and Human Decision Processes*, 40 (1987).

Homans, G.C., *The Human Group* (Harcourt Brace Jovanovich, New York, 1950).

Honey, P. and Mumford, A., *Manual of Learning Styles* (Honey, Maidenhead, 1982).

House, J.S., *Stress Work and Social Support* (Addison-Wesley, Reading, MA, 1981).

House, R.A., 'A path–goal theory of effective leader effectiveness', *Administrative Science Quarterly*, 16 (1971).

House, R.J. and Wigdor, L.A., 'Herzberg's dual-factor theory of motivation and job satisfaction: a review of the empirical evidence and a criticism', *Personnel Psychology*, 20 (1967).

Iaffaldano, M.T. and Muchinsky, P.M., 'Job satisfaction and job performance: a meta-analysis', *Psychological Bulletin*, 97 (1985).

Jones, J.A.G., 'Training intervention strategies', ITS Monograph no. 2 (Industrial Training Service Ltd., London, 1983).

Jones, M., 'Training practices and learning theories', *JEIT*, 3 (1979).

Jongeward, D., *Everybody Wins: transactional analysis applied to organizations* (Addison-Wesley, Reading, MA, 1973).

Jung, C.G., *Psychological Types* (Harcourt, New York, 1923).

Kabanoff, B., 'Equity, power and conflict', *Academy of Management Review*, April (1991).

Kahn, R., 'Organizational Development: some problems and proposals', *Journal of Applied Behavioral Science*, 10 (1974).

Kahn, R.L., Wolfe, D.M., Quinn, R.P, Snoek, J.D. and Rosenthal, R.A., *Organizational Stress: studies in role conflict and ambiguity* (Wiley, New York, 1964).

Kalleberg, A.L., 'Work values and job rewards: a theory of job satisfaction', *American Sociological Review*, 42 (1977).

Kanfer, R., 'Motivation theory in industry and organizational psychology', in *Handbook of Industrial and Organizational Psychology*, 2nd edition, eds M.D. Dunnette and L.M. Hough (Consulting Psychologists Press, Chicago, 1990).

Kanter, R.M., 'Power failure in management circuits', *Harvard Business Review*, July–August (1979).

Kaplan, D., 'Power in perspective', in *Power and Conflict in Organizations*, eds R.L. Kahn and K.E. Boulding (Tavistock, London 1964).

Katz, D. and Kahn, R.L., *The Social Psychology of Organizations* (Wiley, New York, 1966).

Kipnis, D., Schmidt, S.M., Swaffin-Smith, C. and Wilkinson, I., 'Patterns of managerial influence: shotgun managers, tacticians and bystanders', *Organizational Dynamics*, Winter (1984).

Kolb, D.A., 'Towards an applied theory of experiential learning', in *Theories of Group Processes*, ed. C.L. Cooper (Wiley, New York, 1975).

Korda, M., *Power! How to get it* (Random House, New York, 1975).

Korman, A.K., 'Consideration, initiating structure and organizational criteria: a review', *Personnel Psychology*, 19 (1966).

Kormanski, C., 'A situational leadership approach to groups using the Tuckman model of group development', in *The 1985 Annual: developing human resources*, eds L.D. Goodstein and J.W. Pfeiffer (San Diego University Associates, San Diego, 1985).

Kornhauser, A., *Mental Health of the Industrial Worker* (Wiley, New York, 1965).

Kotter, J. and Schlesinger, L., 'Choosing strategies for change', *Harvard Business Review*, March–April (1979).

Kovach, K.A., 'What motivates employees? Workers and supervisors give different answers', *Business Horizons*, September–October (1987).

Krech, D., Crutchfield, R.S. and Livson, N., *Elements of Psychology*, 3rd edition (Alfred A. Knopf, New York, 1974).

Krone, K.J., Jablin, F.M. and Putnam, L.L., 'Communication theory and organizational communication: multiple perspectives', in *Handbook of Organizational Communication*, eds F.M. Jablin, L.L. Putnam, K.H. Roberts and L.W. Porter (Sage, Newbury Park, CA, 1987).

Laird, D., *Approaches to Training and Development* (Addison-Wesley, Reading, MA, 1978).

Landy, F.J., *Psychology of Work Behavior*, 4th edition (Brooks Cole, Pacific Grove, CA, 1989).

Lawler, E.E., Hackman, J.R. and Kaufman, S., 'Effects of job redesign: a field experiment', *Journal of Applied Social Psychology*, 3 (1973).

Lawrence, P. and Lorsch, J., *Organization and Environment: managing differentiation and integration* (Harvard University Graduate School of Business, Division of Research, Boston, 1967).

Lazarus, R.S., *Psychological Stress and the Coping Process* (McGraw-Hill, 1966).

Leon, F.R., 'The role of positive and negative outcomes in the causation of motivational forces', *Journal of Applied Psychology*, 66 (1981).

Lewin, K., 'Frontiers in group dynamics', *Human Relations*, June (1947).

Lewin, K., Lippitt, R. and White, R., 'Patterns of aggressive behaviour in experimentally created social climates', *Journal of Social Psychology*, 10 (1939).

Likert, R., *New Patterns of Management* (McGraw-Hill, New York, 1961).

Likert, R., *The Human Organization: its management and value* (McGraw-Hill, New York, 1967).

Locke, E.A., 'Nature and causes of job satisfaction', in *Handbook of Industrial and Organizational Psychology*, ed. M.D. Dunnette (Rand McNally, Chicago, 1976).

Locke, E.A. and Latham, G.P., *A Theory of Goal Setting and Task Performance* (Prentice Hall, Englewood Cliffs, NJ, 1990).

Lupton, T., *Management and the Social Sciences* (Penguin, Harmondsworth, 1966).

Luthans, F. and Kreitner, R., *Organizational Behavior Modification and Beyond* (Scott Foresman, Glenview, IL, 1985).

McCall, M.W., Jnr, and Kaplan, R.E., *Whatever it Takes: decision makers at work* (Prentice Hall, Englewood Cliffs, NJ, 1985).

McClelland, D.C., *The Achieving Society* (Van Nostrand, Princeton, NJ, 1961).

McClelland, D.C. and Boyatzis, R.E., 'The need for close relationships and the manager's job', in *Organizational Psychology: Readings on Human Behavior in Organizations*, eds D.M. Kolb, I.M. Rubin and J.M. Macintyre (Prentice Hall, New York, 1984).

McClelland, D.C. and Winter, D.G., *Motivating Economic Achievement* (Free Press, New York, 1969).

McDavid, J.W. and Harari, M., *Social Psychology: individuals, groups, societies* (Harper and Row, New York, 1968).

McGrath, J.E., 'Stress and behavior in organizations', in *Handbook of Industrial and Organizational Psychology*, ed. M.D. Dunnette (Rand McNally, Chicago, 1976).

McGregor, D., *The Human Side of Enterprise* (McGraw-Hill, New York, 1960).

Mackie, D.M. and Goethals, G.R., 'Individual and group goals', in *Group Processes*, ed. C. Hendrick (Sage, Newbury Park, CA, 1987).

Mahoney, T. and Frost, P., 'The role of technology in models of organizational effectiveness', *Organizational Behavior and Human Performance*, 11 (1974).

Management Charter Initiative (MCI), *Diploma Level Guidelines* (MCI, London, n.d.).

Marguiles, N. and Raia, A.P., *Conceptual Foundations of Organizational Development* (McGraw-Hill, New York, 1978).

Maslow, A., *Motivation and Personality* (Harper, New York, 1954).

Mayo, E., *The Human Problems of an Industrial Civilization* (Macmillan, New York, 1933).

Miles, E.W., Hatfield, J.D. and Huseman, R.C., 'The equity sensitive construct: potential implications for worker performance', *Journal of Management*, December (1989).

Miller, L., *Principles of Everyday Behavior Analysis* (Brooks Cole, Monterey, CA, 1975).

Mintzberg, H., *The Nature of Managerial Work* (Harper and Row, New York, 1973).

Mitchell, T.R., *People in Organizations*, 2nd edition (McGraw-Hill, Tokyo, 1982).

Morse, N.C. and Weiss, R., 'The function and meaning of work and the job', *American Sociological Review*, 20 (1955).

Napier, R.W. and Gershenfeld, M.K., *Groups: theory and experience*, 3rd edition (Houghton, Boston, 1985).

O'Reilly, C.R., 'Corporations, culture and commitment: motivation and social control in organizations', *California Management Review*, Summer (1989).

O'Reilly, C.R., 'Individual and information overload in organizations: is more necessarily better?', *Academy of Management Journal*, December (1980).

Oldfield, F.E., *New Look Industrial Relations* (Mason Reed, London, 1966).

Olson, J.M. and Zanna, M.P., 'Attitudes and beliefs', in *Social Psychology*, eds R.M. Baron, W.G. Graziano and C. Stangor (Holt, Rinehart and Winston, Fort Worth, 1991).

Ouchi, W.G., *Theory Z: how American business can meet the Japanese challenge* (Addison-Wesley, Reading, MA, 1981).

Pahl, J.M. and Pahl, R.E., *Managers and their Wives* (Allen Lane, London, 1971).

Parker, S.R., *The Future of Work and Leisure* (MacGibbon and Kee, London, 1971).

Paul, W.J., Robertson, K.B. and Herzberg, F., 'Job enrichment pays off', *Harvard Business Review*, 47 (1969).

Pavlov, I.P., *Conditioned Reflexes* (Oxford University Press, Oxford, 1927).

Perrow, C.B., 'A framework for the comparative analysis of organizations', *American Sociological Review*, 32 (1967).

Perrow, C.B., *Organizational Analysis: a sociological view* (Brooks Cole, Belmont, CA, 1970).

Peters, T.J. and Waterman, R.H., *In Search of Excellence* (Harper and Row, New York, 1982).

Pettigrew, A.M., 'On studying cultures', *Administrative Science Quarterly*, December (1979).

Pfeffer, J., *Power in Organizations* (Pitman Publishing, Marshfield, MA, 1981).

Pondy, L.R., 'Organizational conflict: concept and models', *Administrative Science Quarterly*, 12 (1967).

Porter, L.W. and Lawler, E.E., *Managerial Attitudes and Performance* (Dorsey Press, Holmewood, IL, 1968).

Porter, L.W., Lawler, E.E. and Hackman, J.R., *Behavior in Organizations* (McGraw-Hill, New York, 1975).

Pugh, D.S. and Hickson, D.J., *Organizational Structure in its Context* (Lexington Books, Saxon House, 1976).

Pugh, D.S., Hickson, D.J., and Hinings, C.R., *Writers in Organizations*, 3rd edition (Penguin, Harmondsworth, 1983).

Pugh, D.S., Hickson, D.J., Hinings, C.R. and Turner, C., 'Dimensions of organization structure', *Administrative Science Quarterly*, 13 (1968).

Rackham, N. and Morgan, T., *Behavior Analysis in Training* (McGraw-Hill, New York, 1974).

Rauschenberger, J., Schmitt, N. and Hunter, J.E., 'A test of need hierarchy concept by a Markov model of change in need strength', *Administrative Science Quarterly*, 25 (1980).

Reitz, H.J., *Behavior in Organizations* (Richard D. Irwin, Holmewood, IL, 1981).

Renwick, P.A. and Tosi, H., 'The effects of sex, marital status and educational background on selected decisions', *Academy of Management Journal*, March (1978).

Research Bureau Ltd, *Research on External and Internal Influences in Training*, report for the Manpower Services Commission (Manpower Services Commission, Sheffield, 1979).

Reynolds, P.C., 'Imposing a corporate culture', *Psychology Today*, March (1987).

Rice, R.W., 'Construct validity of the Least Preferred Co-worker Score', *Psychological Bulletin*, 85 (1978).

Robbins, S.P., *Organizational Theory: structure design and applications* (Prentice Hall, Englewood Cliffs, NJ, 1990).

Robbins, S.P., *Essentials of Organizational Behavior* (Prentice Hall, Englewood Cliffs, NJ, 1992).

Roethlisberger, F.J. and Dickson, W.J., *Management and the Worker: an account of a research program conducted by the Western Electric Company Hawthorne Works Chicago* (Harvard University Press, Cambridge, MA, 1939).

Saffold, G.S., 'Culture traits, strength and organizational performance: moving beyond strong culture', *Academy of Management Review*, October (1988).

Salancik, G.R. and Pfeffer, J., 'An examination of need satisfaction models of job attitudes', *Administrative Science Quarterly*, 25 (1977).

Sales, S.M., 'Supervisory style and productivity: review and theory', *Personnel Psychology*, 19 (1966).

Sales, S.M. and House, J., 'Job dissatisfaction as a possible risk factor in coronary heart disease', *Journal of Chronic Diseases*, 23 (1971).

Schein, E.H., *Organizational Psychology* (Prentice Hall, Englewood Cliffs, NJ, 1980).

Schein, E.H., 'How culture forms, develops and changes', in *Gaining Control of the Corporate Culture*, eds Kilman et al. (Jossey-Bass, San Francisco, 1985).

Schein, E.H., *Organizational Culture and Leadership* (Jossey-Bass, San Francisco, 1985).

Schein, E.H., *Process Consultation. Vol. 1: Its Role in Organization Development*, 2nd edition (Addison-Wesley, Reading, MA, 1988).

Schermerhorn, J.R., Hunt, J.G. and Osborn, R.N., *Managing Organizational Behavior* (Wiley, New York, 1982).

Schneider, B., 'Organizational behavior', *Annual Review of Psychology*, 36 (1985).

Schreisheim, C.R. and Hinkin, T.R., 'Influence tactics used by subordinates: a theoretical and empirical analysis', *Journal of Applied Psychology*, 75 (1990).

Schwab, D.P. and Cummings, L.L., 'Employee performance and satisfaction with work roles: a review and interpretation of theory', *Industrial Relations*, 9 (1970).

Schwab, D.P., Olian-Gottlieb, J.D. and Heneman, H.G., 'Between-subjects expectancy theory research: a statistical review of studies predicting effort and performance', *Psychological Bulletin*, 86 (1979).

Schwartz, H., 'Matching corporate culture and business strategy', *Organizational Dynamics*, Summer (1981).

Sharplin, A., *Strategic Management* (McGraw-Hill, New York, 1985).

Shaw, M.E., *Group Dynamics: the psychology of small group behavior*, 2nd edition (McGraw-Hill, New York, 1976).

Sherif, M. and Sherif, C., *Groups in Harmony and Tension* (Harper and Row, New York, 1953).

Sillitoe, A.F., *Britain in Figures* (Penguin, Harmondsworth, 1971).

Sills, D.L., *The Volunteers* (Free Press, Glencoe, IL, 1957).

Silverman, R.E., 'Learning theory applied to training', in *The Management of Training*, eds C.P. Otto and R.E. Glaser (Addison-Wesley, Reading, MA, 1970).

Simon, H.A., *The New Science of Management Decisions* (Harper and Row, New York, 1960).

Simon, H.A., 'Invariants of human behavior', *Annual Review of Psychology*, 41 (1990).

Skinner, B.F., *Analysis of Behavior* (McGraw-Hill, New York, 1961).

Sloan, A.P., *My Years with General Motors* (Sidgwick and Jackson, New York, 1965).

Smircich, L., 'Concepts of culture and organizational analysis', *Administrative Science Quarterly*, September (1983).

Smith, P.C., 'Behaviors, results and organizational effectiveness: the problem of criteria', in *Handbook of Industrial and Organizational Psychology*, ed. M.D. Dunnette (Rand McNally, Chicago, 1976).

Smith, P.C., Kendall, L.M. and Hulin, C.L., *The Measurement of Satisfaction in Work and Retirement* (Rand McNally, Chicago, 1969).

Sneizek, J.A., May, D.R. and Sawyer, J.E., 'Social uncertainty and interdependence: a study of resource allocation decisions in groups', *Organizational Behavior and Human Decision Processes*, 46 (1990).

Soelberg, P., 'Unprogrammed decision making', *Industrial Management Review*, 8 (1967).

Staw, B.M., *Psychological Dimensions of Organizational Behavior* (Macmillan, New York, 1991).

Staw, B.M., Bell, N.E. and Clausen, J.A., 'The dispositional approach to job attitudes: a lifetime longitudinal test', *Administrative Science Quarterly*, March (1986).

Steade, R.D., *Business and Society in Transition: issues and concepts* (Harper and Row, San Francisco, 1975).

Steers, R.M. and Porter, L.W. (eds), *Motivation and Work Behavior*, 5th edition (McGraw-Hill, New York, 1989).

Stephenson, T.E., 'Organizational development: a critique', *Journal of Management Studies*, October (1975).

Stogdill, R.M., 'Personal factors associated with leadership: a survey of the literature', *Journal of Psychology*, 25 (1948).

Tannenbaum, R., Weschler, I.R. and Massarick, F., *Leadership and Organization* (McGraw-Hill, New York, 1961).

Taylor, F.W., *The Principles of Scientific Management* (Harper and Brothers, New York, 1911).

Thomas, K.W., 'Conflict and conflict management', in *Handbook of Industrial and Organizational Psychology*, ed. M.D. Dunnette (Rand McNally, Chicago, 1976).

Thompson, J.D., *Organizations in Action* (McGraw-Hill, New York, 1967).

Thorndike, E.L., *Educational Psychology: the psychology of learning, Vol. 2* (Columbia Teachers College, New York, 1913).

Tolman, E.C., 'Cognitive maps in rats and men', *Psychological Review*, 55 (1948).

Training Commission/Council for Management Education (CMED), 'Classifying the components of management competencies' (Training Commission, London, 1988).

Trist, E.L., 'The socio-technical perspective', in *Perspectives on Organization Design and Behavior*, eds A. van de Ven and W.F. Joyce (Wiley-Interscience, New York, 1981).

Trist, E.L. and Bamforth, K.W., 'Some social and psychological consequences of the longwall methods of coal-getting', *Human Relations*, 4 (1951).

Tuckman, B.W., 'Developmental sequence in small groups', *Psychological Bulletin*, November (1965).

Urwick, L.F., 'Executive decentralization and functional co-ordination', *Management Review*, 24 (1935).

Vecchio, R.P., 'An individual-differences interpretation of the conflicting predictions generated by equity theory and expectancy theory', *Journal of Applied Psychology*, August (1981).

Vroom, V.H., *Work and Motivation* (Wiley, New York, 1964).

Vroom, V.H. and Yetton, P.W., *Leadership and Decision Making* (University of Pittsburgh Press, Pittsburgh, 1973).

Wahba, M.A. and Bridwell, L.B., 'Maslow reconsidered: a review of research on the need hierarchy theory', *Organizational Behavior and Human Performance*, 15 (1976).

Wanous, J.P. and Zwany, A., 'A cross-sectional test of the need hierarchy theory', *Organizational Behavior and Human Performance*, 18 (1977).

Wardwell, W.I., Hyman, M. and Bahnson, C.B., 'Stress and coronary disease in three field studies', *Journal of Chronic Diseases*, 17 (1964).

Warr, P. and Wall, T., *Work and Well Being* (Penguin, Harmondsworth, 1975).

Weber, M., *The Theory of Social and Economic Organizations*, ed. T. Parsons (Free Press, Glencoe, IL, 1947).

Wedderburn, D.C., 'Economic aspects of ageing', *UNESCO International Social Science Journal*, 15 (1963).

Weiss, H.M. and Alder, S., 'Personality and organizational behavior', in *Research in Organizational Behavior. Vol. 6*, eds B.M. Staw and L.L. Cummings (JAI Press, Greenwich, CT, 1984).

Wexley, K.N. and Yukl, G.A., *Organizational Behavior and Personnel Psychology* (Urwin, Holmewood, IL, 1984).

White, D.D. and Bednar, D.A., *Organizational Behavior, Understanding and Managing People* (Allyn Bacon, Boston, 1986).

Whyte, W.F., *Money and Motivation* (Harper, New York, 1955).

Whyte, W.H., *The Organization Man* (Penguin, Harmondsworth, 1960).

Williams, A., 'Organizational development', in *Managing Human Resources*, eds A.G. Cowling and C.J.B. Mailer (Arnold, London, 1990).

Woodward, J., *Industrial Organizations: theory and practice* (Oxford University Press, London, 1965).

Yukl, G.A., *Leadership in Organizations*, 2nd edition (Prentice Hall, Englewood Cliffs, NJ, 1989).

Yukl, G.A. and Falbe, C.M., 'Influence tactics and objectives in upwards, downward and lateral influence attempts', *Journal of Applied Psychology*, 75 (1990).

Zalesny, J.D. and Ford, J.K., 'Extending the social information processing perspective: new links to attitudes, behaviors and perceptions', *Organizational Behavior and Human Processes*, 47 (1990).

Zeira, Y. and Avedisian, J., 'Organizational planned change: assessing the chances for success', *Organizational Dynamics*, Spring (1989).

Index